NEVER SAY NEVER

HAVEN HARBOR SERIES BOOK THREE

LILY MILLER

ABOUT THE BOOK

Tucker Collins.

Treasured college football coach by day, Reed Point's most notorious bachelor by night—and the thorn in my side for the past 10 years.

It wasn't always that way. Once upon a time, Tucker and I were inseparable. We grew up next door to each other and he was almost like a brother to me. My closest friend. But as we got older, things started to change. Secretly, I loved his cocky grin and the way his blue eyes would lock on mine. I was resigned to lusting after him from afar until one day he kissed me—only to reject me the very next day.

Since then, I've tried to keep as much distance between Tucker and I as possible. When we do cross paths, which is more often than I'd like seeing as our parents are best friends, that man still knows *exactly* how to get under my skin.

Then one night, Tucker corners me on a date and demands to know who the guy is. I tell him it's just a fling, not that it's any of his business. The truth is I'm leaving town in a few months, so I'm not looking for anything serious. But when I admit to having certain *needs*, Tucker comes up with an agreement.

That's how I end up in a frienemies-with-benefits pact with my childhood best friend. We have a list of rules—no sleeping over, no cuddling and definitely no falling in love. But before long it's taking everything in me not to break every single one.

Catching feelings for Tucker Collins is a very bad idea. There are a million reasons why I should walk away.

But it's hard to leave when I'm having so much fun. Tucker is Reed Point's hottest bachelor. The boy who broke my heart. And my new dirty secret.

Copyright © 2024 by Lily Miller

All rights reserved.

No part of this book may be reproduced in any form or by any electronic or mechanical means, including information storage and retrieval systems, without written permission from the author, except for the use of brief quotations in a book review.

This book is a work of fiction. Names, characters, places and incidents are products of the author's imagination or are used fictitiously. Any resemblance to actual events or locals or persons, living or dead, is entirely coincidental.

Never Say Never

Cover photo: Sarah Martin, Sarah Martin Photoartistry

Cover models: Annamarie Marcello & Zack Landry

Cover design: Kim Wilson, Kiwi Cover Design

Editing: Carolyn De Melo

Publicity: Love Notes PR

PLAYLIST

1. Landslide—The Chicks
2. Skinny Love— Birdy
3. What Could've Been— Gone West
4. I Had Some Help— Post Malone, Morgan Wallen
5. Wind Up Missin' You—Tucker Wetmore
6. Space Cowboy—Kacey Musgraves
7. Cowboys Cry Too—Kelsea Ballerini, Noah Kahan
8. Guy For That—Post Malone, Luke Combs
9. Speakers— Sam Hunt
10. Lies Lies Lies—Morgan Wallen
11. Unapologetically—Kelsea Ballerini
12. half of my hometown—Kelsea Ballerini, Kenny Chesney
13. Didn't I?— Dasha
14. Am I Okay?— Megan Moroney
15. Taste— Sabrina Carpenter
16. Started Stoppin'—Mitchell Tenpenny
17. How Do I Do This?— Kelsea Ballerini
18. I Ain't Sayin'—Jordan Davis
19. if we never met— John K, Kelsea Ballerini
20. Higher—Michael Buble

For Carmen
I wish every girl could have a friend like you. I am sorry that no one dies in this book, but at least I gave you a hot football coach.

ONE

A SPECIAL KIND OF TORTURE

Daisy

"You really should have known better," Briar calls to me from her position on the other side of the net.

I resist the urge to sigh and instead just nod my head. "Yup. Hard to argue that."

She's right. I should have known that going on a date with Scott Dickens was a bad idea. I mean, the date wasn't bad. It just wasn't all that... good. It was kind of like having a cocktail with the human equivalent of an anaesthetic. Not painful, but also not in any way memorable.

Briar strides toward the net that separates us in her lime green sports bra and white pleated athletic skirt. "So did he try to kiss you?" She pauses before her eyes widen in horror. "Oh god, please tell me he didn't."

I watch a shiver pass over her, like kissing Scott is the worst thing she could possibly imagine. Briar can be so dramatic, which is honestly one of the things I love about her. But she doesn't need to worry this time.

Scott is nice.

He is stuffy and ridiculously boring and very, very nice.

We just have zero chemistry.

I want that spark. That sensation in your belly that flutters to life when your gaze catches theirs. That feeling that makes your pulse race, that leaves you breathless.

I've felt that euphoria once.

Stop it, Daisy.

I inhale a long, frustrated breath. With *him*, there was definitely chemistry, but there was also intense aggravation. He only got my pulse racing because he knew exactly how to get under my skin. He enjoyed it. He still does.

"Earth to Daisy!" I blink back to the present when Briar hollers at me from across the pickleball court. "Did he stick his tongue in your mouth or not?"

"God, no. He is way too much of a gentleman."

"You mean he didn't have the balls."

She's right about that too. Scott isn't one of those douchebags who seem hellbent on sleeping with half of the women in Reed Point. Believe me when I tell you I run into my fair share of those guys. Scott is considerate and decent, which is why I agreed to go out with him. He's a doctor at the clinic I work at, he comes from a good family—he's the perfect guy to bring home to meet your mom and dad. So, when he asked if he could take me out to dinner, I decided to give him a chance. I had never really felt any attraction between us, but I thought maybe that part could develop if I got to know him outside of work. Halfway through dinner, I realized that Scott wasn't the guy for me.

The last thing I wanted to do was lead him on, so when he dropped me off at my apartment, I didn't give him the opportunity to try to kiss me. Instead, I politely thanked him for a nice evening and ducked inside, leaving him standing on my doorstep. I guess I am going to have to break it to him that there won't be a second date.

"Scott will make someone very happy one day," I tell Briar, tossing a pickleball in the air and catching it in my palm.

"It's just not going to be you." She shrugs one shoulder. "You tried. Got yourself out there."

For all the good it did me. Sometimes I wonder if I'm ever going to find my person. I've dated a bunch of guys, but I've never experienced that fire-in-my-chest feeling with any of them. Maybe there's something wrong with me.

"3-3-1."

My attention returns to Briar, who announces the score then gets into position to serve the ball into play. We've been playing pickleball since college. Anyone who calls this a game for retirees clearly hasn't played. It's a serious workout and there's a trickle of sweat running down my spine to prove it. We rally back and forth until Briar hits the yellow, plastic ball past the sideline. I jog over to grab it, laughing as she groans loudly in frustration, only to find someone else has already retrieved our ball. My gaze slices from black Nike runners up the very familiar lean, muscular body of the six-foot-two former football player who has snagged my pickleball from the asphalt.

Tucker Collins.

My stomach does a weird flip-flop before I will it to stop.

Steel-blue eyes lock on mine. His honey-brown hair is long and messy on top and trimmed short on the sides. I have felt how soft those thick strands are. I will cut my fingers off before I allow them to touch it again.

I hold out a hand for the ball, noticing for the first time that Tucker is not alone. Standing next to him is Holden Banks. Of course. Some things never change. The two of them have been best friends since childhood, and wherever Tucker goes, Holden is probably not too far behind.

Holden flashes an easy-breezy grin as he steals my gaze. "Daisy-Cakes! Perfect! We're looking to play doubles. You in?" I've known Tucker and Holden since we were all kids, hence the silly nickname.

Heat pricks at the back of my neck and then travels down my spine. These two are entirely too handsome for their own good. And they know it. Just about every girl in Reed Point has shamelessly thrown themselves at them at one point or another.

The last thing I need is to be subjected to their hard bodies flexing and straining and covered in a sheen of sweat as they whack a pickleball. No, thank you. I'll pass on that special kind of torture.

Before I can snap out a response, Briar is at my side.

"Did I hear 'doubles?' We're in!" she tells them with a bright smile. "Let's split up the teams—no offence, guys, but Daisy and I would kill you two."

What I want—which is to get as far away from these two as I can—doesn't seem to matter because all of three seconds later Holden and Briar are headed to the other side of the court. Tucker tosses the ball in the air and catches it again, looking entirely unbothered. In fact, he looks like he's enjoying this, levelling me with that smirk that I know all too well.

Ugh. Fine, Tuck. You win.

Tucker Collins can be irritatingly charming when he wants to be. I've known him my entire life, and I've seen him turn that charm on and off more times than I can count.

"So, you didn't want to lock lips with Dr. Dick?" Tucker's blue eyes pin mine as his smirk stretches into a wide grin. Great. He overheard my conversation with Briar.

"It's Dr. Dickens, dumbass. And don't be mean. Scott is a nice guy."

One dark brow creeps upward. "A little *too* nice, then? Didn't know you had a dark side to you, rebel. Interesting."

I glare at him. "Can we just play the game without you being an ass?"

"We can. But what fun would that be?"

For the last two and half decades, this is how it's been between us. Ever since I can remember, Tucker and I have been riling each other up. You would think that growing up as neighbors and practically siblings, we would have eventually figured out a way to get along. Our families do absolutely everything together—vacations and birthday parties, backyard dinners in the summer, ski trips in the winter. Tucker's mom and dad are my godparents. I'm even named after his mother! Our families are *that* tight.

Tucker and I, on the other hand…

"How did the doc take it when you turned him down?"

"I didn't."

"But you're going to."

I can't help the aggravated sigh that escapes me. Tuck has always been protective of me—overly protective, in my opinion. It's frustrating. There was a time that I loved the attention from him; I couldn't get enough. Now I just wish he would learn to stay out of my private life.

"Tucker, I'm pretty sure we've been over this before, but who I choose to date is none of your business."

Why do I let him rile me up like this? It's not like I have feelings for Tucker. The thought of kissing him makes me nauseous.

Except for that one time. If I let myself, I can still remember the way his lips felt, soft and pillowy against mine. But that is ancient history. A moment, a blip. There's no way I'd let that happen again.

"You will always be my business, Daisy. We're family. It's my job to make sure you're not dating some douche-canoe."

If I was annoyed before, now I am livid. It takes effort to unclench my jaw as I glare at him. "For starters, Scott is a doctor. He might be a bit dry, but he is not a 'douche-canoe.' Second, you and me... we're not family."

Tucker flinches and for a second, I worry that my words have caused him pain. Immediately, a guilty feeling takes hold of me. Tuck is right, as much as I hate to admit it. For all intents and purposes, we are family. His mom and dad are second parents to me. His older sister Addy is the sister I've never had.

His gaze holds mine and I can feel my cheeks flush, betraying me. We're interrupted by the sound of Holden loudly clearing his throat from across the net.

"Ready to get this game going or what, Daisy-Cakes?" I look over to see Holden with his game face on. I nod. I'm ready to get this game and this entire afternoon over with. Pronto.

I take my position and then swing my racket through the air, serving the pickleball as hard as I can. I grip the handle of my paddle as Briar volleys the ball back to our side of the court and then I smack it back across the net with more force than necessary. The ball bounces off the asphalt just inside the sideline, making it impossible for Holden to reach it.

"Sniper," Holden says with an easy laugh as he retrieves the ball.

Too bad the shot wasn't aimed at Tucker's head.

TWO

I LIKE FUCKING WITH HER

Tucker

I take a long pull from my water bottle as my gaze travels over the curves of the feisty brunette with her back to me. I know I should put some distance between us. In fact, I should stay as far the fuck away from her as possible. Instead, I'm standing here watching her like a creep.

I'm such an asshole for ogling my god-sister. But it's so difficult to back off when all I want to do is get my hands on her. Let's face it, I've never been any good at staying away from Daisy. Especially when she's dressed like that.

My eyes wander over Daisy as she talks with her friend Briar at the net. Her heart-shaped ass is barely covered by a pair of athletic shorts while her midriff is bare thanks to a hot as fuck black sports bra. Her long, golden-brown hair is pulled off her face in a ponytail. The exposed skin above her breasts glistens with sweat.

I grip my water bottle with enough force to pop a blood vessel. What was she doing with a guy like Scott Dickens? He's at least five or six years older than her and as dry as the

Mojave dessert. I'm sure he's a nice enough guy, but he isn't even close to being Daisy's type. How do I know? Because I know everything about Daisy Carter. I know her drink order at Dream Bean, how she likes her eggs. I know what makes her laugh, and what scares her. If I had to guess, she was bored out of her mind before Dr. Dickhead pulled out her chair at the restaurant. Because Daisy likes adventure. She likes a thrill.

"Daisy doesn't seem very happy to see you," Holden says from the bench beside me as he swipes a towel over his face. "What did you do to her?"

With a snort, I tear my attention from her. "You know me and Daisy. It is what it is."

Holden shakes his head. He has had a front row seat to my relationship with Daisy for decades. He knows how it works. He also knows she is off-limits. I made that clear in fifth grade when she paid him a little attention.

"You two are like oil and water," Holden says. "Always have been."

I shrug. I get what Holden is saying, but he has it wrong. Daisy and I are more like moths to a flame. We may not always get along, but we are irresistibly drawn to each other even though we know the heat could kill us.

My gaze casually slides back to Daisy and our eyes catch. Lust crackles through my body. "I like fucking with her. It's fun."

"You'd like to fuck her," Holden says with a grin. "There's a difference."

I try to rearrange my expression to look like that couldn't be further from the truth. Holden may have his suspicions about me and Daisy, but I'm not about to confirm them. The last thing I need is my best friend knowing I have a thing for the girl who was practically raised as my sister. He would never let me live it down.

"I wonder what your mom and dad would think about that?" he continues, clearly enjoying pushing my buttons. "I bet family dinners would get pretty entertaining. Do they know you're picturing Daisy naked when you're asking her to pass the potatoes?"

"Lucky for me you're full of shit, because if I was into Daisy, they'd blow a gasket. I don't have a death wish."

My parents would flip their lids. Daisy can say we're not family all she wants, but deep down she doesn't believe it. Family isn't always blood. It's the people you choose to go through life with.

Holden lifts a brow as he studies my expression. "Maybe it's time I shoot my shot then."

It takes a every bit of my willpower not to snap his arms off his body. "What the fuck did you just say?"

The dude laughs. Doubles over and fucking laughs. "Relax, Tuck. If you're trying to convince me that you're not into her, you're doing a pretty shit job."

He's enjoying this way too much.

"I've known Daisy my entire life. We grew up together," I remind him. "That doesn't mean I want to fuck her."

A smug grin tips the corners of his mouth as he picks up his racket and stands up. "Sure, man. Whatever you need to tell yourself."

Holden laughs again as he strides toward the girls at the net, leaving me where I'm standing at the edge of the pickleball court.

"Can we get you a snack to go with your water, Tucker, or can we get back to the game?" Briar deadpans.

You bet I'd like a snack. Her name is Daisy.

With a swagger, I stride onto the court, racket in hand,

ready to get back to the game. Unfortunately, my game has gone to shit.

And I know exactly why.

Daisy.

I've been this fucked up over her since before I can remember. In all these years, it's never changed.

THREE
COCKY IS HOT

Daisy

I turn the volume on the radio up and then put my sunglasses on, hoping to mask my frustration. I can feel Briar lasering a hole into the side of my head from where she sits beside me in the passenger seat of my Mini Cooper. I let out a sigh, and that's all it takes for her to turn the volume back down.

"Tucker Collins strikes again, huh?"

I shoulder check before backing my car out of its spot outside the pickleball courts. "He is such an ass. He ruins everything."

I force myself to ease up on the white-knuckle grip I have on the steering wheel, trying to wipe all six-foot-something of that man from my brain. A powerful cocktail of frustration and lust spirals through me. Tucker drives me crazy. How else can you explain the heat that simmers at the back of my neck or the lump that forms in my throat whenever he's around? The physical effect he has on me is a giant pain in my ass. Just like Tuck. We have nothing in common, he treats me like a kid, and most of the time we can barely stand one another. And yet, whenever we're together, it feels like fireworks.

But that's just my body's mixed-up response to how much he aggravates me. Nothing more. I am one hundred percent not attracted to him.

"What did he do this time?" Briar asks.

"Oh, he was just inserting himself into my life, as always. He overheard us talking about Scott and went on and on about my questionable taste in men. He wouldn't let it go."

"Well, he was sort of right on this one. You said it yourself, there were zero sparks," she reminds me, then adds, "Those only seem to ignite with Tucker."

I whip my head in her direction, eyes narrowed.

Briar holds up her hands as if to defend herself. "I'm kidding," she says, her gold-rimmed green eyes wide with innocence. "Kind of." She winks at me, then flips her sun visor down to look at her reflection in the mirror. She frees her hair from its ponytail, shaking the short, platinum-blonde waves loose.

I decide to ignore her comment, grumbling under my breath instead. I'm not in the mood to argue about this. No, thank you. I have much better things to think about than *him*.

A phone call pops up on the screen on my dash and I'm surprised to see it's my dad. My parents are on vacation in Florida, their annual spring golf getaway with Tucker's mom and dad.

"Hey, Daddy."

"Hey, princess. How's my girl? Staying out of trouble?"

A genuine smile curves at my lips. I am very close to my dad. He's my biggest cheerleader and always has been. "Always. How's Florida?"

"It's fine. Can't complain. Your mom says hi."

"Tell her I say hi back. What's up? Shouldn't you be golfing?"

"We just got back to the house. It's hot as heck out there today. Anyways, I'm just calling to ask a favor for Aunt Daisy. Would you mind running over to her house today to pick up an Amazon delivery from her doorstep? You've got your key, right? You can just leave it inside."

Addy is away with her husband Jonathan and while Tucker doesn't live too far from his parents' place, I'm not surprised his mom is asking me instead of her own son. She and my Uncle Mark never trust him to get anything done. Tucker's dad has been hard on him since we were kids. I can't even count the number of times the two of us would get into some harmless trouble together and Tuck's dad would blame him entirely. I, on the other hand, seem to do no wrong in Uncle Mark's eyes.

Tucker's parents have always adored me. Tuck and I were born in the same hospital on the same day, and we were raised practically as siblings. Aunt Daisy was there when I took my first steps, and my dad was always in the stands at Tucker's baseball or football games. Our parents have a thousand stories of the two of us growing up side by side, and they like to tell them to us often.

Tucker and I may have grown up together, but in some ways our lives were quite different. Whereas his parents could be demanding, mine were always kind and supportive. I love Aunt Daisy and Uncle Mark, but I have seen firsthand the pressure they put on Tucker. My mom and dad, on the other hand, have only ever wanted me to be happy.

The Collins' house looked much like ours from the outside—big, luxurious homes nestled in perfectly manicured gardens. But while Tucker's house looked like a show home inside, mine was filled with family photo galleries.

Our families just had different priorities. The Collins' like expensive things, and my Uncle Mark worked all the time so they could afford the best. My parents were more concerned with making memories than making money, and it showed.

"Of course. Let her know it's not a problem."

"Thanks, sweetheart."

I end the call and shoot Briar an apologetic look. "Sorry about that," I say, but she doesn't seem to hear me. She's leaning against the headrest with a far-off look in her eyes.

"Hello? You okay?" I ask, wondering where she has disappeared to.

"What?" She returns to the present with a heavy sigh. "Sorry. Just trying to decide which one I'd marry and which one I'd fuck."

"What are you talking about?"

"Tuck or Holden."

I groan.

"Tucker's tats, baby blues and biceps or Holden's curls, mysterious gaze and killer jawline," she says wistfully, with one foot pressed into my dashboard. "How's a girl supposed to choose?"

"They're both egotistical and cocky."

"Cocky is hot."

"They've both slept with half of Reed Point. Still hot?"

I look over in time to see Briar smirk. "Well, they're obviously good at—"

My hand flies up like a stop sign between us. "Spare me your disgusting fantasies."

"Fine, I'll stop," she laughs. "You obviously have a *thing* when it comes to talking about Tucker."

I don't have a *thing*.

Okay... maybe just a small one.

Tucker and I have fallen into a pattern of provoking each

other, which usually ends in us not talking for days. But that wasn't always the case.

When we were little, we did everything together. Swimming lessons, preschool, endless hours spent on his couch watching movies. Our family photo albums are full of pictures of us together: our first day of kindergarten, the day we graduated elementary school, the two of us celebrating our birthdays together. Most of my childhood was spent with Tucker and his older sister Addy. We were thick as thieves... until we weren't.

I remember the day I first noticed him in a different way. It was so cliché. We were 15 years old. We were spending the afternoon swimming in the pool at his place, as we often did in the summer. Tucker pushed himself up to sit on the edge, feet still in the water. I was lying on a floatie trying to get a tan. I was half-expecting him to kick a spray of water in my face, but when I turned my head to glance in his direction he was just sitting there quietly, looking at me. Something about his expression made my pulse speed up and my chest tighten. It was the first time I thought of Tuck as anything other than a friend.

After that day, there was a shift between us. We'd still hang out, have lunch together at school, sneak out and meet in his backyard at night, lying on a pool lounger and talking for hours. But the air between us felt different. Charged.

No one has ever made me feel unsteady on my feet like Tucker. No one has made me feel this deep connection, this intense attraction. I've always felt a pull toward him, and for a while I thought he felt it too. I thought maybe he wanted more.

I blink away the memories when I pull up to the two-bedroom apartment Briar and I share just four blocks from the beach.

"We should go to Cucina Caliente for dinner tonight," Briar says as we head up the walk to our building. "I am craving tacos. Also, the place will be packed tonight. Maybe we can find you a hot dentist since the nerdy doctor didn't pan out."

"I'll pass," I tell her, heading up the stairs to the second floor. "I'm going to do some research for my trip and then I have to head over to Aunt Daisy's."

Briar shakes her head. "It's Saturday night. You're not leaving for months; you have lots of time to plan. It would do you some good to get out."

Not a chance. Tucker and his buddies are always out drinking on Saturday nights. Reed Point is a small town, and I don't have the energy for another run-in with him today. I also have zero desire to have a front row seat as a bunch of girls throw themselves at him.

"Have fun without me. I'm still a hard pass."

"Big mistake, Daisy. It might help relieve some of that sexual tension you've got brewing inside of you," Briar says with a wink as I unlock the door to our apartment.

A snort escapes me. "Yeah, right."

"Okay, fine. Well, at least lock your door and get that toy out that you hide in the top drawer of your nightstand. Trust me, you'll feel better."

I roll my eyes. "You think an orgasm is the answer for everything. If that were the case, there would be world peace."

"Ooh, you may be onto something. If I ever run for president, that will be my platform. Orgasms for peace!" Briar says, flashing a peace sign at me.

I shoot her a smile to appease her. "I think it needs a little work, but you've got my vote."

I escape to my bedroom before Briar tries to physically

drag me out of the apartment with her. I strip out of my sports bra and shorts and jump in the shower, determined to scrub all thoughts of Tucker from my mind. After I'm dressed, I settle onto my bed with my laptop. I've been planning my next adventure for a while now, eager to cross Italy off the long list of places I want to visit. Last year, I travelled to South Africa and two years before that I spent a few weeks backpacking in Costa Rica. I love finding hidden places, meeting new people, exploring different cultures. I want to see as much of the world as I can.

The next couple of hours pass in a blur as I lose myself in creating an itinerary for my trip: a few days in Rome, a farm stay in Tuscany, a train to Venice. When I realize my stomach is grumbling, I close the lid of my laptop and quickly heat up some leftovers from the fridge before heading over to Aunt Daisy's.

It's after 8:00 p.m. by the time I step outside of my apartment building into the cool fall night air. I'm wearing jeans and a cropped T-shirt and am thankful that I threw on a baggy cardigan before heading out. Arriving at the Collins' 15 minutes later, I find Aunt Daisy's package tucked beside the beautiful potted Hydrangeas that sit on the doorstep. I scoop it up and then twist the key in the lock and walk through the large front doors of the stone mansion. I stride through the foyer with its vaulted ceiling and gigantic chandelier toward the back of the house, dropping my keys and the package on the kitchen counter.

Grabbing a glass from the cupboard, I move to the sink and turn on the tap—and then freeze when the sliding glass door opens and Tucker walks into the kitchen from the backyard. He's wearing just a pair of swim shorts—bare chest, water dripping from his slicked back brown hair down his muscular torso. Our eyes meet and it only takes two seconds for the tension between us to skyrocket. The two of us are in this kitchen every Sunday night for dinner with our families. So why does this feel so awkward, being here alone together?

We stare at each other in silence for a moment before I clear my throat and attempt to appear as if my pulse isn't racing beneath my skin. Tucker runs one hand through his dark, wet hair as his other hand trails down his chest to the shorts he's wearing deliciously low on his hips. The sight of his sculpted abs, his tattoos and the dusting of hair leading into his shorts sends a wave of lust through me. I swallow hard. It's been a while since I've seen Tucker shirtless, and in that time, he's filled out. My eyes wander to his torso, where droplets of water trail slowly down his smooth, golden skin, and I fight the urge to reach out and touch him.

I hate to admit it, but Tucker Collins is complete perfection.

"What are you doing here?" I blurt out, regaining the ability to speak.

"What am *I* doing here? What are *you* doing here? Last time I checked this is *my* parents' house."

Needing to move, to put distance between us and stop standing here and staring at him, I walk back to the counter where I dropped my keys. "Your parents called and asked me to stop by to bring in a package that was delivered today." There's a beat of silence, the tension so thick it's suffocating.

I can't read the look in his eyes. Is he upset that I'm here? Annoyed?

"So, what are you doing here? It's Saturday night. Shouldn't you be out with one of the girls from your fan club?"

"I was supposed to have a date," Tucker says, and jealousy sinks its sharp claws into me.

"What happened? She cancelled? Came to her senses?" I ask, attempting to sound unaffected.

His eyes search mine as if he's trying to chip away at me, to read the thoughts in my head. "Wasn't feeling it so I called it off."

It's only when my chest falls, and I exhale that I realize I was holding my breath. "Oh."

It's all I can get out before he's crossing the kitchen, eating up the space between us. "Since we're both here, what do you say we stay and watch a movie? It'll be like old times."

My skin heats.

When I don't answer, his chin tips downward and he looks at me through thick, dark eyelashes. "Come on, Daisy. It'll be fun."

TUCKER

MY EYES ARE ALL OVER THE ONLY GIRL WHO HAS EVER BEEN able to make my heart stop in my chest. The one girl I should *not* be having filthy thoughts about. But Daisy, damn her, is looking fucking amazing in fitted jeans and a crop top that shows off just the right amount of smooth, golden skin. Her ass looks incredible in those jeans, and it has my cock stirring. I've imagined fucking that ass a time or two. My fingers ache to touch her. Her body is perfection, long and lean from years of running. As I drink her in, I try to convince myself that I am not attracted to her one tiny bit. I'm used to being around pretty girls. But it's pointless. No matter how hard I try to get her out of my head, in the end it's always Daisy.

Daisy Carter is a triple threat— smart, funny, and ridiculously sexy. And I'm not the only one who has noticed. For as long as I can remember, she's turned heads. Back when we were in school together, guys would follow her around like love-sick puppies, hoping they had a shot with her. I'd see them eyeing her in class or offering to carry her books for her; I'd hear the whispers and cat calls that she did her best to ignore. Daisy was always polite to them—that's just who she is—but I made sure those assholes never got too close. Any guy who tried to make a move on her had to deal with me. My dad drilled it into my head that it was up to me to look out for Daisy, to protect her from guys who only wanted one thing: to get in her pants. Fuck that. It wasn't going to happen as long as I was around. If Daisy was off-limits to yours truly then she was off-limits to every other guy at Reed Point High School too.

Daisy is still standing a couple of feet away from me, and I take it as a good sign that she hasn't already bolted out of the house. Having her so close, her blue-green eyes on me, is all it takes to send a bolt of lust right through me. It would be so easy to kiss her right now. I take a half step back, hoping the space will help calm my racing pulse.

My eyes drop to the Amazon package sitting on the counter. *Of course,* my parents would call Daisy when they needed a favor. Why would they ask their own son? I shake my head at the ridiculousness of it all. Do they really think I'm not capable of driving the 10 minutes to their house to pick up a box off their doorstep? I feel my jaw clench, frustration rising. I don't know why it surprises me.

My dad has never made it a secret that he thinks I'm a screw-up. He's your classic Type A over-achiever. After earning a degree in accounting, he joined his father's firm, where he spent almost a decade working his way up the ladder. Eventually, my grandpa retired, and my dad stepped in as CEO. He always assumed I would follow in his footsteps, but I had zero interest in joining the family business. My dream had always been to play professional football, but when an injury made that impossible, I knew I wanted to do the next best thing: coach. When I told my dad that I planned to get a degree in exercise science and then teach and coach football at the college level, he lost it.

After graduating from college, I accepted a job at Reed Point University and my dad refused to speak to me for months. He just couldn't comprehend that being happy and fulfilled matters more to me than making millions. Now I'm the athletic director at the school and head coach of the football team. I have an epic job that I enjoy going to every day. I love seeing my athletes meet their potential. I love the smell of the turf. I love constantly learning and sharing my passion for the sport. I get that my dad had other plans for me, but he has to understand that those are his dreams and not mine.

Daisy is leaning against the counter, looking at me like she's trying to figure me out.

"So, what do you say, Daisy? We can watch *Wedding Crashers* like old times. It was always your favorite. I think you made me watch that stupid movie 40 times with you."

"Yeah, I guess I did," she says with a laugh. "I was a little obsessed."

"I'm pretty sure I still know every word thanks to you."

She blinks, her big eyes locked on mine. "I didn't think you were paying attention."

I've gotten used to Daisy having her guard up around me, to the constant sarcastic banter between us, but right now the vulnerable look in her eyes makes the air in the room feel thick. My mouth turns cottony. It's so hard not to tell her that I see everything when it comes to her. I always have. But that would be dangerous and would only lead to trouble.

I crack my neck from side to side in an effort to relax. "So, did you break up with Doctor Dud?" My vision practically blurs red when I think about the two of them together.

"Why do you do that?"

Daisy crosses her arms over her chest and my eyes drop, admiring her tits. I've seen her in a bathing suit, and I know they're each a perfect handful.

"Do what?"

"You always have something snarky to say about the guys I date."

She's right, I do. And that isn't going to change. I feel completely out of control at just the thought of her with some guy who doesn't deserve her. It kills me. But I'm not stupid enough to tell her that.

"What are you talking about? I couldn't care less who you date, Daisy."

Her gaze is locked on mine. Her head tilts to the right like it always does when she's pissed off at me for something. It's cute as hell but I hate being the guy to upset her. She just makes me crazy and trading jabs with her is the only way I've been able to keep her at an arm's length.

"You realize that you are full of shit, right? You've been this way since high school and I'm sick of it. You're not my brother, Tuck, so stop acting like it."

The tension between us kicks up, the air in the room growing thicker by the second. Daisy keeps her eyes pinned on mine for another beat before she huffs out a breath, grabs her keys from the counter and turns to walk away. I slip my fingers around her wrist before she's able to get far. "Where are you going? We aren't finished talking."

My fingertips press into the warm, soft skin at her wrist and my breath catches in response to the feel of her. Daisy's cheeks are flushed pink; I notice the sharp rise and fall of her chest. My fingers stay firmly around her wrist, in no rush to let go.

I know it's careless. I shouldn't be this close to her. The attraction I feel for Daisy has always been a problem. When I'm around her, I can't think straight.

I let go of her wrist and she blinks, then glowers at me. "You aren't the boss of me, Tucker, so explain to me why you seem to think you are? Scott is a nice guy. It's not like I have a track record of dating dog killers."

"Setting aside the fact that he's about as interesting as a rock, you work with the guy," I growl. "I thought you were smarter than that, Daisy."

Anger flashes in Daisy's eyes as she lifts her chin to hold my gaze. "How many times do I have to say this, Tucker? It is none of your business who I date. And frankly, dating advice from you—the king of meaningless sex with dumbbells— is laughable. I'll date whoever I want, and you don't get a say in it. I mean it, Tucker. You aren't my dad, you aren't my brother, and you do not get a say in who I choose to be with."

Rage flows through my veins like boiling water, just like it always does when I think about her with another guy. There was a time I thought *I'd* be that guy, but that dream got shut down pretty quick. I shove that thought from my mind, knowing it's pointless to think about the past. I can't stop the jealousy that flares up in me when I think about the fact that some other guy is going to get to take that place in Daisy's life. I'm not naïve enough to think that she will be single forever. It's only a matter of time before someone wins her heart. I'm surprised it hasn't happened yet.

I take a step closer to her, erasing some of the distance she's put between us. "I am the closest thing you'll ever have to a brother, and that's not changing, so you might as well get used to it."

A look of irritation crosses her face. "Why are you even here, Tucker? It's not like you to turn down one of your groupies. What's going on with you?"

Good question. Since when do I turn down a date? Since *never*. I am always in the mood for sex. I love women, and if I'm being honest, women love me. So why am I standing here arguing with Daisy in my parents' kitchen on a Saturday night instead of hooking up with the girl I met at the bar? I could have taken that girl home and fucked her for three hours straight without a care in the world. No strings, no complaints. She would have left with a smile, and I'd have fallen asleep in my empty bed. A perfect fucking Saturday night.

Except...

Daisy Carter is in my head.

I've been lusting over her all day, like a starved animal with a ribeye steak in its sights.

I have learnt to push my feelings for her as deep down as I can, but lately that's been harder to do. Every time I see her, the urge to touch her, kiss her, feel her lips on mine again is getting harder to control. It feels like I need every ounce of willpower I have not to put my hands on her.

"I came over to swim some laps. Cool down." I clear my throat. "And I wasn't expecting to see you here. But it figures my parents would have you doing their favors."

I see some of the fight leave Daisy as her expression softens. My parents have always treated Daisy as if she's their own kid. In their eyes, she can do no wrong whereas I can't seem to do anything right. I've gotten used to it. Daisy can be their precious "bonus" daughter for all I care. I'm over it.

That's what I keep telling myself, anyways.

"It's not a big deal, Tucker. It's Saturday. I'm sure they just thought you were busy. They probably thought you were coaching a game."

Silence settles in the air between us.

"Tuck?"

"Yeah?"

"I'm sorry your dad is the way he is with you."

I shrug. "You know him. He thinks he's better than me, and he likes to remind me of that every chance he gets."

Daisy tucks a few strands of her thick, honey-brown hair behind her ear. "You know it's him and not you. You're the best coach they've ever had at Reed Point University. He's just too stuck on you refusing to take over his firm to notice."

"That is the nicest thing you've said to me in a long time," I tell her, surprised at the shift in her tone.

"Well, it's true," she says with a soft smile. She looks at me a moment longer, then pushes off from the counter. "Okay, I'd better get going."

With that, Daisy turns and walks toward the door.

I watch her leave, wishing with everything in me that she'd stay.

FOUR

GUARANTEED TO BE A GOOD TIME

Daisy

Ten more minutes.

This day has felt like an eternity. Beside me, the clinic's newest employee, Hazel, hums quietly as she enters a patient's data into the system. What she lacks in experience she makes up for in enthusiasm—I swear even the sound of her typing is cheerful. I am trying my best to be upbeat and welcoming, but I'm pretty sure I'm failing miserably.

My run-in with Tucker on Saturday has me very distracted. On top of that, I still need to deal with the situation with Scott. I've managed to avoid him all day, pretending to take a call when he arrived this morning and at one point even ducking behind a corner when I saw him on his way out for lunch.

I feel like a coward—I know I need to gather the courage and tell him we're better off as friends, but I hate the idea of hurting him. I'm a people pleaser and always have been. But I have to just deal with it. Maybe tomorrow, though? That sounds like a good plan to me.

I quickly tidy my desk, getting ready to make a break for it, when I hear Scott's voice directly behind me.

"Can I talk to you for a second, Daisy?"

I wince. *Shit.* I paste a grin on my face and follow him as he motions to an examination room across the hall, a knot forming in my stomach.

You can do this.

Make it short and sweet.

Get it over with.

But before I have a chance to open my mouth, he takes a step toward me with an awkward smile. "I had a really great time with you the other night. I wondered if you would like to go out again this Friday?"

He exhales and the tension in his shoulders seems to relax. My muscles, on the other hand, are pulled tighter than the strings on a guitar. "Scott, I—"

"Why don't I pick you up at seven?" he says, before I can finish. "We can go to Catch 21."

I find the courage to scrape out the words. "I think we need to rethink things, Scott. It's just that I work for you, and I think it's best that we keep our relationship professional."

His eyebrows pull together in surprise.

"I thought you had a good time. It felt like you were feeling it as much as I was."

"I like you," I say gently. "But I'm not the girl for you. I hope you can understand."

"I see." He looks up at the ceiling. "I guess I misread things."

I hate this. And I'd also like to keep this job for the next four months before I leave on my trip. "I really enjoy working for you. I hope it won't be awkward. I'm sorry."

"It's fine. Don't be sorry," Scott says, his expression softening. "It won't affect things around here. I need you. Hazel is taking longer than I hoped to get the hang of things around here. Do you think you can get her up to speed before you leave?"

I heave a sigh of relief at the change of topic. "We have a ways to go, but yes, I'll make sure of it," I answer, hoping that I sound convincing. He hired Hazel to take my place while I'm away but so far, she has spent more time fawning over Scott than she has actually working. The girl has a serious crush.

"I know you will," he says with a nod. He steps aside, motioning toward the examination room door. "See you tomorrow, Daisy. Go ahead. I'll lock up."

I say goodnight and head out, thankful to have the conversation over with. I'm looking forward to a date with my couch and some leftover Thai food. Maybe a warm bath or a walk along the beach if I can find the energy. At the apartment, I find Briar in our kitchen wearing a tight jean skirt, a black tube top, and black ankle boots. Her platinum hair is in waves around her face and her lips are painted with a shiny, pale pink gloss.

"Wow," I say, looking her up and down as I drop my purse and keys on the counter. "It's Monday night. Where are *you* going?"

"*We* are going out," she corrects me. "You have 20 minutes, and I am not taking no for an answer, so don't even bother trying. I'm starving, and I have no interest in cooking. Besides, it's Marg Monday at Cocina Caliente."

I cast a wistful glance at the couch as Briar ushers me to my bedroom, where she plucks out a selection of short dresses from my closet, tossing them on the bed. I sigh in defeat. When Briar is determined, I know I don't stand a chance.

"You can wear this," she announces, shoving a spaghetti

strap dress toward me. It's not overly dressy but also does not give off the I-put-zero-effort-into-getting-dressed vibe. "And wear your Jimmy Choo wedges. They make your legs look nine feet long."

The shoes are one of my best-ever thrift store finds, right up there with my treasured pair of perfectly fitting vintage Levi's. Briar and I go thrifting pretty regularly. It's like a treasure hunt—nothing beats the straight up euphoria I feel when I find something I truly love tucked into the racks. But I'm not in the mood for Jimmy Choos tonight.

"What's wrong with jean shorts and a T-shirt?" I ask, flopping down onto my bed.

Briar levels me with a look that lets me know she is exhausted with my excuses. When she crosses her arms over her chest, I know I'm wearing the damn dress.

"Come on, Daisy. Let's have some fun. It's just dinner. We'll eat tacos, drink two-dollar margaritas and if we're lucky, meet our future husbands."

"Fine. I'll go," I groan. It will probably be good for me to unwind a little after my uncomfortable chat with Scott.

"Good." She smiles as if she knew all along that I would cave. "I'll drive. Holler when you're ready. I'm going to send a quick text to my brother and check in on my mom while you're getting dressed."

"Say hi to him for me," I say before she winks and turns for the door.

I've known Briar since college; we met at a party in the second semester of freshman year and immediately hit it off. I admired her confidence, her over-the-top fashion, and boisterous personality. With Briar, it's guaranteed to be a good time. She's turned out to be an incredible friend too. In our sophomore year, we shared a dorm together and then after graduation, we decided to rent an apartment close to the beach.

Sadly, Briar's stepdad passed away six months ago from a heart attack and her mom has been really struggling. She lives just outside of Vancouver, British Columbia so Briar relies on phone calls and text messages to keep in contact. I know she's toyed with the idea of moving closer to her mom, but for now her brother living nearby is given Briar the peace of mind she needs.

Twenty minutes later, I join Briar in the kitchen, wearing the little black dress with the wedges, my hair pulled back into a bun at the nape of my neck.

"You clean up good," Briar says with an approving nod. She grabs her keys, and we head out. The drive to the restaurant takes six minutes—one of the perks of living in a small town. But when we push open the big, wooden door to the colorful hot spot we're told it will be a 10-minute wait.

Once we've been seated, it's another several minutes before our server arrives. "Sorry for the delay, ladies," she says apologetically as she hands us our menus and slides a basket of taco chips with salsa and guacamole into the center of the table. "It's always like this on game night. Take your time with the menu. I'll be right back."

My gaze flicks over to the bar and the giant TV playing the Rangers' game. That explains it.

"Oh good, we can watch the game," Briar says, rubbing her hands together.

"Since when do you like hockey?"

"I've always loved it."

"The game or the hot guys on skates?"

"What game?" she shrugs her shoulders reaching for a taco chip.

"Puck Bunny."

Briar's lips tip up in a mischievous smile as she pops the chip into her mouth. She shrugs, not bothering to argue the nickname. Just then her eyes land on something over my shoulder and she leans toward me conspiratorially. "Check out the table in front of the bar," she tells me, eyebrows raised. I take a quick glance in that direction and the smile falls from my face when I spot Holden, Jake Matthews, and Grayson Ford. My gaze nervously moves around the table looking for Tucker, and I exhale in relief when I can't find him.

Grayson and Jake are close friends with Tucker and Holden. While Tuck and Holden are notoriously single, the other guys have settled down. Grayson is married to Sierra, Jake's sister, who owns a bakery here in town. Jake is married to a woman named Everly and last I heard they have a baby on the way. I don't know either of them very well, but they seem like nice guys, although Jake has this serious intensity to him that always makes me feel a little off balance.

All of them are handsome, but Holden is probably the prettiest, with his perfectly styled dark hair and sea-green eyes. He's also the one that gets the most attention from the opposite sex, but I think he is officially off the market since meeting his girlfriend Aubrey last year. Holden was single for a long time—ever since his high school girlfriend broke up with him after graduation. They had been pretty serious, so that messed him up for a long time. Eventually, though, the carousel of girls vying for his attention got him out of his funk. He and Tucker are roommates and I can only imagine what has happened in their little beach house on Haven Harbor over the years. Scratch that. I don't want to imagine it. Now that Holden is with Aubrey, that leaves the title of Reed Point's most notorious bachelor to Tucker.

"Where's Tucker?" Briar asks as if reading my mind, nodding in the direction of the boys' table.

I raise a brow. "How would I know?"

"I don't know. You guys are family or whatever. I thought maybe you'd have talked to him."

"I have better things to do than keep tabs on Tucker," I huff, and it comes out sounding more defensive than I had intended.

Briar gives me an amused look, but thankfully we are interrupted by someone at the table next to us who says something about hot sauce. When my eyes lock with his, I'm momentarily at a loss for words. The guy is gorgeous.

"Daisy, the hot sauce," Briar says, coming to my rescue.

"Oh, right," I stumble. "Hot sauce. Sorry. Here you go!" I quickly grab the bottle from the table and shove it toward him.

Hot Guy smirks, then takes it from my hand, lifting his chin in a nod. "Thanks," he says. "I'll give it back. I promise."

I watch him twist the cap off the bottle with his large hands and nicely manicured fingers. *Why is that so attractive?* I've always had a weakness for guys with nice hands.

When I realize that I'm staring, I reluctantly rip my attention away from Hot Guy and his hands, which honestly deserve to have their own Only Fans page. I shove a chip in my mouth, trying to regain my composure. Clearly, I need to release some tension. When my gaze lands on Briar, her mouth falls open.

"That guy is so hot," she whispers. "Holy fucking shit... you need to make a move."

"What if he has a girlfriend?"

"What if he doesn't? Just go for it. Make eye contact and hold it. If his gaze doesn't immediately snap back to his friend, then it's a sign he's interested. Trust me, the eye lock works every time."

Briar is right. What's the worst that can happen? Well, his equally hot girlfriend could show up and interrupt my pathetic attempts at flirting. I shudder with anticipated embarrassment. It's been a *very* long time since I've even thought about picking up a guy at a bar.

"Hey, thanks," Hot Guy says from beside me, interrupting my thought spiral. I take the bottle of hot sauce from him. "With how busy this place is tonight, I thought it would be quicker if I just borrowed yours. Is it always like this on a Monday?"

"It's not. It's the hockey game. Gets people off their couches, I guess." I nod my head at the big screen. "You haven't been here before?"

"First time. Just in town for the week at a hotel conference. We're from Lake Tahoe. My name is Will, by the way," he says, then nods to the guy sitting beside him. "This is Cam. And you are…"

"Daisy. My name is Daisy… and this is Briar. It's nice to meet you."

Briar echoes the sentiment and the four of us settle into easy conversation, chatting about our jobs, the restaurant, where to find the best coffee in Reed Point. Before long, the two of them are sitting at our table and ordering us a round of drinks.

My face feels hot from the sexual tension crackling in the air between us. Looking at Will, I find myself thinking that maybe what I need is a couple of hours in bed with a hot guy. No strings. Forget the feelings. Just a good time and a release from all of the stupid thoughts I've been having about Tucker.

This guy could be the distraction I need to finally get Tucker Collins out of my system.

Will stretches his arm across the back of my chair, the tips of his fingers grazing my shoulder when he does. "We gotta get going," he says, sounding reluctant to leave. "Daisy, um... any chance I could get your number. We're in town for most of the week, maybe we could meet up for a drink? I had a good time with you tonight."

Without thinking too hard on it, I agree and watch him punch my number into his phone.

When they're gone, I turn my attention to Briar, who is staring at me with her eyes wide. "I am screaming inside for you, girl!"

"Don't get too excited. With my luck, he won't even call."

"I saw the way he was looking at you. He is going to call.

By the time I'm back home and hopping into bed, I have convinced myself that a steamy night with Will is exactly what I need. A little adventure before I leave.

But when my head hits the pillow, it's not Will who comes to mind as I drift off to sleep, but a honey-haired, sapphire-eyed football coach I've known all my life.

FIVE

NO-STRINGS SEX

Tucker

I kick my runners off at the door and walk into the house I share with Holden on Haven Harbor. I find Holden and Grayson sitting on the couch eating steaks and watching the game. Their eyes stay locked on the big screen mounted above the fireplace as a Ranger takes a shot on net and narrowly misses, ending the second period and prompting a string of curse words from Holden.

"Florida is lucky they have Luv between the pipes tonight. That should have been a damn goal."

Holden glares at the TV. "We should be up by four. They're playing like jackasses. I need another beer." He tosses the remote onto the couch before getting up and heading to the kitchen.

"Hey. Grab me one too," I say as I sink into the leather armchair.

"How'd work go? Big game this weekend, right?" Grayson asks.

"Yeah, it is," I say, dragging a hand through my hair.

The Reed Point Outlaws are riding a 4-game winning

streak, and we have a home game on Friday. The season will be over before we know it then we'll be playing for the conference championship and a spot in the national championship. We need this win. We need them all but heading out on the road with a W on the books is a confidence boost. When players lose their confidence, an entire season can go down the toilet, which is exactly what I'm trying to avoid.

"You'll get the win," Holden says as he returns to the couch, handing me a beer as he sits down. "The team's been looking great."

"Thanks, man. So, how was dinner with Jake last night? Any shenanigans to report?"

I don't miss the look that passes between the two of them.

"What happened? What did I miss?"

Holden snickers at Grayson. "He's either going to care or he's going to really fucking care."

"Oh, he's going to really fucking care all right, but he'll play it off like he couldn't care less," Grayson laughs, like I'm not sitting right here listening to their stupid conversation.

"What the fuck are you two idiots talking about? What did I miss?"

Holden finally looks at me and lets out a long exhale, as if preparing to be the bearer of bad news. It suddenly clicks who they must be talking about. They're talking about Daisy. My spine instantly stiffens.

"Seriously, man, maybe you want to finish that beer before we get into it. That vein in your neck looks like it's about to explode," Holden says.

"Just break it to him." Grayson urges.

"You do it."

"Jesus," I say. "Enough. Can someone just tell me?"

"We saw Daisy at Cocina Caliente. She was with some

guy we didn't recognize. They looked like they were really into each other."

My mouth falls open, but I close it again before I say something I might regret. "What do you mean, you don't know who the guy is?"

"Wasn't anyone from around here. None of us recognized him."

Reed Point is the size of a shoebox. Everyone knows everyone. So, whoever the guy was, odds are he's from out of town. So how the hell does Daisy know him? And how *well* does she know him? My heart pounds behind my ribcage.

"Did she go home with him?" I ask, my right foot bouncing in a steady rhythm against the hardwood.

"Dude, you need to chill," Holden cautions.

"Answer me," I warn. "Did she go home with the guy or not?"

"No. Relax, man. He left before she did." Grayson shakes his head. "Seriously Tuck, when are you going to admit you have a thing for her? Do yourself a favor and find your balls. Do something. You need to fuck the girl out of your system."

"Fuck you." Daisy is not a girl you fuck and walk away from, and I'm pissed he would even suggest it. I would never cross that line. "At least my balls are attached to my body. Sierra has yours in a fucking vice grip."

Jake's sister Sierra moved to a place here on Haven Harbor a little over a year ago, and Grayson has been batshit crazy about her since the day they met. There were a few bumps along the way for the two of them, but today they are very happily married. Gray got the girl of his dreams, and as an added bonus he gets to bug Jake mercilessly about it every chance he gets.

Grayson grins and puts his hands up. "Take it easy, Tuck. You don't have to be a dick about it. Forget it. You're not into

Daisy... whatever. But if that's the case, then stop being a cockblock. You're an overprotective ass when it comes to her."

I've had enough of this conversation. I'm hungry and I'm annoyed and I'm being an asshole. "Is there an extra steak for me?"

"Of course, it's on the grill. There's a baked potato for you too."

"Thanks," I mutter, walking toward the back deck. I stop in my tracks and turn back to Grayson. "I'm sorry. I didn't mean that. Sierra's the best. You know I'm happy for the two of you."

"We're good. I know. But I stand by what I said. You need to fuck your stepsister out of your system."

"She's not my stepsister," I groan. "She's my god-sister. There's a difference."

Sort of.

"All the more reason," Holden says with a smirk. "I'm with Gray on this one, for what it's worth. I think it would do you some good to bone her."

"Not a fucking chance."

Closing the patio door behind me, I lean against the balcony railing and drag a hand over my face. Obviously, I haven't done a very good job of hiding my feelings for Daisy. If I'm being honest, there's nothing I'd like more than to fuck Daisy's brains out.

The guys are right about one thing: I definitely need to get this girl out of my system. Just the thought of her with this other guy is enough to drive me fucking crazy. Maybe they have a point; maybe the reason I'm so hung up on her is because she's always been off limits. Maybe if we did bang, I could move on without this constant ache in my chest every time I think about her.

Or maybe it would just make me want her more.

TIPPING BACK MY RED SOLO CUP, I TAKE A LONG DRINK OF THE cold beer then wipe my mouth with the back of my hand. I'm wiped today after being up half the night tossing and turning, but I give myself a quick mental pep talk, trying to return my focus to the evening ahead. It's not as easy as it sounds. If I'm not thinking about the game the Outlaws need to win on Friday or our upcoming road trip, I'm thinking about Daisy.

If anything can stop this endless cycle of unwanted thoughts, it's tonight's party. It's one of my favorite nights of the year in Reed Point.

My gaze roves over the packed pier and the dock party that's in full swing. The dock glows with hundreds of string lights and colorful paper lanterns that sway above the crowd. It's an annual fundraiser hosted by the Reed Point Fire Hall. They throw a bash at sunset, complete with a beer garden, BBQ and a live band. The tickets sell out every year weeks in advance and there's always a mix of locals and boaters who sail in from neighboring towns, dock their boats and spend the night in the marina for the weekend.

This party is guaranteed to be a blast. I might feel like crap, but my plan is to drink enough to get over it.

As I empty my cup, my eyes land on Becca Livingstone, who's standing close to the stage where the band is warming up. When I catch her eye and smile in her direction, she whispers something to her friend and then makes her way through the crowd and directly to me.

Becca is a lot like me. And that is why I like her.

She's fun, she's straightforward and she understands no-strings sex, which makes her the perfect girl to fool around with. We've been hooking up for years and she's phenomenal between the sheets; so good she'll fuck the hell out of my cock until I've come twice in under an hour.

She's not shy, she's a giver and when we're done and we've both come, she's putting on her clothes and heading out the door. She might be just what I need to forget the brunette I can't stop thinking about.

She eats up the space between us until I can feel her warm breath against my neck.

"Hey Tuck," she murmurs.

"Hey, Bec. Having fun?"

"Of course, I am. But I bet I'll have even more fun now that you're here."

Her eyes drink me in as she moves in for a hug, and I wrap my arms tightly around her curvy figure as her ample breasts press firmly to my chest.

"You busy after this?"

"Not too busy for you," I say, watching her lips tip up in a sultry smile.

"Good," Becca purrs, going up on her toes to press a kiss to the side of my mouth. Just then I spot Daisy on the dance floor, and that's all it takes for my cock to twitch to life. I move a little to my left to get a better view. She has on a simple gray dress that stops mid-thigh and the pair of Converse sneakers that she wears almost exclusively. My dick might have been half-hard only a second ago, but now it's granite. Daisy looks incredible.

How the hell does she make a T-shirt dress look so damn hot? She's just fucking gorgeous.

It's the way she's never cared about other people's opinions of her, even when she was a teenager and would walk into stuffy events at the country club our families belonged to wearing wild, thrift store clothes while the rest of the girls were draped in brand names from head-to-toe. It's the way she's always been fearless, like when she jumped out of a plane after graduation or the time she bungee jumped off of the High Steel Bridge in Washington. It's the way she never hesitates to call me out when I'm being a dick.

Every little, spontaneous thing about Daisy Carter turns me on, and that has made my life fucking hell. Living in the same small town as Daisy, running into her when I'm out with the guys, attending family dinners together every single Sunday—and wanting her the entire time. I deserve a fucking medal for the self-restraint I have shown.

I've been so busy staring at Daisy that I didn't even notice the tall dude beside her. The one who is now putting his hand on her shoulder and leaning down to whisper something in her ear. I see red.

Who the fuck is that, and why the hell is he touching her?

I squint to get a better look at the asshole next to her. This must be the guy Grayson and Holden told me about, the one they saw with Daisy at the restaurant the other night.

Dammit to hell.

The guy looks like a douche. If he puts his hands on her one more time, he and I are going to have a talk.

"I see you found your stepsister," Holden says quietly as he appears with a drink in each hand. He passes one to me and I immediately take a long swig.

"She isn't my stepsister," I grumble, watching Daisy tilt her head back and laugh at something the prick says to her. "Is that the guy?"

"That's the one she was with at Cocina the other night," Holden says. "Honestly, they look good together."

His words are like a kick to my groin. "Shut the fuck up, Holden."

Becca laces her hand through mine, a reminder that she's still here. "Tuck, what do you say we go chill on my uncle's boat over there? I've decided I'm ready to get out of here."

She tugs gently on my hand, but my feet don't budge.

"Tuck?" she coos. "I want you so bad."

I tear my gaze away from Daisy to deal with Becca, who is staring up at me with heavy-lidded eyes. If I were to follow her right now, it would mean a wild night of sex. But I can't leave here until I find out who this guy is, and what's going on between him and Daisy.

"I'm sorry, Bec. Something's come up. I'll have to catch you later."

"You're joking, right?" she asks as I untangle my hand from hers.

"I'm not, unfortunately."

She rolls her eyes at me and stomps away, clearly pissed. With Becca gone, I return my focus to Daisy and to the guy's hand that has just moved from her shoulder down to her waist.

That is all I need to see. I chug the rest of my beer, then shove the empty cup into Holden's chest and stalk directly over to Daisy and the dickhead.

SIX

WHAT IS HE SO MAD ABOUT?

Daisy

"I'm really glad we did this," Will says, squeezing my hand.

"Me too. The dock party is one of my favorite nights of the year."

A warm breeze whips over the waves, bringing a taste of the ocean with it as Will's olive eyes meet mine. A half-moon in the sky softly illuminates the pier with the help of a few dozen string lights.

I wasn't sure what to expect, but I've been having a good time with Will so far tonight. He texted me the day after we met at Cocina Caliente, asking if he could take me out. When I mentioned the dock party, he said he was in. We decided to meet at the restaurant at the marina for dinner and then walk over to the dock party together.

We picked up our conversation where we left off the other night, getting to know each other a little more over dinner. He talked about his family, most of whom still live in San Francisco, where Will grew up. It turns out he has an adventurous side as well—he told me all about a rock-climbing trip to Yosemite he's planning for the spring, which sounds amazing. You'd have to be blind not to notice how handsome Will is, with his infectious smile and deep green eyes, but it turns out he's easy to talk to as well.

Will and I are just coming out of the beer garden when I notice a familiar figure barrelling through the crowd of partiers toward us. Tucker's hands are squeezed into tight fists at his sides as he practically pushes people out of his path.

What is he so mad about?

Will. Of course. This is textbook Tucker. He must have seen me with Will, and now he's here to insert himself into my personal life yet again. My suspicions are confirmed when he reaches us and immediately wraps a hand around my waist, dragging me toward him. My hip presses against his thigh, and I can smell the intoxicating, woodsy scent of his cologne.

"Tuck, what the hell are you doing?" I demand, trying to ignore how good it feels being this close to him.

"Is this guy bothering you?" Will asks, eyes narrowed at Tucker.

"I'm not bothering her," Tucker growls, glaring right back at him. "She's family and I need to have a word with her, if you don't mind."

Will looks from Tucker to me. "You good?"

Tucker's hand on my waist tightens. My pulse speeds even though it shouldn't. I can't remember the last time he had his hands on me like this.

I nod. "I'm good. Sorry about this."

Tucker turns me to face him, our bodies dangerously close as people party and dance all around us. Tension thickens in the salty air.

His blue irises lock on mine and my breath catches in

my throat. He's moved us a couple of feet, putting other partygoers in between us and Will.

"Who is this guy and why have I never seen him around?"

I laugh in response. "Are you serious? Not that it's any of your business, but I met him this week at Cocina Caliente and he's a really nice guy. We're having a good time—or we *were* until a minute ago," I say, feeling the heat from Tucker's body seep into mine.

His nostrils flare. "In other words, you know absolutely nothing about this guy. For all you know he could be a—"

"Drop it, Tucker!" I spit out, anger getting the best of me. "You don't get a say. Not now. Not ever."

"I will always get a say, Daisy." He moves even closer so that there is only an inch of space between us. Arousal erupts in my center, and I exhale a breath, trying to keep it at bay. "What if he hurt you? Jesus, Daisy... you don't know this guy. You're drinking. You should know better than this."

Rage rushes through me, and I straighten my spine and glare up at him. We're toe-to-toe. I watch Tucker blink a couple of times before his eyes drag down my body, like he's just noticed how close we are. I jab a finger into his chest, where it connects with hard muscle, and the contact sends a shiver over my skin. "I'm not stupid, Tucker. And I've had enough of the big brother act! I am a grown woman, and I am capable of making smart decisions. I will date who I want to date. I will make my own mistakes. And you don't get a say. Leave me alone!"

Tucker scowls, and there's a noticeable tick in his jaw that matches the pulse beating on the side of his neck. Again, that spike of arousal blooms in my belly. Tuck is hot when he's angry and he is definitely mad right now. His hand wraps around the finger that I have stabbing into his ribs and heat hammers into my skin.

"Daisy—"

"No. I'm so done with this," I say, exhausted by this never-ending argument with him. My eyes sting, but I manage to keep my composure. The last thing I need is for Tucker to see me cry. "You don't listen, and I'm tired of repeating myself. Have you ever stopped to think about how these over-the-top outbursts affect me? If you weren't such a controlling ass maybe you would see that you ruin any potential relationship I might have. Any time a guy shows a little interest in me, you show up to scare him away. And for what? Just to make me miserable?"

I extract my finger from his hand with a sigh, the anger starting to drain from my body now. "Will is a good time," I tell him. "I'm not going to marry him, Tucker. I'm not looking for anything serious and neither is he. I'm leaving for Italy soon, and I just want to have some fun before I go."

Tucker's eyes go wide. "'A good time?' What is that supposed to mean?"

"It means exactly that. I'm not looking for anything serious right now. I'm not leaving a boyfriend behind while I'm gone."

"Great. So, stay away from guys all together," he says flatly. "Why do you need to have... fun?"

I shake my head in disbelief that I am having this conversation with him. "Do I really need to spell it out for you?"

"Yeah, I guess you do."

"A girl has needs, Tuck. Guys aren't the only ones."

I watch as his expression changes from confusion to shock, and when he fails to say anything, I cover my face with my hands in embarrassment. He's infuriating. I shouldn't have admitted that. I should have just walked away. I kick myself for letting him get to me yet again.

Tucker gently peels my palms from my face and then lifts my chin so that my eyes meet his. As much as I want to look away, I can't.

"You're like a sister to me, and I worry about you," he says quietly. "It would kill me if anything ever happened to you. I would pummel any guy's ass to the ground if they did anything to hurt you."

My spine stiffens. I'm like a sister to him. That is how Tucker sees me, and that is how he will always see me. I need to remember that.

"Look, I know what guys are like," Tucker continues. "They want one thing. I just don't want you to fall into that trap and get hurt."

Slowly, I pull my hands away from his, needing to put space between us. I'm tired of the mixed-up emotions I feel when I think about Tucker. I'm so tired of him having the power to wreck me. Hoping that the disappointment I feel isn't showing on my face, I turn away from him without a word. I've said enough already tonight.

I snake through the crowd, finding Will waiting for me where I left him. I don't have to turn around to feel the heat of Tucker's stare. And even after everything he just said to me, I love having his eyes on me just as much as I hate it.

Tucker

I'm a wreck.

It's been three days since the dock party, and I can't get that conversation with Daisy out of my mind.

I replay it over and over again, and I feel the same jealousy raging in me as I did that night. I couldn't control myself when I stalked over to her and demand we talk. Was it my finest moment? Not even close. But I couldn't bring myself to give a shit.

When Daisy asked why I wouldn't just leave her alone, I told her the truth: I was worried about her. I didn't want her making a mistake she would regret with some loser she barely even knows. But deep down, I know it's more than that. The truth is, I wish it was me who was holding her hand. I want to be the guy who makes her blush and giggle. Fuck, I want to be the guy who makes her come. I've imagined her big, beautiful eyes flutter shut as my mouth sucks one of her perfect tits into my mouth, the shape of her hips under my palm, and the sounds she would make when my cock slowly sunk inside of her. At this point, it's practically all I think about.

And that fact alone scares the ever-freaking shit out of me. It's getting harder and harder to ignore the illicit thoughts I keep having about Daisy. Speaking of hard, I've woken up the last three mornings with a raging hard-on. I get horny as fuck knowing that she has *needs* and wants to have some *fun* before she leaves on her trip because I keep imagining that I'm the guy who is giving her exactly what she wants.

Why *can't* it be me? I'm not looking for a relationship, and neither is Daisy. She's leaving in a few months— there would be an expiry date. As long as neither one of us caught feelings, what could go wrong? With any luck, we could share orgasms, scratch an itch, and then she could leave me in her dust when she boards her plane.

But I guess Daisy already has a guy who can do that for her. A heavy dose of jealousy and anger bubbles up inside me when I think about her with him again. The way she was looking up at him, the way his hands kept finding her. Then I think about the way I hurt her that night. I can't handle seeing Daisy upset but knowing that I was the person who made her feel that way cracked my fucking heart in two. And while she wanted to smack me, all *I* was doing was trying not to kiss her.

I shove my hands through my hair and look out my office window to the field below. Pride blooms in my chest at the sight of the green and gold banner above the scoreboard, the Outlaw logo emblazoned on the turf and the 17,000 stadium seats. It's not large compared to other U.S. college stadiums, but it's mine. I live for the glare of the stadium lights, the feeling of the manicured pitch under my feet and the loud, raucous energy of the crowd. Before our games even begin, you can hear the chants, feel the beat of the pounding drums from RPU's marching band. And when the boys hit the field, it's almost impossible to hear myself think over the roar of the fans.

This team. This school. This feeling is what I live for. There is nothing I love more on this earth.

A knock at the door pulls me from my thoughts and I turn to see our assistant coach, Jesse Workington, standing in the doorway. He's wearing the coaching staff's signature black polo with the Outlaw logo on the chest. Jesse and I go way back; we were both Outlaws long before we became coaches for the school.

I wave him in, and he joins me at the window, standing silently for a moment as he takes in the familiar view. His sandy blond hair is dishevelled, and he has a week's worth of scruff covering his jaw. I recognize the tension in his tall frame, a sure sign that he's just as wound up over this weekend's game as I am.

"I came to check in on you, coach," he says, clapping me lightly on the shoulder.

"You sure I shouldn't be checking in on you?" I respond with a sly grin.

He smiles but it doesn't quite reach his eyes. "The Vikings have been dominating this season. They aren't going to make this easy."

He isn't wrong, but we are the better team. I leave him at the window and sink into the chair behind my desk. "We didn't play our best against the Panthers last game. There were too many mistakes. Hopefully we are more focused on Friday. We need this win."

The frustration in the locker room after last week's game was palpable. Everyone is on edge, knowing the stakes and what it means if we lose the next four games. We've spent all week going over film, hashing out our strategy to win our last home game then the remaining games on the road. We need every fucking victory we can get before we end out the season.

A crease forms between Jesse's brows as he slumps into the chair across from me, like maybe he isn't so sure we can pull out the win. "I think we should call an extra practice."

"There isn't any time." I shake my head. "But let's bring them in after practice on Wednesday to review the playbook."

"Okay. Fine by me."

"How are things otherwise, at home?"

"They're fine. Caitlyn is feeling good, a little nervous but I guess that's to be expected when you're going to have a baby in less than six weeks."

"I still can't believe you're gonna be a dad."

"Some days, I can't believe it either."

Jesse married his high school girlfriend. They've been

together since senior year. He proposed to her on her 21st birthday, married her a year later. They bought a little house about a half hour drive from Reed Point. "Is she coming to the game?"

"Planning on it, God willing," he answers, looking up at the ceiling.

"It's all gonna be fine."

He nods, pushing up from the chair "I just wanted to check in with you, make sure you're good. It's going to be a crazy week."

"I'm good. Gonna finish up here and head home. You should too."

Jesse nods and heads for the door, leaving me alone with my thoughts. I scrub a hand through the stubble on my jaw, anxious. The game. The season. Daisy. The spinning cycle of thoughts immediately returns; I feel like I'm going out of my mind.

I stuff my phone in my pocket and grab my gym bag. I really should be going over the playbook, but I need to get my nerves in check first. I head straight for the locker room, where I change into a T-shirt and athletic shorts and then head for the gym.

I'm relieved to find the facility empty. Normally I enjoy running into students here, but today I just don't have the energy for small talk. I pop in my ear buds and sink down on a weight bench, The Rolling Stones playlist reminds me of my dad as always. His favorite song is *Start Me Up*.

Pain and bitterness burn in my stomach when I think about the arguments we've had over the years—none more intense than on the day I broke the news that I wouldn't be following in his footsteps. My dad was angry. My mother sat in silence. I wanted to scream at them both for not thinking I was enough, for not supporting me in following my own dreams. I wanted them to know how inadequate they had always made me feel and how tired I was of carrying that burden.

But instead, I went next door to Daisy's house, to the people who had always felt like a second family to me. There were no questions, just love and support. Daisy's mom and dad had always treated me like I was their own and some days it felt like they understood and appreciated me more than my own parents did.

Daisy grew up knowing that she was loved unconditionally. Her childhood was spent in a house that was filled with warmth and fun. Every birthday and anniversary were celebrated, every accomplishment was noticed. Meanwhile, I have spent most of my life trying to prove to my perfectionist parents that I'm not a screw-up. Ours is a deeply flawed relationship, and sometimes I wonder if that's the reason I've avoided getting serious with anyone.

Despite my disdain for relationships— the thought of being tied down to one woman gives me hives— I would do anything for Daisy. I have always felt protective of her. I've never met anyone else who I have felt this fiercely connected to. I cannot imagine a life without Daisy in it.

We were seven years old when I pushed a kid in our class for pulling her hair. We were 10 years old when I told off some twerp for trying to steal her sandwich. And we were 16 when I finally found the balls to kiss her, and it was even better than I had ever fantasized.

After the kiss, she didn't shut down or run away. She opened her eyes and stared back at me, like she was daring me to kiss her again. Her confidence was sexy as fuck, tempting me to take her up to my bedroom and take the kiss further, and damn if I didn't want to. I had spent a long time battling the lust I felt for her, and that kiss only proved the attraction wasn't one-sided.

I'll never forget the soft smile on her lips when her eyes fluttered open or the four words she said to me when we broke the kiss. *That felt so good.* The expression on her face hit me like a punch to the gut. I had never seen her look at me like that before. Instead of playing it cool and worrying about what the kiss meant to me, she admitted how it felt to her.

It is a trait of Daisy's that I loved then and still do; a real, raw vulnerability that my stupid heart has always a had a soft spot for. It still does.

I tried to forget it and move on. I fooled around with women—a lot of them—and hoped to make a genuine connection along the way. But I have never been able to shake the dream of being with Daisy.

It doesn't help that we see each other at least once a week, or that her name comes up in almost every single conversation I have with my parents. Daisy has always been so deeply intertwined with my life, but I've done my best to keep a safe distance, because depriving myself of the one thing I really want is the only option.

But since that conversation on the dock, I can't get this idea out of my head. It's crazy, but it could work. Daisy wants to have *fun* before she leaves, and I can't stomach the idea of a stranger putting his hands all over her. That is not going to fucking happen.

Maybe I can be her good time until she leaves on her trip. Better it's me than some other guy who doesn't deserve her and who won't treat her right.

Maybe it could work. But it will have to wait.

First, I have a game to win.

SEVEN

TUCKER COLLINS DETOX

Daisy

I hurriedly walk through the doors of Dream Bean café, sighing when I see the lineup of people in front of me. I join the line, checking the time on my phone because I need to get back to the clinic. But I also really need my Americano.

When I left Hazel at the office, the phones were ringing off the hook and appointments, not surprisingly, were running 15 minutes behind. I absolutely knew Hazel was in over her head, but I had already skipped lunch, and a coffee break was non-negotiable if I was going to survive the rest of the day.

I spent most of last night tossing and turning. It was Will's last night in town, so we went out for dinner and a movie. At the end of the night, I said goodbye and gave him a hug, but that was where it stopped. When I closed my apartment door, I was frustrated at how relieved I was. When I first met Will, I was pretty sure that I wanted a one-night stand with him—okay, maybe a four-night stand—but in the end, I couldn't bring myself to do it.

There were plenty of opportunities, but every time Will made a move, I could feel my body shutting down. In the moment, I couldn't explain it, but last night as I lay in bed alone staring up at the ceiling, it clicked into place. Will is missing the tattoos that are inked on Tucker's arms. He's missing the playful smirk that spreads across Tuck's face when he's teasing me. And Will definitely doesn't turn me into a quivering, crumbling mess like Tucker does every time I notice him watching me. And that's a problem. A huge one.

I've never been able to understand what happened with Tucker and I after we kissed all those years ago. I was pretty sure I loved him back then. So much so, I would have done anything to be with him. That night, I had gone to bed feeling a high that set my soul ablaze. I replayed the kiss over and over in my mind, remembering the look in his eyes and how it made me feel. I was sure he liked it as much as I did. I *felt* it. At least, I thought I did. But what a stupid girl I was. The next day Tucker told me it was a mistake, said that we were friends and nothing more. He didn't want me. It felt like a curse, knowing what it felt like to have his hands on me, his mouth, then to be told I could never feel that way again. I was crushed for a very long time. I'm not sure I ever got over the sting of his rejection.

I built that kiss into something that it wasn't, and all these years later, I continue to allow him to take up way too much space in my mind.

Somewhere around 1 a.m., I decided it had to end. I would stuff every salacious thought I've ever had about Tucker into the darkest, deepest trenches of my brain. To do that, I need space. No more private chats at parties, no more Sunday dinners with him and his family. I'm on a

Tucker Collins detox until I know without a doubt that I can be in the same room as him and not be turned on by his charm.

But first, coffee. A lot of it. I inch forward in line, trying not to think about the chaos that is probably unfolding at the clinic right now. The door opens behind me, and I turn to see—

You have *got* to be kidding me.

Tucker.

The universe has a really awful sense of humor sometimes. *Damn it*, I mumble under my breath.

"Daisy."

He has a way of saying those two syllables like a love note.

He's wearing a short-sleeved Outlaws polo, and his team baseball hat is pulled low on his forehead. I let my eyes roam over the tattoos on both of his arms, the ones I can see so clearly when I close my eyes.

Tucker joins the line behind me, the scent of leather and soap filling my nostrils. It's masculine, strong. Uniquely him.

Stop it, Daisy. I remind myself that I'm still mad at him after the stunt he pulled at the dock party. And I've officially started my detox.

"Tuck." I scowl before turning my back to him, taking another step forward in line.

"I know you're mad at me. Let me buy you a coffee. Think of it as a peace offering."

I cross my arms over my chest, giving him a view of my back. My annoyance deepens. "I'm absolutely mad at you. And I don't need you to buy me anything."

"If this is about the dock party, I'm not going to apologize for worrying about you."

I clench my jaw and ignore him, praying the person in front of me would hurry along with their order.

"Fine. I'm sorry," he says.

"Sorry for what?" I ask, wanting to hear him say it.

"Really, Dais? 'I'm sorry' isn't enough?"

"No."

"Okay, fine," he grumbles, taking a step forward so that he's standing right next to me, forcing me to look up at him. "I'm sorry for acting like you can't take care of yourself."

"And?" My voice softens just a little.

Tucker arches an eyebrow. "And I'm sorry for interfering with your love life."

"Great. Don't do it again."

He gives me a small nod, and for once, Tuck actually looks remorseful. I can't help feeling victorious; maybe I finally did get through to him this time.

"I'll still buy you that coffee to make it up to you. What'll it be? Your usual Americano?" he asks, throwing an arm around my shoulders and hauling me into his side. It takes an effort to peel his muscular arm from my body, but enjoying the heat of Tucker's skin is definitely not part of my detox.

"Tall, please." With my body now a safe distance from his, I relax a little.

"Have time to drink it here?" He waves a hand toward an empty table near the window.

"I need to get back to the clinic."

"Come on. What would 10 minutes matter?"

"A lot."

He gives me a disappointed look before turning his attention to the guy at the counter. After he gives him our order, we walk over to the counter to wait for our drinks.

Tucker seems noticeably stressed. He anxiously checks

his phone, then scrubs a hand though his thick hair and over the back of his neck. My gaze lands again on the ink on his arms. I shouldn't like his tattoos as much as I do. I remember sitting at family dinners, my eyes searching his forearms for his latest tat, wanting to ask him about each one.

I force myself to look away, mentally shaking the thought from my mind. I will not look at Tucker that way again. Ever.

"Busy day at the clinic?"

"Very." In all the years I have worked there, I have never felt this overwhelmed. At one point this morning I had two phones going, a lineup of three patients waiting to be checked in and a 5-year-old who had vomited on the waiting room carpet. Hazel, of course, was nowhere to be found. I'm assuming she was wherever Scott was.

But as stressed as I am, Tucker looks worse. His eyes are tired, lacking their usual intensity.

"Are you okay?"

He shrugs nonchalantly. "Yeah, I'm fine."

I've known him long enough to know he's lying. "Are you gonna make me drag it out of you?"

"Drag what out of me?"

"Whatever it is that's eating at you."

"Just a big game tonight. I guess I'm wound a little tight."

"It's going to be great, Tucker. The Outlaws play their best ball under pressure. And they've got a great coach," I add.

"That they do," he says with a smirk, that playful spark returning to his eyes. It hits me square in my chest, but I refuse to get sucked in by him.

"Get over yourself." I roll my eyes at him as I shove my phone in my back pocket.

"So, are you coming?"

"Where?"

"To the game tonight."

Normally I wouldn't hesitate, but I'm not sure going to cheer on Tuck's team fits with my self-imposed Tucker Collins detox. Faking a headache might be the better idea.

"I'd like to, but I have a list a mile long of things I need to get to."

"Daisy—"

"The groceries aren't going to buy themselves," I deadpan, crossing my arms over my chest.

He tilts his head at me pointedly, eyebrows raised. Something about the way he looks at me feels so familiar, like we have shared a moment like this a thousand times before. No matter what has happened between us, no matter what else is going on in our lives, Tucker and I know each other almost as well as we know ourselves. He pushes my buttons, and I allow him to get under my skin. It's what we do. But underneath all of that, we are a constant in one another's lives.

He waits for me to say something, not breaking eye contact. Wordlessly, I stare back until he caves and breaks the silence.

"It's a big game, Dais. I really hope you'll be there. But if not, then I'll see you when I pick you up for dinner on Sunday."

Just then, the barista calls Tucker's name, placing our drinks on the bar. He picks them up and turns to me, his eyes catching mine as he smiles. It's not forced or awkward. It's the smile I remember from when we were kids that assured me, we were okay.

I smile back as I reach for the cup in his hand, and his fingers brush against mine as I take it. My skin tingles at the contact. He pauses, his eyes dropping down to my lips before returning to my eyes.

Neither of us move. This can't be happening. He isn't going to kiss me in the middle of the coffee shop. Or is he? My heart drops to my stomach.

Tucker reaches out and softly places his hand on my forearm. "Daisy."

The years since that kiss seem to unravel and I am back on that day, on his parents' couch, when I was just a girl, and he was everything I ever wanted.

I'm not sure which of us breaks eye contact, but I manage to speak first. "I think I should go," I say quietly. I watch Tucker's hand fall from my forearm and pretend I'm not affected by the loss of his touch. I yank my purse up onto my shoulder, dismissing the pesky flutter in my belly. I need to get out of here before I give into temptation and break my pact with myself.

"I'll see ya," I say in a hurry.

"I'll leave tickets for you and your parents at will call," he calls as I slip out the door.

Then I'm walking away from him. I need air. I need to breathe. I need to be as far away from his damn blue eyes as possible.

THE STADIUM IS PACKED WITH OUTLAW FANS WEARING GREEN and gold. The excitement coursing through the air so thick tonight it's palpable, the whole place is buzzing with anticipation. I join the rest of the fans who are on their feet cheering wildly as the team files out of the tunnel one by one, followed by Tucker and the rest of the coaching staff.

My heart bottoms out when I notice the tension in his

jaw, the focus in his eyes, the undeniable love he has for the game written all over his face. At Dream Bean this afternoon, his need to win was evident but tonight as he stalks to his position on the sidelines, there's no mistaking just how badly he wants it.

It doesn't surprise me. I know Tucker better than anyone. Coaching is his life, and he will do everything he needs to do to make sure the Outlaws take this victory. So far, he's done a damn good job; the team leads the state in points and are the favorite to win the conference championships.

The burst of pride I feel for my friend is so strong it nearly brings tears to my eyes. I've always loved coming out to support our football team, but never more than when Tuck took the job as their head coach.

My plans to stay at home tonight went awry when my mom called and mentioned that Tucker had left tickets for us at will call. I tried to squirm my way out of it, but she pushed, and I relented. My parents are just back from their vacation, and it's been a couple of weeks since I've seen them. My detox would have to wait one more day.

So, thanks to Tucker, we are sitting in the third row behind the team. We have our own little cheering squad: me, Briar, my parents and my Aunt Daisy and Uncle Mark.

I'd been relieved when my dad told me that Uncle Mark would be at tonight's game. It isn't often that Tucker's dad makes the effort to show up and support him. But this is a huge game; it seems like the whole town is in attendance tonight.

"I'm so nervous, I can hardly stand it," my mom says, leaning into me so I can hear her over the roar of the crowd.

"You and every other Outlaws fan," I reply, my own

nerves twisting a knot in the pit of my stomach. "How's Aunt Daisy doing?"

I lean forward to look over at Tucker's mom, who's wearing an Outlaws jersey with her wide-legged linen pants and silver Gucci loafers. She always looks perfectly polished. Her light brown hair is styled in a long bob at her shoulders and the diamond choker that Uncle Mark gave her for their 20th wedding anniversary is around her neck.

I remember that night. My family had joined the Collins' for a two-week vacation in Hawaii. Uncle Mark paid for everyone to go to a fancy restaurant for dinner to celebrate the milestone and Aunt Daisy's jaw had dropped when she opened the jewelry box.

Things with Tucker were still normal then; we swam in the ocean together during the day, walked down the boardwalk for shaved ice after dinner. At night, he and I would sneak out of our hotel rooms to swim in the dark. We'd only drag ourselves out of the pool when we started shivering, or when we were caught by a security guard. I wonder if Tucker remembers that trip.

We hadn't kissed yet. That would happen six months later, but we both came up with endless excuses to touch one another. Tucker was my first crush, and even all these years later, no one else has even come close to making me feel the way he does.

"It's nice to see her supporting Tucker," Mom says, looking at Aunt Daisy. "He'll appreciate it. Your Uncle Mark, on the other hand, looks like he'd rather eat glass than be here. Stubborn ass."

I roll my eyes before returning my gaze to Tucker, tracing every curve of his beautiful face. I have memorized every line. After tonight, Operation Detox resumes, so I figure it's okay to get my fill in now.

"I wish he'd ease up on him," I say to Mom, shaking my head. "Stop being so serious all the time."

"I wish he would too, my darling. But it's just his nature. It's part of the reason he's so successful."

Maybe my mom is right, but I'd be willing to bet Uncle Mark would be happier if he spent more time laughing and less time being so stressed about everything. Will he ever realize that he got it all wrong with Tucker? Will he ever just let his son make his own choices and live his own life?

The game passes in a nail-biting blur, and by the fourth quarter, the Outlaws are leading the Kodiaks 13-10. Both teams have played their hearts out tonight, but Tuck's team almost has it. Their only job now is to defend our lead and hold them off for a few more minutes.

The whole place erupts as the clock runs down. Fans are on their feet, cheering, waving flags as our quarterback looks for his receiver then sends the ball soaring high over the field.

I steal a quick glance at Tucker, who is standing impassively, eyes locked on the field as he adjusts his baseball cap on his head.

With my heart beating wildly in my chest, I will the ball to land straight into the arms of our wide receiver. "Come on," I murmur to myself, saying a silent prayer, positive I'm not the only one talking to God in the stadium right now. And when he catches the ball and heads straight for the end zone, the cheers of the crowd are deafening.

Touchdown.

We still have a field goal to kick, but it doesn't matter. The Outlaws win.

He did it! Of course he did. Tears of joy prick at the back of my eyelids as I watch Tucker do what he was born to do.

On the sideline, he throws a fist in the air as the assistant coach, Jesse, tackles him from the side.

Briar throws her arms around my neck, and then both of us are jumping up and down. My mom joins us in a group hug, followed by high fives from my dad and my aunt. We are all here for Tucker. We always will be.

I look to the field to find Tucker standing in the middle of a throng of people, staring up at me. The moment our gazes lock, his eyes wrinkle at the corners and his thousand-watt smile spreads across his face. On a normal day, Tucker is handsome. But *this* Tucker—joyful and filled with pride—is magnetic.

I smile back and we stare at each other in silence for a moment, the sounds of the crowd slipping away, until Jesse tugs at his arm and points him in the direction of a local reporter.

Tucker turns away and a rush of breath escapes my lungs. This is *bad*. I gather my jacket and bag, returning my attention to Briar and my parents. I need to get out of this stadium and away from Tucker. I need to go home and forget all about the way he just looked at me.

I take one last look at the field, my heart racing when I spot Tucker walking across the turf toward the tunnel. Butterflies erupt in my belly. How has he always managed to make me feel this way?

His stride is confident, but relaxed. It's so Tucker. Just as he's about to disappear into the tunnel, he turns back toward the stands, searching the crowd until his eyes find mine. A ghost of a smile touches his lips and then he's gone, off to the locker room to celebrate with the team.

And all I can think is, *I wish.*

I wish it didn't have to be this way. I wish things with

Tucker could have been different. I wish this didn't feel like a goodbye.

EIGHT

AWKWARD FAMILY DINNERS

Daisy

I started my day with a renewed commitment and calm energy. A five-mile run along White Harbor beach, followed by a croissant and an Americano on my porch while I scrolled through Airbnbs in Rome. After that, I showered, taking time to blow dry my hair as I listened to a podcast. It felt like I could breathe for the first time in weeks. I had officially started my detox yesterday morning, muting Tucker's socials—not that he ever posted much of anything on them anyway— and focusing my energy on trip planning. The sooner I started this withdrawal, the sooner I'd be over him.

And the sooner I could move on with my life.

I emerge from the bathroom to find Briar in the kitchen unloading the dishwasher.

"Hey, wanna hit the pickleball courts this afternoon?" I ask, opening a cupboard door and taking the stack of plates from her hands.

"I wish, but I can't," she says. "I bit the bullet and bought myself a plane ticket to Vancouver this morning. I leave in a few weeks, and today is the only day I have to do some shopping. I want to get my mom a few things before I leave."

"Briar, that's great. I'm glad you're going. It will do you some good to see her."

"Yeah," she agrees, putting the last of the coffee mugs away. I slip onto one of the bar stools lining the counter, and she wipes her hands and then takes the seat across from me.

"How long are you gone for?"

"A week," she sighs. "I need to be back for work. I have a performance review." Briar works in sales and marketing for a huge food company that is famous for its cheese. "I wish I could have stayed a little longer."

"You'll make the most of it. I know you," I say, looking at my best friend. "Have you told your mom?"

"That I'm coming?" she asks. I nod. "I'm going to call her now before I go to the mall."

"She's going to be so happy."

"Yeah, that's the plan."

Briar pins me with an inquisitive look. "So... what's the deal with you and Tucker?"

"There is no deal," I tell her.

"It sure looked like there was something going on with the two of you. You couldn't take your eyes off each other."

"What are you talking about?"

"You know exactly what I'm talking about. After the game Friday night, he looked like he wanted to celebrate with you... in his bed... horizontally." My stomach torpedoes to the tips of my toes remembering his eyes on mine. I'm surprised that Briar noticed, I thought maybe that moment between Tucker and I had been all in my head.

"It's not like that. It was nothing." I spin the ring on my index finger, not entirely comfortable at the turn this conversation has taken.

Briar huffs out a laugh. "Do you really believe that?"

I slide off my stool and walk toward the cupboard for a glass. "Uh huh. He was excited at the win. We were all excited! His family was there. Hell, my family is his family. He was probably looking at all of us."

"Whatever you say."

I turn the tap on, allowing the water to run cold before filling my glass.

"But... how would you feel if he *did* want something more with you?"

I take a sip as her question tumbles around in my brain.

How would I feel? I'm not sure how to answer that. I can admit to the undeniable attraction I've always felt for Tucker, but anything beyond that—anything resembling a relationship—is hard to imagine.

Her question feels too big.

"He doesn't." When it comes to Tucker, the only thing I'm sure of right now is that I need space so that I can stop having these feelings for him. "Besides, we're family. It just seems wrong."

I've never told anyone about our kiss, not even Briar. I've kept that secret close to my chest for over 10 years and because of that it feels as if that brief moment belongs to me and Tucker only. Our secret. I have no delusions about what it meant, but every time I think about his lips on mine, I smile. There's no way I could ever forget it.

Briar's expression softens as if she knows there's more to it than what I've told her. "For what it's worth, babe, I think you'd be playing with fire with that one. You're looking for love. A ring and a white picket fence. The whole deal. Maybe not right this second, but that's the path you want to be on. Tucker seems like the type who would rather set himself on fire than commit to one woman. Why waste your time? Imagine if you did sleep with him and then realized it was a mistake. Family dinners would get awkward real fast." She stretches out the word *real*.

She's right, of course. The rational part of my brain knows this, but there's another part that gets excited at the thought of having Tucker's arms wrapped around me, his naked body pressed against mine, him buried deep inside of me. But sleeping with Uncle Mark and Aunt Daisy's son would be a surefire way to complicate our family dynamic.

"Daisy, are you okay?" Briar cocks her head at me, looking concerned.

I inhale, bringing myself back to the present and to my best friend. "Yeah, I'm fine. I think I'll go get some groceries. The fridge is looking pretty sad."

"Okay," she says. "If you're sure. I'll be in my room. I'm going to call my mom."

I open the fridge to survey its contents, making a mental note of what I need to get. It's Sunday, so maybe I'll stop by the farmer's market and pick up some fresh produce and bread before hitting up Whole Foods. I'm closing the refrigerator door when I hear a knock at the apartment door.

I swing the door open to find ocean-blue eyes staring back at me. *Tucker*. I'm speechless. *What is he doing here?*

I am not prepared to see him. Especially when he looks like that. God, he looks good. His tall frame fills the doorway. He's wearing a gray Henley and a pair of jeans, his chiselled jaw covered in dark stubble.

"Don't look so happy to see me."

I stay where I am, careful not to give him an opening to come into my apartment. "Tucker, what are you doing here?"

"I told you I'd pick you up for dinner."

"You what?"

He stares back at me as if I've lost my ever-loving mind, with the hint of a smirk that causes an annoying spark of arousal deep in my belly. "When did you say that?"

He gives me an exasperated look. "I told you at Dream Bean. I guess you were too busy hating my guts for it to register."

Not picking up on my cue, he smiles as he squeezes past me and walks into the living room. I shut the door behind him and immediately feel the charge in the air. The room gets smaller, the air thicker, and I find myself wishing Briar would walk out of her bedroom to break the tension.

He stalks toward my couch, shifting the two mismatched throw pillows over before taking a seat.

"What are you doing?" I ask.

"Waiting."

"For what?"

"For you to get changed so we can go to Mom's for dinner," he says before grabbing a book off my coffee table. It's a National Geographic travel book that I found in this cute thrift store in Cape May. I had to have it when I flipped through its pages and saw the stunning photos of ancient towns nestled into Italian hillsides, narrow canyons carved into bright red sandstone, golden temples perched on lush, green mountains. I wanted to see it all.

I went to South America right after graduation, it was one of those Contiki tours. It was the first trip I took without my parents, and I had the time of my life. That was the trip that sparked my need to travel the world.

"Well, don't get too comfy," I tell him, crossing my arms over my chest. "I'm not going for dinner. I told my parents I'm sick."

Tucker gives me a look. "You don't look sick."

"I'm not."

"Then why would you tell them that?"

"I'm busy and I'm tired and I don't feel like going," I lie with a shrug, hoping he will stop asking questions and get the hell out of here.

His ocean-blue eyes meet mine and he fixes me with a calm, steady gaze. "I want you to come with me."

Something in the way he says it knocks the wind out of me. My response is barely audible. "Why?"

He exhales a deep breath, then looks down at the book in his lap before returning his gaze to me. "Because they like you. They'll talk to you and ignore me. I need that tonight."

"Your parents like you too, Tuck."

"Daisy," he says with a sigh, "With the road trip coming up and the end of the season, I'm too anxious to deal with my dad tonight." My chest aches at the hurt in his voice. "When you're around, it's just... easier."

Tucker is normally stoic. He shies away from emotion or opening himself up, so this admission is important. "Okay. I'm going to go get dressed," I nod my head in the direction of my bedroom. "I won't be long."

I watch the tension in his shoulders release, and I know I've made the right decision. I close my bedroom door behind me and sit down on the edge of my bed, taking a moment to gather my thoughts. This is the opposite of what I promised myself. I had vowed to keep a safe distance from Tucker, but this just feels different.

He needs me.

I quickly change into a vintage skirt, tank top, and a light sweater that falls off one shoulder and twist my hair into a messy bun at the nape of my neck, then join Tucker back in the living room. He's on the couch where I left him, still flipping through my travel book.

"Do you ever think about traveling?" I ask. The Collins'

vacationed often when Tuck was growing up, but as far as I know he hasn't gone anywhere on his own, beyond the occasional golf or fishing trip with the boys.

He flips a page of the book before responding. "I remember being envious of you when you went on that trip after graduation."

"You were? I didn't know that," I say as I sit down next to him, his knee an inch from mine. My stomach climbs into my chest as I breathe in his woodsy scent, remembering what happened the last time I was on a couch this close to him. It has been ages since that day— Tucker was just a boy with a slender frame and no facial hair— but something about this moment brings me straight back.

"There's a lot you don't know." He flips another page, looking lost in thought, and I wonder what he means. Before I have the chance to ask him, he turns to look at me.

"I want to be the guy you have fun with until you leave," he says, looking at me with sudden intensity.

Pardon me?

"What?" I must be losing my mind, because there is no way Tucker just said what I think he said.

"You heard me, Daisy."

"No, I don't think I did," I stammer. "I couldn't have heard you right."

His already dark eyes turn three shades darker. "You heard me just fine. You want to have fun before you go. You have needs and so do I. Neither of us are looking for a relationship, so it makes perfect sense," he says. "We care about each other. We can have safe, consensual sex with no strings and neither one of us gets hurt."

"You must be out of your mind."

"Not really."

He actually thinks this is a good idea. "What are you

always saying? I'm like a sister to you, right? You really think I'm the right person to be having sex with? Have you thought about our parents? They would lose their ever-loving minds."

"They never have to find out," he says. "And it's not like we're related. We grew up together, yes. As friends. So, we wouldn't be doing anything wrong."

Technically, he's right, but he knows as well as I do that we were raised like siblings. The two of us have always been seen and treated as family.

He raises a brow as if he doesn't understand why I'm hesitating. My heart thuds in my chest and I am hyper-aware of the place where our knees are still touching. Are we really having this conversation? I feel like I'm in a fever dream.

"Why do you need me for sex?" I ask in an incredulous tone. "You have every girl in Reed Point wanting a turn with you."

He cocks his head instead of responding to my question. "I want you to think about it, Daisy. It's not such a bad idea. I'm a better option than some guy you just met. You know me; you don't know anything about that other dude."

"He left."

Tucker's eyes narrow. "What do you mean, he left?"

"Will. The guy you saw me with at the dock party. He was only here on business. I knew he was leaving from the start." Which made him the perfect guy to enjoy for a little while. "And no, I didn't, before you ask. I couldn't bring myself to sleep with him. It didn't feel right."

As soon as I say it, I know it was a bad idea to admit to Tucker that something stopped me from going all the way with Will. It was only two days ago that I vowed to forget all about Tucker Collins, and now here we are, casually discussing a friends with benefits scenario. What is happening?

"Why?" he asks, refusing to let it go.

"Why what?"

"Why couldn't you sleep with him?"

My mouth goes dry as a bone as tension simmers in the air between us. Part of me wants to spill my guts, to tell him everything. But I can't do it, so instead I just say, "I wasn't attracted to him."

I release a slow breath and force my racing heart to relax. When Tucker speaks next, his voice is low and laced with heat that wraps itself around my chest.

"Then I have one more question... are you attracted to me?"

NINE

FRIENDS WITH BENEFITS

Tucker

I'm sitting next to Daisy on her couch, a little too close, the question I just asked her a little too raw. But I need to know her answer, and my body buzzes in anticipation as I wait for her response.

I'm close enough to her to see the blush that creeps over her cheeks, the rise and fall of her chest; I hear the slight hitch in her breathing.

Finally, her lips part, an answer on the tip of her tongue. "You're a good-looking guy, Tuck. Who wouldn't find you attractive?"

A smile curls the edges of my lips. The satisfaction her answer brings me is almost enough, but I want more. "I'm sure there has to be someone who thinks I'm not hot, but I haven't found them yet."

When Daisy rolls her eyes, I can't help but laugh.

"Seriously, Tuck. You are your own biggest fan." My laugh only gets louder as she grows more annoyed. "You're such an idiot."

"An idiot who *you* find attractive. Another reason this is going to work."

"What is going to work?"

"Friends with benefits."

She shakes her head, but her eyes don't leave mine. "You realize it's a terrible idea, right?"

I admit it's wild, but I couldn't care less. I only care about making Daisy mine, even if it's just until she leaves. The attraction I feel for her vibrates through me. I want to mold my body to hers and take her right here on this couch. "Daisy, if you need a release, I want it to be from me."

Shock flashes across her face before she quickly shakes it off. "We can't, Tucker. This is crazy. I can't sleep with you. Your parents are my aunt and uncle."

"But they're not."

"They basically are!"

I'm prepared to argue with her all night if that's what it takes. Daisy is coming up with all of the reasons we *shouldn't* do it, but I can't help but notice that she hasn't said that she doesn't want to. "We can keep it between us. And when you leave, that will be the end of it. No strings, no one gets hurt. Our parents never need to know. No one needs to know. It can be our secret. We've always had secrets."

All these years later, I still remember the rush of sneaking out of my house at night and meeting Daisy in my backyard. The high I felt at having something that was just ours. When she's quiet, I press on, sensing her hesitation starting to wear down. "I promise you won't regret it. I'll give you more orgasms than you've ever had in your life."

I realize that Daisy is not looking for a relationship, and if she was, she wouldn't be looking for one with me. We can barely have a conversation without it turning into an argument. But she *is* looking to have her needs met, and I am definitely the right guy for that job.

Her eyes widen, betraying her. She's considering it. I'm so close to getting the answer that I want. "What do you say? You set the pace," I say, but add, "But if we do this, I don't share. Nobody fucks you but me."

"And what about you? Same goes for you?"

"Same, Dais. It's just you and me. Well? What do you say?"

My stomach is a jittery mess of nerves. I want this so fucking bad, I can taste it. I want Daisy Carter. I want her all to myself. I want her to belong to me. I think I always have.

Her ice blue eyes meet mine again as she blows out a breath.

"Okay."

One word. One simple word, and my body erupts in chills. I search her gaze for any indication that just she's messing with me, but her blue eyes are clear and confident. "Okay?"

"I said okay, Tuck. Friends with benefits until I leave and then it's over."

My body relaxes as the air that was trapped in my lungs releases in one long exhale. *Fuck me.* I will finally have what I have always wanted. Daisy.

"But I have rules," she says firmly.

"Tell me."

"No flirting"

"Gotcha."

"No cuddling."

"Got it."

"No sleepovers."

"Done."

"No dates. No beach walks. No dinners, coffees, desserts..."

"Dais," I say, laughing now. "We have been best friends since the day we were born. I think we can handle getting a cup of coffee together."

"No. Those are my rules. Take them or leave them."

"Fine. It's a deal. Now it's my turn."

"Your turn to do what?"

"To tell you *my* rule."

She rolls her eyes but smiles at me. "Why do you get a rule? This whole thing was your idea."

"Exactly. My idea, so I get a rule too," I say with a smirk. "No falling in love with me, Dais."

She immediately looks exasperated—it's an expression that I have grown very familiar with—but then her face softens, and a smile tips her lips. "Fat chance, Collins. That will never happen."

"Never say never."

The pink blush of Daisy's cheeks brightens. She clears her throat, then reaches over to grab her travel book from my hands. "Okay, we should get going, we're already late," she says nervously, just as her hand accidentally grazes my fucking dick.

I bite the inside of my cheek at the feeling of Daisy's hand over the ridge of my cock, which has been half hard ever since it thought there was even a slight chance it could get inside Daisy.

"I'm so sorry," Daisy stammers, trying to grab hold of the book a second time only to graze my dick again. Her eyes widen. "Oh my god, I didn't—"

Before I have a full-blown erection, I grab the book from her now shaking hands and set it on the coffee table.

I clench my jaw and count backwards from 10 and when

that doesn't work, I imagine filing my tax return, dead kittens, a chainsaw to my nether region, trying to ease the bulge in my pants.

"Honestly, I didn't mean to—" Daisy's face is the shade of a tomato as she shakes her head, her bottom lip trapped under her teeth. She looks so fucking cute, which is doing nothing to help the situation in my briefs. This girl only needs to breathe, apparently, and I turn into a horny teenager who can't control his dick. "I... am so sorry. We should probably get to your parents' place."

"Daisy, you don't need to apologize, but I need a minute."

When she realizes why, her eyes squeeze shut in embarrassment. "Oh, god."

"Yeah."

Her eyes drop to my lap, and she swallows. Her chest sharply rises and falls. If I wasn't so sure that I infuriate her, I would think she's turned on by my arousal.

The room goes silent.

The air feels charged.

If I were to kiss her right now, it feels a lot like she would kiss me back.

"Oh. Hey, Tucker. When did you get here?"

Briar pads into the room, grabs her sneakers from the entryway and then drops into the chair across from us to put them on. The moment is lost, the tension between me and Daisy is gone, and what's left of my hard-on deflates in seconds.

THE DRIVE TO MY PARENTS' HOUSE IS PAINFULLY QUIET. IN fact, Daisy has barely said two words since we left her place, and it has me worried. Is she having second thoughts?

Her gaze is fixed out the passenger window, her hands in her lap, her fingers twisting at the opal ring she's worn on her index finger since she was a kid. Halfway into the 15-minute drive to my parents' house, I turn up the radio in an effort to drown out the silence between us. A Morgan Wallen song floats through the speakers. We pass Daisy's parents' house, and I pull through the gates of the sprawling estate where I grew up. I park behind my father's Aston Martin then round the front of the car to open Daisy's door.

She smooths her hands over her skirt before tucking a lock of hair that's fallen loose from her bun behind her ear. "We can stay as long as you want," she says softly. "If you need to get out of here, just say the word." I nod, grateful that she understands how uncomfortable I can get around my parents. With my hand at the slope of her back, I follow her inside, noticing the way her skirt clings to the curve of her hips.

Inside, Daisy's mom is the first to greet us, embracing us both as soon as we enter into the kitchen. "My babies are here," she coos, one hand on my shoulder, the other hand on Daisy's. "You both look so good. How was your day?"

"Good, Aunt Vic," I answer politely. "Nice to see you."

"Thank you, honey. It's good to see you, too," she says, reaching up to cup my jaw. Aunt Vic is always happy. She's the most upbeat and positive person I have ever met. "What a game on Friday night, Tucker. The Outlaws looked great out there. You sure made us all proud."

"Yeah, the team played well. Thank you for being there," I tell her, flicking my gaze around the kitchen. My mom is at the stove and my dad is sitting at the kitchen table drinking whiskey with my Uncle Randy.

"Daisy, love your skirt. Another one of your thrift store finds?" Aunt Victoria takes a step back to admire Daisy's ruffled skirt. She's always appreciated Daisy's eclectic style and taste in clothing. Like her daughter, she couldn't care less about name brands—a characteristic that I admire in both of them.

"It is. Thanks, Mom. I found it at the store I was telling you about downtown." Daisy smiles. "Something smells good. What are you cooking up, Aunt Daisy?"

"Chicken piccata and roast potatoes," my mom says, wiping her hands on a dish towel as she turns to face us. "Hi, you two. Come here."

She hugs me and then embraces Daisy. "There's beer and white wine in the fridge. Help yourselves. I need to get the potatoes out of the oven."

"Where's Addy and Jonathan? Are they not coming?" I ask, opening the fridge to grab a beer. I reach for the bottle of Riesling for Daisy, knowing it's what she likes. She'll drink one glass before switching to ice water with a lemon slice. After dinner she'll drink a cup of camomile tea.

"She'll be here. You know your sister, she's always late. But Jonathan can't make it."

I pour a glass of wine for Daisy and hand it to her. "Thank you," she murmurs, taking a sip. Watching Daisy swallow down the wine I poured her gives me an instant hard-on. So does the way her tongue licks a path across her bottom lip. "Take a breath, Tuck. Let's go say hi to our dads."

She nods in encouragement, her blues eyes sparkling. I'm captivated by her. My hands itch to touch her, or better yet, to carry her up to my old bedroom and act out one of my teenage fantasies with her. My heart thunders in my chest knowing I'll get to have her soon.

"Maybe I should drink three of these first," I joke, taking a swig of my beer.

"Nice try. Come on. Let's get this over with." She leads the way to the kitchen table, where my father's gaze is immediately laser focused on me.

"There he is!" Uncle Randy gets up from his chair to clap me on the shoulder. "You sure were incredible out there on Friday night. What a game. You must be feeling like a king." If I didn't happen to glance over at my dad I would have missed the clenching of his jaw, the way his eyes narrow at the compliment.

I nod at my uncle. "The team played exceptionally. I'm glad you were there to see it."

"Hi son." My dad greets me, a tone of annoyance in his voice. He pushes to stand and embraces me in a stiff hug. "Your hair is looking long, time for a cut, don't you think?"

I drag my hand through my hair, which is much shorter than the shoulder-length style I had a year ago. My father *really* despised that one. The passive aggressive comment pisses me off, and I let it get the best of me. "Not even going to congratulate me on my win, huh?" I ask, grinning despite the edge in my voice.

"Maybe I will after I say hello to my girl," he says, opening his arms wide to Daisy. For a second, I wonder what it would feel like to have a father who's proud of me, but I quickly push the thought away. I accepted a long time ago that my dad is who he is. Wishing he would change is just a waste of time.

"I'm glad you made it for dinner, honey." Dad says to Daisy. "Your aunt said you weren't feeling well."

My eyes catch Daisy's with a knowing smirk, and her cheeks pinken. "I had a headache, but I'm feeling much better."

"I'm glad. Now, maybe you can talk your friend here into getting a proper haircut? There's a girl at the club I would like to introduce him to, but he needs to clean himself up first."

I can tell he has more to say, but Daisy interrupts him.

"It's the style, Uncle Mark. It looks nice. We'll leave you two to whatever it was you were talking about," she flashes both of our fathers an easy smile. "Tuck, you were going to show me that photo on your phone." She tilts her head toward the living room, and we make our exit before either of our dads can argue.

I'm not surprised by my father's feeble matchmaking attempts. At 26 years old, my parents want me to settle down and get married and have a slew of babies. They have prospects all lined up—girls at the country club, or the daughters of my dad's golfing buddies. I'm pretty sure my dad is only interested in having grandchildren as a way to further secure his legacy.

Daisy and I walk past the kitchen to the spacious living room. A massive crystal chandelier hangs from the vaulted ceiling, and a baby grand piano sits in the corner of the room. Glass doors open to the expansive backyard and pool, the scent of freshly cut grass wafting into the large space.

"Thought I'd better get you out of there," Daisy teases. "I was worried you were about to tell your dad what bridge he could jump off."

"I was *this* close," I answer, holding my thumb and index finger an inch apart. "I don't know why he gives a shit about my hair. Add it to the list of disappointments, I guess. He's such a controlling asshole."

"You know he's wrong about you," she says quietly. "You're doing incredible things with that team. You're amazing at what you do."

I was so happy when I saw Daisy in the stands at Friday's game. I'm not sure she knows how much her support means to me.

If anyone understands the toll that my father's criticism has taken on me over the years, it's Daisy. I've developed a few different coping mechanisms, self-deprecation being a big one.

"Yeah, I am a fucking phenomenal coach, but I'd definitely make the world's shittiest accountant. I guess us athletes aren't always the sharpest tools," I say with a wink.

Daisy frowns, shaking her head. "Don't do that. I hate it when you do that. You could do anything you want and be successful at it, Tuck. But coaching is your passion, and you're lucky you discovered that early on." She pauses. "And for the record, your hair suits you. I like it."

"Are you flirting with me, Dais?"

"No."

"Come on, just admit it... you think I'm hot."

I'm grinning, but part of me wants—no, needs—to hear her say it. Daisy just rolls her eyes. "What is wrong with you? I thought agreeing to your friends-with-bennys pact would make you stop pestering me."

"Well, you thought wrong."

I glue my eyes to hers with a smirk before leaning into her, my mouth inches from her ear. "We're leaving immediately after dessert, Dais. We're making our pact official tonight, before you can back out on me."

"What makes you think I'm going to back out?" she replies. "You should know me by now. It's been... what... 26 years?"

"Careful, or I'll drag you upstairs with me right now." She cocks her head to the side, levelling me with a look that seems like a challenge. "I swear to god, babe, I'll do it and after I'm done with you, you'll be begging me for more tonight."

Just then, the front door swings open and my sister Addy hurries into the living room looking frazzled.

"Hey, so sorry I'm late." She's dressed in all black, with large gold hoops and her curly hair pulled back in a ponytail. "I had to drive Jonathan to the airport."

Jonathan is in tech sales and often travels for work. It's a crazy schedule, but Addy seems to have gotten used to it in the two years since they tied the knot.

"What did I miss?" She slips an arm around my waist and gives me a quick squeeze as a hello.

"Just dad being an ass."

Daisy gives me a *be-nice* look, but my sister ignores me.

"And you, we need to talk. I heard you went on a date with Dr. Dickens! I want every dirty detail."

I force myself to bite my tongue. I know nothing happened between Daisy and Dr. Dick, but the thought of her with another guy still makes me want to punch a wall. Thankfully, my mom interrupts the conversation when she announces that dinner is ready.

We take our seats at the table in the dining room off the veranda outside, Daisy to my left, her parents and my sister across from us and my mom and dad at either end. We sit next to the sliding glass doors, a trellis of bougainvillea, my mother's favorite flower, just beyond the glass. There are two salads and platters of chicken, potatoes, and green beans in the middle of the table. It's enough food to feed three more families. My mom is a great cook, and she's always happiest when she is feeding the people she loves.

"How's the trip planning, Daisy? Do you have everything booked?" my mom asks as she scoops some beans onto her plate.

"I have some of my stays booked so far, but I'm still figuring out the route I want to take and the places I want to visit. Three months seems like a long time, but there's so much I want to see."

I don't like thinking about Daisy being so far away for so long. There are too many variables. She could get hurt. She could meet someone, fall in love and never come back to Reed Point.

"That's fantastic," my mom says, pouring herself a glass of wine. "You are going to have such a wonderful time."

"It's so important to see the world," my dad adds. "I wish Tucker had the same adventurous spirit as you. My work has given me the opportunity to travel a lot, but Tucker hasn't ever shown an interest. Probably one of the reasons he settled on teaching."

I grip my fork with enough force to snap it in two. "I didn't settle on anything. It was my choice to go into teaching."

He sighs like I'm being a petulant child. "And make a quarter of what you would have made if you worked for me."

"And be miserable," I snap back, immediately embarrassed at my outburst. My aunt tries to move us past the tension that has settled heavily over the table, complimenting my mom on the chicken and then turning to make small talk with Addy. I feel Daisy's hand slide discreetly over my thigh, a gentle show of support and a reminder not to engage with my dad's bullshit.

"Mrs. Whittaker was in last week," Daisy says interrupting the tension in the room, smiling at her mom. She has always been a natural at making conversation, and putting people at ease, and I know that's what she's trying to do now. "She said to tell you hello, Mom."

"Oh, that was nice of her. How is she doing?"

"She looks great for 85. Her kids are throwing her a birthday party this weekend. They've invited 50 people."

"Isn't that sweet of them."

"Did I see her at the game on Friday?" Daisy's mom takes a spoonful of potatoes before passing them to me.

Daisy nods. "She hasn't missed an RPU game in years. I think she's your number one fan, Tucker."

If I didn't know my father as well as I do, I might have missed the tick in his jaw. It's his tell that he's annoyed, and his next comment confirms it. "I will never understand why people seem to find college football so entertaining."

"Oh, honey. You may not be into football, but I would say that most of the country is," my mom tells him gently, doing her part to make her guests feel comfortable.

My father apparently doesn't give a shit who's uncomfortable, though, because he doesn't let it go. "Grown men throwing a ball around a field doesn't seem that exciting to me."

"Excuse me," I grit my teeth, pushing my chair back. I'm seeing red, my pulse thumping under my skin. Realizing that I need to get away from my dad before I say something I regret, I leave the table and head into the kitchen.

I'm so tired of his bullshit. I show up every Sunday for my mom, but sometimes I don't know how much longer I can do this.

I should have known tonight was going to be a disaster. Over the years, I have learned that my dad hates to see me succeed in a job he feels is beneath a Collins. I think he's been waiting for me to fail at it, or to hate it and be forced to admit to him that I made a mistake. Fat fucking chance.

Anger is radiating off me when Daisy finds me at the kitchen counter, pouring myself a glass of whiskey. "Make it two," she says, and I grab a second glass from the cabinet and pour her a shot.

I slide the glass along the island counter to her and we both knock back the amber liquor.

"Your dad can be a real asshole sometimes."

"I'm aware," I say, slamming the shot glass down on the counter.

"I told him as much when I got up from the table."

"You didn't have to do that," I say, feeling terrible that I somehow dragged her into this bullshit.

"Of course I did. You would have done it for me." I nod, knowing without a doubt that she's right. "I have your back, Tuck. Always will."

I raise my eyes to meet Daisy's and find her looking back at me with the same sincerity and care that she has shown me all my life. I want to explain to her what she means to me, but I'm afraid that if I try, I will screw it up. Instead, I reach for her hand and pull her out of the kitchen and down the hall to my father's office where I lock the door behind us.

In a moment of weakness or maybe it's pure lust, my hands cup either side of her face, taking in her pink cheeks and the heavy rise and fall of her chest.

I want her. Need her. Crave her.

And I can't wait another second.

TEN

ALL APPENDAGES ARE INTACT AND IN EXCELLENT WORKING CONDITION

Daisy

Tucker takes a step closer, our mouths now only inches apart, and I am brought straight back to the bittersweet moment that I have never quite been able to erase from my mind. The way he took my face in his hands, the way my heart rate skyrocketed when he leaned in closer. I remember what it feels like when he pressed his lips to mine and how badly I wanted it.

Tucker's gaze falls to my lips, and I know he's remembering that day too.

My heart is thumping so hard in my chest that it almost hurts. It's been 10 years, but I still remember that kiss like it was yesterday. And now my entire body is trembling with an intense need to feel that way again. I am hungry to have his lips on mine, greedy to ease the ache that I haven't been able to figure out how to ease.

Finally, Tucker's mouth descends on mine, and I feel lightheaded. With skill, his mouth moves over mine, and he groans into the kiss. The feel of his lips is perfection. It feels right. The kiss is laced with hunger and desperation, and it's everything I have ever wanted it to be. My hands move to his chest, where I flatten my palms over his pecs, savoring the feel of hard muscle.

Tucker is kissing me like he's waited 10 years to kiss me again. He's kissing me like there's nothing in the world that makes more sense, like he couldn't have waited another second to have his mouth on mine.

He sucks on my bottom lip before pulling back and looking at me with an intensity I've never seen before. It's like he's seeing me—really *seeing* me and what we could be — for the first time, but then his eyes darken and his mouth crashes to mine again. There's nothing gentle about the kiss, and when his tongue sweeps over the seam of my lips asking for entry, I give it to him.

His tongue strokes against mine, over and over like he can't get enough. His lips are soft, but his mouth is controlling, possessive. I am kissing the boy I had a crush on and the man I didn't think I could ever have. Everything around us fades away.

I tell myself to remember every second of this kiss, every flick of his tongue, but when he backs me up against the door, I can feel his thickening erection pressing against my abdomen and my brain short circuits. *He's hard for me. For me. I made Tucker hard.*

Needing more, my hands move to his hips before sliding around to the curve of his back, eventually slipping under the hem of his T-shirt. His skin feels so soft and warm, and I remember every one of those summer days when I was forced to look at Tucker in his swim shorts and wonder what his skin would feel like. Now that I know, I never want to stop touching him.

A wave of goosebumps washes over me as I remember what Tucker said to me earlier... *We're leaving after dessert,*

Dais. We're making our pact official tonight, before you can back out on me.

My need for him only intensifies at the thought. My hands grip his flesh while my tongue strokes the inside of his mouth, leaving no corner untouched. The kiss is frenzied and frantic and Tucker groans, his erection trapped between our bodies as he pushes me harder against the door of his father's office.

It feels wrong to be kissing Tucker in here of all places but there's no way I can stop. I've been dreaming about this kiss for a decade.

His hand moves from my hair and then he's massaging my breast over the cotton of my tank top. My head tips back and I feel my nipple pebble under his touch. I breathe hard, squirming my pelvis into his thigh, searching for some much-needed relief.

"Jesus, Daisy," he growls against my neck as his hand squeezes my breast then pinches my nipple through the thin cotton of my shirt. He sucks hard on the sensitive flesh of my neck, earning him a moan and most likely leaving me a mark. The thought shoots a lightning bolt of arousal straight between my thighs. Just the thought of being marked by Tucker is a fantasy come true.

"You taste so fucking good." He drags his nose along the column of my neck until my eyes are on his, those blue eyes searching mine for a silent beat. It's long enough for the two of us to be brought back to the present, our hold on one another loosening as we untangle from each other and take a step apart.

Biting my lip, I can't help the laugh that escapes me. "Your dad would lose his mind if he knew what we just did in here."

"Worth it," he smirks.

Bringing my hand to the spot on my neck where his lips just were. I move my fingertips over the sensitive flesh and Tucker looks at me sheepishly. "You gave me a hickey, didn't you?"

"Maybe," he says, smiling now.

"Tucker, what I am supposed to do now? We need to go back downstairs and finish dinner."

His eyes trail down my neck and then over every inch of my body before he reaches to the nape of my neck and frees my hair from the elastic band, gently shaking it loose with his fingertips.

"What are you doing?"

He drags my hair over one shoulder. "I'm making sure I'm the only one in this house who knows what we just did in this room." With that, Tucker leans forward, pressing one last soft kiss to my mouth, making me dizzy, before he unlocks the office door. "After you, rebel."

The sound of my old nickname falling from his lips sends a million butterflies fluttering in my belly. I'm senseless over just a kiss with Tucker. He has always owned a piece of my heart. He always will. What will happen when we take it further? But that's too much to think about right now. I need to get back to dinner before someone finds us in here.

Tuck unlocks the office door and pushes it open, motioning for me to lead the way. I take a deep breath and walk to the dining room, rejoining our families at the dinner table. I take my seat, hoping nobody spots the mark on my neck or hears the hammering of my heart.

Tucker and I managed to make it through dinner without incident. Lucky for us, his dad was deep into a story about a very wealthy client he landed at the firm when we sat back down so he was too busy talking about himself to bring up the fact that Tuck had stormed away from the table earlier.

I had no choice but to follow him, my feet pushing me from my chair and straight to him in the kitchen. I had just wanted to make sure he was okay, just like he's always done for me. He was there for me the day my grandma died. Again, when my parents had to put our dog down when he was old and blind and could barely walk. He ran his fingers through my hair then while I cried against his chest. I will always do whatever I can to make Tucker hurt a little less.

I finished my meal in silence, hyper-aware of the bruise on my neck. I'm not sure I heard a word of what was said at the table. Between worrying about the mark and replaying what happened in Tucker's dad's office over and over in my mind, let's just say I was very, *very* distracted. As promised, as soon as we finished dessert, Tucker was standing up and apologizing for having to leave so soon. We said our goodbyes and then made a quick exit to Tucker's truck. I slid into the passenger seat, still reeling.

This is such a bad idea. Was I delirious when I agreed to this insane plan of his? Every part of me is screaming that we are playing with fire, but still, I can't say no.

"Do you really think it's smart to travel all the way to Italy by yourself?"

Tucker's question jars me from my thoughts and with a frown, I turn in my seat to face him. "I've been crazier places. I'll be fine."

He scrapes a hand through his thick dark hair, and the muscle in his jaw fires.

"What's going on?" I search his expression to figure out what he's thinking. "What's bugging you?"

"It's just far, Daisy, and you're going to be gone a long time. Don't you get homesick?"

"Nope."

"That's it? Just 'nope?'"

There's a crease between his brows like he can't figure me out.

"I won't be gone forever. And it's not like I'm off the grid. There's email, FaceTime. I'll keep in touch with my parents," I explain, but that crease only seems to deepen. "What? Do you think it makes me heartless to leave home for so long?"

Tucker smiles casually, but the look in his eyes betrays him. "You could never be heartless. But you *are* stubborn as hell."

"Thanks, I think," I laugh. "Anyways, you're one to talk. I recall a camping trip where you stayed in that ice cold lake until your fingers were literally blue rather than just admit that you were freezing. I'm surprised you didn't lose an appendage."

"Don't worry, Dais. All appendages are intact and in excellent working condition," he says, a mischievous grin taking over his stupidly handsome face. It's enough to knock the air from my lungs.

"You are such an idiot, Tuck."

He places a hand over his heart, looking at me with mock sincerity. "Aw, Daisy. You're going to make me cry."

"You, cry? You would never." I roll my eyes. "You didn't even cry when you left the gate open, and your dog got out."

"Correction: I didn't cry in front of *you*."

"Pul-ease. You didn't even like that dog."

"And you did?" he says. "He yapped nonstop. And he shit

in the house all the time. You try stepping in dog shit with your bare foot."

The look of disgust on Tucker's face makes it clear that he is very vividly recalling the sensation. He glances over at me, and we both crack up.

Tucker has always been able to make me laugh. When we were kids, we would laugh non-stop about anything and everything. If I was having a bad day or a hard time, I could always count on Tucker to cheer me up with a stupid joke or prank; it's one of the things that I've always loved about him. He doesn't take himself too seriously. He's fun to be around.

That's one of the things I've missed the most over these past years, since our relationship became so complicated. I can't remember the last time we've laughed together like this. It makes me realize how much I've missed it.

It also makes me realize how this friends with benefits pact could very easily go wrong. I survived Tucker breaking my heart once, but there's no way in hell I'd survive it a second time.

That's why when Tucker pulls up in front of my house five minutes later, I lie to him.

"Briar just texted. She had a rough night and wants to eat ice cream and chill. Is that cool?"

Tucker frowns, then shoots me a curious look. "Yeah, yeah, that's cool. Of course." His fingers tap the leather of the steering wheel.

His hands are incredibly sexy, and even though I want nothing more than to go inside with Tucker and finish what we started in his dad's office, I know I need to take a minute and really think about what I'm getting myself into. But it still really sucks.

I'm sure Tucker sees right through me. He's known me forever. I've seen him in braces, and he knows what I looked like when I went through that awkward stage and cut my hair short and died it pink. So, I am well aware that I'm probably not fooling him.

"Thanks for the ride. Good luck on your road trip."

"Thanks. I'm going to need it. I'll call you when I get back."

Call me? The thought of Tucker wanting to check in and reconnect after returning home makes my stomach feel all fluttery. But then I remember that he's not going to be calling me because he misses me. He'll be calling because of the pact. Because he wants sex.

"It's fine, Tuck. Don't worry about it. I'm sure you're going to be busy with semi-finals coming up."

"Yeah, I probably will be. It's going to be intense. My schedule for the next month is going to be insane."

"I'm sure it will be," I manage to squeak out around the utter disappointment that I feel bubbling to the surface. I let myself get swept up in what happened between us at his parents' place tonight. Tucker made it very clear that this pact he proposed had nothing to do with a relationship or with actual feelings, but here I am already letting myself think that he cares about me. When will I learn? It feels like I've been brought right back to the day he pushed me away a decade ago. "I better go. Thanks again."

I reach for the door handle, but before I can push it open, I feel Tuck's warm hand on my wrist. "Daisy, wait."

I shift a little in my seat to face him, ready for him to tell me that he regrets the kiss in his dad's office, and it can't happen again. Just like the last time. "What is it?"

"Can I tell you something?"

I nod.

"I know you and I haven't been super close for a while, not like we used to be. And I know I haven't always been that nice to you. But I... want that to change. I miss the way things were."

He gives me a half-smile, making it so difficult to be upset with him. I wish it was easier to ignore these stupid feelings I have for him, but when he says stuff like that and looks at me the way he is, I'm powerless. I always have been. Maybe one day I'll be able to look at him without my skin erupting in goosebumps. It's a curse to love someone as much as I love Tucker and not be able to have him.

"I miss the way things used to be too."

I'm not sure why, but suddenly the energy in the truck changes. The air all around us grows thick, and Tucker's gaze has been glued to mine for what feels like minutes.

"Tucker, you're staring." The words come out breathlessly and the way they sound surprise even me. Slowly, he leans across the console, so close that his face is inches from mine.

"Daisy. Close your eyes."

"Why... what are you—"

"Close your eyes, Daisy-Cakes." His voice is low and smooth.

My eyes flutter closed and then I feel his hand slide into my hair. His fingertips grip the back of my head, and a chill runs up my spine.

"I'm going to kiss you again if you're okay with that." His voice is confident, bordering on cocky as his breath breezes over my lips.

"Kiss me," I whisper without opening my eyes. I lean over the console, a little closer to getting what I want, and that's all it takes for his mouth to find mine as a wave of lust crashes over me.

Eventually, Tucker pulls away, his hand still tangled in

my hair. "And Dais," he says as my eyes slowly open. "Next time I won't be able to stop myself from doing a lot more."

My chest heaves at the thought of being naked with Tucker, his hands on my skin, easing the ache between my thighs. Feeling the growing tension between us, I force myself to open my car door before he has my clothes off and I'm riding him in the driver's seat. I say goodbye then slip out of the truck and up the walk to my apartment.

I'm still turned on when I climb into bed and dig out my favorite toy from my nightstand to ease the sexual frustration that Tucker left me with.

ELEVEN

YOU'RE AN EIGHT AT BEST

Tucker

Our three-week road trip wrapped up with a game last night against the Cougars. We ended up winning two out of our three games— not bad for a road trip — although I still can't seem to wrap my head around the one loss. We didn't play our best. We looked tired and made rookie mistakes. But right now, I need to focus on the last game of the season.

There is no way we are going to lose the next one. I'll make sure of it. And I don't want to just win, I want to annihilate the other team. I want stats that will break every Reed Point record. I want this team to earn its way into the state's hall of fame.

I reach for my coffee, tipping it back to get every drop, then I pull up today's itinerary on my phone, double checking what time I need to be out front of the hotel to get on the bus.

I haven't slept much since we left Reed Point. My mind has been constantly racing. It's been 21 days of strategizing and reviewing plays and making sure the team is ready to hit the field. And when I haven't been doing that, I've been thinking about Daisy. She has had my mind spinning. What is she doing? Is she thinking about me? Is she having second thoughts about our pact?

I look out the hotel room window to the pool below, where some kids are taking turns jumping off the low diving board. I suddenly flashback to a day when I was about 10 years old. Daisy and I had walked through the forest behind our houses to the stream where we often ended up on hot summer days. She had on a polka dot tank top with striped shorts, her long hair was tied off her face with a big, yellow bow.

Daisy clambered down the large rocks to the streambed and I followed closely behind her, both of us slipping off our shoes to wade through the water in our bare feet. She glanced back at me to make sure I was there and just then she slipped, twisting her ankle as she fell into the cool, clear water. I remember the sound of her shriek, and the way it made my heart stop.

I was next to her in a flash, lifting her into my arms and helping her to the edge of the water. Her shorts were soaked, and her ankle was already swelling but she tried to tell me that she was fine. I knew from the way her lower lip was quivering that she wasn't.

I hated to see Daisy sad. I hated even more to see her hurt. I was barely bigger than her at that point, but I managed to get her back up the rocks and to her house. I would always take care of her. There is nothing that could ever change that.

I snap back to the present when my phone vibrates with a call from Jesse.

"Hello?" I answer, grabbing a sweatshirt from the pile of clothes on the bed and adding it to my half-packed suitcase.

"Hey, Tuck." Only two words and I know something is off with Jesse. There's an edge to his voice—fear— and right away my shoulders tense. "I'm renting a car and heading home as soon as possible. Caitlyn is in labor, and the doctors think she's going to have the baby today," he says, his voice sounding shaky.

It's not often I see Jesse's feathers ruffled. The guy thrives under pressure. We all do to some extent, it's part of the job, but Jesse is always cool as a cucumber, taking everything the game throws our way in stride.

But not today.

"I'm going with you," I say, quickly starting to stuff the rest of my things into the bag. "I'm not letting you drive. I'll meet you in the lobby in five."

"Okay, I'm not going to argue. But hurry, okay, Tuck? I need to get to Caitlyn."

I hang up and am downstairs within four minutes. I find Jesse already outside, lifting his suitcase into an Uber. He looks like hell. After I shove my stuff in the trunk, I get in the backseat with Jesse for the 15-minute ride to the nearest car rental company.

"I'm going to make some phone calls, so the team knows we're not on the bus with them going home."

"Thanks," he mutters as his fingers fly across the screen of his phone, no doubt texting Caitlyn.

"How's she doing?" I ask as I wait for our assistant athletic director to answer my call.

"She's at the hospital. She's already been admitted." He takes off his ball cap before dragging his hands through his hair.

"You'll make it in time. It's going to be fine."

"She wasn't supposed to have the baby for three more weeks. What if—"

"No what-if's, man. Everything is going to be okay."

We pull up in front of the hospital two hours later. I told Jesse we should stop at his house and pick up some clothes and toiletries, but he was in a rush to get to Caitlyn. His mother-in-law kept him updated the entire drive, and as of 10 minutes ago Caitlyn was still in labor.

"You're gonna be a dad the next time I see you," I tell him as we make the turn into the hospital parking lot. "That's some cool shit, man. Send me a pic, okay?"

I've barely stopped the truck when Jesse throws the passenger door open and hops out, calling out his thanks as he takes off running through the hospital doors.

I'm itching to get home, but first I drive to the car rental place and drop off the vehicle, and then call for an Uber back to the stadium. By the time I am pulling my suitcase up to the front door of my house, I'm wiped. I pause for a moment to take in the view of the beach across the road. I've lived here for years now, but it never gets old. I check my phone quickly, but there is still no news from Jesse.

My mind again wanders to Daisy. I wonder if she wants a family. She is so carefree, still intent on travelling the world and going on new adventures. Thinking back, she's never been one of those girls who talked about how many kids they wanted or the baby names they liked. Maybe she doesn't really see herself settling down and having children.

"Are you going to stand out here by yourself all night?"

I look up, startled by the sound of Holden's voice. "I'm coming in. I'm exhausted. Just needed a minute."

"Too tired for a beer on the porch with me and Jake?"

It's been a long day, but a beer with the guys sounds

good, so I deposit my suitcase inside and then head out to join Holden on the porch. As I'm easing into the Adirondack chair, Jake walks across the lawn from his house next door with a beer in his hand.

"Hey. Where's Grayson?" I ask.

Grayson lives next door to us with Sierra, Jake's sister. They got married last year and are expecting their first baby. It's wild when I think about how my best friends are mostly all husbands and fathers now. Jake's wife Everly is also pregnant, and they have an 8-year-old daughter, Birdie. Everly had Birdie with her ex, who is a real piece of work, but Jake loves that little girl like she's his own. The three of them moved onto Haven Harbor last year, moving into Sierra's house after she decided to move in with Grayson.

Now it's just Holden and I who have stayed strong. Holden has been with his girlfriend, Aubrey, for a while now, but I'm not sure how much longer that will last. They've been fighting like cats and dogs lately.

"Gray is probably banging Sierra's brains out," Holden jokes, unable to pass up the opportunity to rile Jake up.

"I will fuck you up if you say shit like that again," Jake says, glaring at him.

"Like I'm wrong? The walls in these old houses are pretty thin, man," Holden says, laughing.

Jake makes a move in Holden's direction, and he throws both hands up in self defense. "Okay, okay," he pleads. "I'll stop."

I shake my head then take a swig of my beer, looking out at the ocean. I wouldn't trade this view for anything.

"So, what happened on the road?"

"We won two out of three."

"Atta boy. Must feel good to be Coach Collins right now. Man, you win the Division 2 national championships, and this town just might erect a motherfucking statue of your ugly mug in the center of the town."

"Just what we need," Jake mumbles under his breath.

"Damn right, I deserve a monument. I'm a 10."

"You're an eight at best," Jake says. "A waste of stone, if you ask me."

"Good thing no one is asking."

"Hell, your dad would love that," Holden says, sitting back in his chair. "Man, I'll pay for the damn thing myself just to see the look on his face."

"Yeah, my dad would shit."

"He can fuck a coffee table," Jake says. "Everyone knows what an incredible coach you are. If he can't see it, you're better off without him."

Holden and Jake have always had my back. Holden and I have been friends since we were kids. We went to high school together and played on the same baseball team, then ended up going to the same college as well. After graduation, I needed a roommate, and Holden was the first guy I thought of. We moved into our little place on Haven Harbor and that's when we met Grayson, who lived next door. Not long after that we met Jake and the four of us have been like brothers ever since. These guys show up for me like family, without me ever having to ask.

"I gotta run," Jake says, pushing up from his chair. "Ev just texted. She has a craving for a McDonald's sundae."

"A craving?" Holden asks.

"Did you forget she's pregnant, dummy?" I mutter, checking my phone again for a message from Jesse. Still nothing.

"How can I? *Every*one is pregnant," Holden says, stretching out the word. "There's something in the water, Tuck. I wouldn't drink it."

I shake my head. I'm happy as hell for my friends, but I'm in no rush to start a family. Grayson, Jake, and Jesse are going to make phenomenal fathers.

I'd probably just fuck it up. That is, if I'm anything like my own dad.

TWELVE

DEEPEST DARKEST SECRETS

Tucker

I crack a beer in silence.

Holden is out with Aubrey and the house is eerily quiet. Haven Harbor doesn't get a lot of traffic, especially at night after the beach crowd has packed up and gone home.

I take my beer to the couch, turning on the TV, flipping through channels as I think about Jesse and his brand-new baby. Caitlyn gave birth not two hours after he arrived at the hospital—a healthy baby boy they named Noah, after Caitlyn's dad.

The three of them came home from the hospital a day later, but Jesse is taking the week off work to be with his wife and son.

My phone buzzes on the couch beside me, and I pick it up to see a text from Holden.

> Holden: Where are you, bro?

> Me: At home. Where should I be?

> Holden: If I were you, I'd be hauling ass to the Seaside lobby bar. Your girl is here, and I doubt you'd like what you see.

> Me: My girl? Wtf are you talking about?

> Holden: Daisy is here and she's getting a lot of attention. Bunch of guys... they're wasted. I'm keeping an eye on her, but Aubrey and I have to head out soon.

My jaw clenches.

> Me: Be there in ten.

> Holden: Good call.

I throw on a hoody and then head out to my truck. Ten minutes later, I'm walking into the Seaside Hotel, hoping that I look calmer than I feel. My stomach is in knots.

I swallow the ball of cotton under my tongue, wondering where Daisy is. It's been three weeks since I've seen or talked to her. Twenty-two days since I marched her into my dad's office and kissed the hell out of her up against the door. Twenty-two days since she kissed me back. And ever since then, I haven't been able to get her off my mind. I'm like a starved man. By now, I should have forgotten all about the way she felt in my arms. But I haven't.

I realize that Daisy isn't mine, and that it drives her nuts when I act overprotective of her. I know she's not interested in a relationship with me and to be honest, I'm not sure I'm the guy to give her what she needs. But the girl is in my head and knowing she's out here with a bunch of drunk guys doesn't sit well with me. I told myself a long time ago that I would take care of her, and that's what I plan on doing.

LILY MILLER

The lobby of the hotel is quiet when I arrive. I walk across the polished Italian marble floors past plush velvet armchairs and uniformed bellhops to the bar. It's dimly lit, the glow of crystal chandeliers reflected in the large mirror that runs the length of the room.

I immediately spot her. She's wearing a short blue dress, her hair half-tied back with a thick, white ribbon. She's perched on a barstool next to Briar, a martini in hand, her long legs crossed at the knee.

Holden wasn't lying. There's a group of dudes hovering around them, most of them looking really fucking intoxicated. My hands ball into fists at my side as I gauge the scene. I spot Holden sitting with Aubrey at a table several feet away and decide to check in with him before I do something I might regret.

"That didn't take you long," Holden smirks as I join them, taking the empty chair next to him with my eyes still on Daisy. "I figured you'd drop everything and bust it over here."

I frown. "Any of them put their hands on her?"

"Not yet."

Daisy hasn't noticed me yet, so I take the opportunity to stare. She's so fucking beautiful. The thin straps of her dress expose her smooth, tan shoulders. I watch her raise her drink to her lips, and the way her blue eyes sparkle as she smiles at something Briar says. She's always smiling, and I swear it's contagious. Even when I was in the worst mood, Daisy would just have to smile, and my face would mirror hers. I would instantly forget about everything else.

"So, what's your plan?" Aubrey asks.

"I'm going to let her have her fun."

"Okay," Aubrey says, eyebrows raised. "You're here as her bodyguard then?"

"It's complicated."

"That's a fucking understatement," Holden mutters.

Aubrey looks to Holden, then back to me, her interest piqued. "What's the deal with you two?"

"It's a long story. Daisy and I grew up together. I've known her forever. I just want to make sure she's not taken advantage of by some sleazebag."

Aubrey is silent for a moment before she shifts her gaze to Holden, who's reclined back into his seat, listening to me with a cocksure smile. "You could just tell her how you feel about her."

I shake my head. "It's not like that. We're friends. That's all." My stomach churns. I know there is nothing going on with Daisy and me. I'm still surprised she agreed to it, but the pact is a short-term thing. It may get her into my bed, but nothing more than that.

I watch Daisy slip off her barstool, the corner of my mouth ticking up when she ignores the guy who's trying to get her attention.

I tell myself to stay in my seat as I watch her cross the bar toward the restrooms, but it's like telling a moth to stay away from the light; I can't help myself. I'm getting up from my seat as soon as she disappears from my sight.

"Took you long enough," Holden says, smiling smugly, but I ignore him, already well on my way to see Daisy.

My adrenaline is pumping when I watch her slip into the restroom. Leaning against the wall, I feel my heart rate pick up as I wait for her, and it strikes me that I've never been this excited to see a girl.

After what feels like forever, the bathroom door swings open, and Daisy walks out. Her eyes are on her dress as she straightens the fabric at her hips, but when she looks up, the energy in the air between us crackles. I take a small step toward her as she walks closer. Then her eyes—as blue as the depths of the ocean—land on mine.

"What are you doing here?".

"Having a drink with a friend?" The moment the words fall from my lips, her expression shifts. *Got it,* her eyes say.

"I didn't realize you had gotten home from your road trip."

I flinch, knowing why her gaze feels like ice water running down my spine. I should have called her while I was away. Texted. Anything. I realized that after I got back into town, and honestly, I don't even have a good excuse for disappearing on her. When it comes to football, I just get so deep in the zone that it's hard to focus on anything else. But it doesn't mean I didn't think about her every single day.

We're silent in the dimly lit hallway for a few heartbeats, standing two feet away from each other as I scrub my hand over the scruff on my jaw.

"I'm sorry I didn't call."

"I didn't expect you to."

"Well, I'm still sorry I didn't."

She glowers. "It's fine."

I know that scowl intimately. It's the same one she wore the day I told her the kiss was a mistake and couldn't happen again.

She pushed me away after that day, and she's doing it again now.

"It's not fine. I can tell you're upset."

Her jaw hardens. "Don't flatter yourself, Tuck. I'm not some Tucker Collins groupie sitting around waiting for you to text me. We have a pact, we're not in a relationship. We don't owe each other anything."

I swallow as my chest tightens. "Do you remember when we were 16 and I kissed you?" I ask, taking one step closer to her so that we're standing toe-to-toe in the darkened hallway. I reach out and tip her chin up until our eyes meet.

Daisy closes her eyes for a moment and when they open again, I can see she's fighting something. "Never in a million years did I think you would kiss me," she says softly, like she's back in that moment all those years ago. She looks sad, or maybe it's regret. But we both stay rooted in place, her eyes locked on mine. I fight the urge to pull her into me and kiss her.

"I wanted to kiss you that whole summer. It took me months to work up the courage. It's all I could think about. I was so worried you wouldn't even kiss me back."

Her eyes widen at my confession. "I thought it meant nothing to you."

"Daisy, it was everything."

A million more words left unsaid hang in the air between us, but where do we even start? Years of distance has taken its toll on us. Daisy's walls are built so high, I'm not sure she even considers me a friend at this point.

I wonder if it hurt her as much as it hurt me when I had to push her away. I wonder if she ever really understood the reason why.

But suddenly, none of it matters. I just want a second chance. I want to try again.

"We used to swim at night."

"Yeah," she says. "We used to spend a lot of time together."

"When was the last time?"

"That I swam at night?"

I smile. "Yeah."

"With you."

Her answer surprises me. "Do you miss it?"

It's a loaded question. Maybe Daisy can tell by the look

on my face that what I really want to know is... *Do you miss me?* I want to know. No, I need to know.

"I missed it for a long time."

What does that even mean? Has she stopped thinking about all those nights we spent together? Has she moved on? Her answer has my heart emptying out onto the tile floor beneath my shoes.

Then she lifts her gaze to meet mine, and I can see that there are tears in her eyes. "Why did you push me away?" Her voice is barely a whisper. If my heart was on the floor a second ago, it's now been stomped over and broken into a million tiny pieces. I've never let myself think about how much I hurt Daisy years ago. It was easier to think that she was just mad at me. But the look in her eyes right now makes it clear that it went way beyond anger.

I never told her at the time what had happened after I left her that night because I thought that if I did, she would hate my dad. They have always been so close, and I didn't see the point in ruining their relationship too. So, I did what my dad demanded, even though it was the hardest thing I've ever had to do. And I hated him for it.

"I didn't have a choice," I tell her now, deciding on a half-truth. "If I did, I never would have stopped kissing you. I wanted you to be mine so badly."

Daisy looks at me like she's waiting for more. One tear falls down her cheek, and then another, and without thinking, I reach over and smooth them away with my thumb as her breath hitches in her throat.

"I didn't want to hurt you, Daisy. And that's exactly what I ended up doing."

"You were my best friend. And somehow, I ended up losing you over a kiss."

"A really fucking amazing kiss."

She closes her eyes, vehemently shaking her head. On instinct, I run the back of my knuckles from her wrist up to her shoulder. Is she remembering what it felt like to be 16 again, kissing me for the first time, all of the nerves and excitement?

"I thought about that kiss constantly, Daisy." My throat burns as the confession falls from my lips. "How perfect it felt. How good you tasted. I went to bed every night for months and fucking replayed that kiss in my brain." I swallow. "I've never forgotten it."

Recklessly, I take a step toward her, my hand sliding from her shoulder to her cheek. My body hums with excitement being this close to her.

"Neither have I, Tuck."

With her confession, I feel free. Daisy looks over her shoulder at the darkened, empty hallway, as if making sure that no one is watching us. Then her bottom lip drops, and her breath turns shallow and when her eyes meet mine a moment later, I swear I see desire.

My heart races behind my ribcage as I think about kissing her. My childhood best friend. But we're in a busy bar; anybody could walk by and see us. We live in a small town, and by morning half of Reed Point would be talking. Do I even care anymore?

Fuck.

My feet stay firmly where they are, my body only inches from hers. I think of our pact; making out in public places is almost certainly against the rules that we've put in place. And I realize now that sticking to those rules is going to be a lot harder than I realized. There's one rule in particular that seems almost impossible. *Don't fall in love.*

"I want to kiss you, Dais. I want to kiss you so fucking bad."

"Not here."

I don't miss how her skin erupts in goosebumps. She reaches for my hand and the moment she touches me heat crackles up my spine, a million memories of every time I've held her hand since we were kids flashing through my mind. The times she reached for me when we climbed rocks at the creek. The times we lay side-by-side at the pool, my fingertips tracing the lines on her palm until our hands eventually intertwined.

And then we're turning for the exit, her hand in mine and my heart in my throat. I swallow the knot in my throat as we hurry through the hotel lobby and out onto the street. I pull her down a quiet side street to where I parked my truck, and as soon as we get there, I spin her to face me. I reach for her, gripping her face in my hands. There isn't a moment to think about where we are or what we're doing, I just kiss her with everything in me.

She stiffens for a split second and then melts into me, her hands gripping the fabric of my shirt, both of us breathing in the kiss like it is everything we've ever wanted. Everything we ever needed.

I tell myself it's just a kiss.

I tell myself it's just a pact. No strings. No emotions.

But deep down, it feels like so much more.

I breathe her in, deepening the kiss, pulling her to me, feeling like she can never be close enough.

My pulse begins to slow, and my heart rate steadies when her hands slide up my chest to my neck. I slow down the kiss, my tongue finding hers in sensual, calculated strokes. I could kiss Daisy like this for hours.

I'm not sure how long we stay like this, kissing in the dark with the moon and the stars above us, but eventually, it ends, and my forehead is against hers.

"I have to go, Tuck," she sighs into my mouth. "Briar is going to wonder where I am."

I nod before pressing my mouth to hers one last time, still holding her tightly to me. I finally release her, taking a step back, and that little bit of space allows me to take my first deep breath since I hauled her outside.

I walk Daisy back to the hotel, my stomach tied in knots wondering how I am ever going to survive this damn pact with my heart in one piece.

I haven't even fucked her yet and I'm already in over my head.

THIRTEEN
DO YOU WANT TO TASTE IT?

Daisy

My chest aches the entire drive home.

I stare blankly out the window while Briar drives the quiet street that curves along the shore. The beach is mostly empty now, the reflection of the moon shimmering on the dark waves. It was Briar who insisted we go to the hotel bar tonight. She said she was worried about me, that I was too tense, and I needed to let loose. She was probably right. I've spent the last 22 days trying to figure out what is happening between Tucker and me. First, he kisses me, and then he just... disappears. Not a phone call. Not even a text.

I couldn't make sense of any of it. We went from barely being able to stand one another to making out in his dad's office. I'm still not over the way his lips controlled mine, the way time stopped. It was just... us. Then Tuck left on his road trip, and it felt like he pushed me away all over again. I have whiplash from the mixed signals and the back and forth of it all. It's practically all I've been able to think about. I keep reminding myself that this pact Tucker came up with is just about sex for him—I'm sure he hasn't been losing sleep over it, so why should I? So, when Briar suggested a night out, I reluctantly agreed.

The last person I expected to see there was Tucker.

Tonight left me feeling even more confused. I had to stop my jaw from hitting the floor when he admitted that he never stopped thinking about the kiss all those years ago. I assumed it meant nothing to him, so to find out that I was wrong about that made my heart expand in my chest.

But then why did he push me away?

What did Tucker mean tonight when he said that he didn't have a choice? Was it because he needed to focus on football? Or that he didn't want a girlfriend tying him down in high school? I've been wracking my brain all night and those are the only explanations I have been able to come up with. What else could it be? My entire body needs to know– but going back to that time in my life feels like pouring salt on an open wound. But for us to be able to move forward– relationship or not– we need to face our past.

"So, tell me what happened tonight." Briar finally breaks the silence in the car.

"With Tucker?"

"Obviously. I saw him drag you outside. What is going on with you two?"

I stare out at the streetlights instead of at my best friend because it feels easier. Briar has always been able to read me like a book. There's no point in lying to her, she'll be able to see right through me.

I exhale deeply, still avoiding eye contact. "We... have a pact."

I'm quiet for a full 20 seconds before I'm able to glance in her direction, and when I do, the smirk on Briar's face is enough to make me drop my head into my hands.

"What kind of pact?"

LILY MILLER

I tell Briar everything, just like I've always done since we became best friends in college. I tell her about my past with Tucker, about how we used to sneak out at night when we were kids, about the kiss in his living room, and everything that has happened since he came up with our friends-with-benefits pact.

When I'm done explaining my pact to have sex with my god-brother, I turn in my seat to face her. We've just pulled up to our apartment and Briar puts the car into park, then looks at me with wide eyes.

"That's all of it," I tell her, shaking my head at how crazy it sounds saying it out loud.

"Woah. That is a lot for even me to unpack."

"I know."

"Daisy, are you sure you've thought this through?"

I laugh, my head falling back against the headrest. "If I did, do you think I would have said yes?"

"You two have always been incredibly close."

I nod, then look down at my hands in my lap. "Tucker has always been in my life. When I think back to every big moment, he was there next to me. It really broke me when our friendship fell apart, Bri."

"It sounds like you're happy to have him back in your life."

"I am. But I just can't stop wondering what happened to make him push me away back then."

"You're going to have to ask him. Only he knows the answer to that."

I nod, knowing she is right, but with the semi-finals coming up, it will have to wait. Suddenly, headlights shine through the back window of Briar's car. When the lights turn off, we both look over our shoulders in unison to see Tucker parked behind us.

I whip my head back around. "What is he doing here?" I whisper to Briar.

"Probably wants to get started on your pact." She smirks.

I swat at her arm. "*Not* helping! What do I do?"

"Deep breaths," she says calmly. "He's still in his truck. You have time to gather your thoughts, but you better make it quick. And Daisy... follow your heart. It's never let you down before. It won't now."

I nod, then follow her advice and take a couple of long, slow breaths, trying not to freak the fuck out. Briar shuts off the engine and we both slip out of the car. "I'm going inside. I won't wait up. Call me if you need anything."

Then Tucker is by my side under the glow of a streetlamp. *Fuck*, he is beautiful. In the dim, golden light, I notice the turquoise ring around his irises, the coarse layer of scruff covering his jaw, the Roman curve of his nose.

He rakes his hand through his thick, chestnut hair, pushing a few strands back off his forehead. "Hey," he says, his hands stuffed into his pockets.

"Tucker, what are you doing here?"

He rocks back on his heels and there's a gleam in his eyes. "There's somewhere I want to take you."

"It's almost midnight. Can't it wait until tomorrow?"

"No," he responds, his lips quirking up in a smile. "Do you have to be at work tomorrow morning?"

"No, but where on earth do you want to take me at this time of the night?"

"Do you trust me?" The tone in his voice is soft. When I don't respond, his head tilts to one side. "Daisy?"

"Of course, I do."

"Then one hour, Dais. That's all I'm asking for. I promise you'll like it."

A few minutes later, I'm sitting next to Tucker in his

truck with the scent of his cologne obliterating my senses and a Sam Hunt song floating softly through the speakers. I recognize the route he's taking, heading toward the street we grew up on and our childhood homes. Considering how our relationship has changed over the last few weeks, it feels a little strange.

When he pulls his truck down the long stone driveway of his parents' place and cuts the engine, I glance at him and notice the smirk on his face.

"What are we doing here?"

"It's been a long time since you swam in the dark. I thought we should change that."

The pool. That's all it takes for my heart to riot against my chest. It has been 10 years since I last snuck out of the house to meet Tucker here. We were just kids then.

"We don't have swimsuits," I point out, my mouth as dry as cotton.

His smile widens and even in the darkness, his expression pins me in place. My stomach does a belly flop. I've known this man all my life and he has always had this effect on me.

"We don't need them. Come on, Dais." He slips out of the truck, rounds the front of it and extends a hand for me once he's opened my door.

I bite my bottom lip as I place my hand in his. He tugs me out of the truck, closing the door behind me, then he's walking us through the gate at the side of his parents' house to the backyard. That's when I realize my aunt and uncle are probably asleep inside.

"Tuck!" I say suddenly, careful to keep my voice down. "I'm not skinny dipping with your parents 20 feet away. What do we do if they wake up?"

"No need to whisper, rebel. They're not here, so you

don't have to worry… they won't be home until late tomorrow."

My heart races in my chest, but I keep my hand in his as I follow him to the backyard where he turns on the outdoor heat lamps. A million memories flood my mind of all the hours Tucker and I spent in this same swimming pool under this same midnight sky.

I stop breathing when Tucker drops my hand and lifts his T-shirt over his head, dropping it onto a lounge chair. His runners go next along with his socks, and he's standing bare-chested in front of me in nothing but a pair of jeans. Even in the darkness, I can see how much he's changed since we were kids. His shoulders are broad, pecs defined with a fine dusting of chest hair that ends at his ribs then begins again above the waist of his jeans. My eyes unabashedly roam his muscular chest, his inked arms, the grooves of his sculpted abs.

Tucker Collins is literal perfection.

"Are you coming in?" His fingers move to the button on his jeans, and it feels like I might combust right here on the pool deck. He shoves his jeans down his legs and steps out of them, leaving him in just his dark navy briefs.

My brain short circuits at how good he looks. And it's impossible for him to hide what he's packing behind the thin fabric of his boxer briefs that hug the imprint of his thick cock.

"Daisy. Are you coming?"

My nerves kick up, but somehow my answer is sure. "Yes."

"In your dress?"

My heart thumps inside my chest. I've gone skinny dipping plenty of times before, but never with Tuck. In all the years we've known each other, he's never seen me undressed before. I take a deep breath as I toe out of my shoes, then reach for the zipper of my dress with trembling hands. As I slip the straps from my shoulders, I glance at Tucker to find his eyes are glued to me. I let the straps of my dress fall slowly down my arms. My dress slides over my hips and thighs to land in a puddle at my feet, leaving me standing in front of Tucker in nothing but a strapless bra and matching lace thong. My skin pebbles as the cool night air blows over me.

"Jesus, Dais." His eyes roam greedily over my body.

And then his fingers hook into the waistband of his briefs, tugging them down his thighs until he's completely naked.

Lord, help me.

His cock is thick and heavy, proudly on display for me with neatly groomed dark hair and tight balls. I shouldn't be staring, but I can't look away. A pulse throbs between my legs when I notice his dick twitch.

"Do you want me to close my eyes?" His gaze tips to my chest.

My shaking hands reach around to my back where I find the two hooks on my bra.

"Good girl." His eyes are pinned on mine. "Go slow for me, Dais."

That's all it takes for the apex of my thighs to react in arousal. I swallow thickly and with an exhale, I unclasp my bra, the garment falling from my chest onto the deck. Tucker's gaze dips to my chest, his Adam's Apple bobbing in his throat. He makes no attempt to hide the fact that he's staring at me, and I try not to blush. When his eyes drag up my torso to meet mine, his lips are parted.

"Fucking perfect."

The pulse between my legs begins to throb at his praise.

The look of pure appreciation in Tucker's eyes is all I need to find the courage to hook my fingers into the lace at my hips and shimmy my thong down to my ankles.

Then we're both bare for one another, our eyes exploring every inch as if we're seeing each other for the first time. Because we are. As intimately as I've known Tucker, we have never seen one another without clothes.

I'm surprised that I'm not covering myself with my hands or taking off for the pool. I like the way it feels, having his eyes take in every part of me. His arousal is evident when his length begins to harden even more.

"I have never seen anything more beautiful," he says quietly, and my skin heats all over at the compliment. The rasp in his voice has my heart pumping. I have the sudden urge to run my fingertips slowly over every muscle of his torso, his inked arms, his thighs.

"I mean it, Dais. You are perfect. Come on, just like old times." Then he's turning for the pool, diving into the clear water, coming up for air in the deep end. When he surfaces, he floats on his back for a few seconds like he doesn't have a care in the world before he starts to tread water, dragging his hands through his wet hair.

"Get in here, Daisy. The water is perfect."

Walking to the shallow end of the rectangular pool, I take the three steps down, sucking in a breath when the cool water hits my stomach. Then I push off the bottom of the pool, slicing my body through the water, holding my breath for as long as the air in my lungs will take me. It feels exhilarating to be naked in the turquoise water under a vast inky sky. My muscles relax and when I break the surface, the nerves that were fluttering in my belly earlier are gone and things between Tucker and I feel like they did when we were young.

"I forgot how warm your parents keep their pool," I say, my mouth barely above the surface.

"Do you remember when I used to swim underneath you and grab your feet?" He's treading water a few feet away, his eyes on me. "You used to scream, and I'd have to pull you under so you wouldn't wake up my parents."

"It blows my mind that we never woke them up," I say, laughing at the memory. "We must have snuck out here 50 times, but we never got caught."

Tuck shrugs his shoulders. "Heavy sleepers," he says, before a mischievous smile takes over his face. Then he's diving under the water and swimming directly to me. I shriek when I feel his hand take hold of my foot.

"Tucker Collins—" I manage before he pulls me under with him.

We're laughing when we both come up for air, then he's wrapping one arm around my middle and pulling my body into his. My legs instinctively wrap around his hips while my arms snake around his neck. His free hand grips my ass to hoist me higher in his arms while my breasts press firmly into his hard pecs. We stop laughing when the hard length of his erection presses into the V of my thighs.

Arousal flares in my core at the feeling, intensifying as the tip of him bobs between my legs where I'm spread open while he treads water to keep us afloat.

"Jesus," he growls.

Then his mouth descends on mine, lips crushing together in a searing kiss.

And it is the single hottest moment of my life.

My core pulses with need. My hands hold on tight to his neck. My mind is drunk with lust as my thighs squeeze his waist like I'll never let him go.

The kiss is soul-deep, his mouth devouring mine. The

feeling of his erection nudging my entrance with nothing between us is incredibly arousing. The energy between us feels like it's hit a boiling point.

As his tongue glides against mine, his legs work to get us to the shallow end, and when his feet hit the bottom of the pool, he breaks the kiss, eyebrows pulled together like he's not quite sure this is real. It feels surreal to me too.

"Tonight, you're mine, Dais," he growls before leaning in to kiss me again. "Unless you tell me to stop, then we stop. Do you understand?"

I understand. Tucker is mine for tonight, but he'll never be mine to keep. And if this is all I will ever get, I can be fine with that.

"I'm yours tonight, Tuck. Do whatever you want with me."

His blues eyes turn green before his hand cups my jaw, then he presses a soft kiss to my lips. Will I ever get used to his mouth on mine? Whether it's a quick peck or the kind of kiss that lingers, every single time Tucker kisses me, heat rushes down my spine.

He breaks the kiss and lazily floats to the edge of the pool with a smirk on his face. I stay where I am in the crystal-clear water, staring at him.

Tuck stands so I have a view of his torso, and I greedily take in his bronzed skin and his rigid muscles. "Come here, Daisy."

I follow his command, moving closer until I'm standing in front of him. He grabs me by the hips and lifts me up onto the edge of the pool. His eyes lock on mine, pinning me in place as water drips down my body. His big hands grip my thighs, spreading me wide. My cheeks burn, hyper-aware that I'm spread open for him, and as vulnerable as it feels, I force my legs to remain that way, never breaking eye contact.

Then he runs his tongue over my seam, slow and eager, and I groan, arching my back, letting my head fall back in ecstasy.

"Is this okay?" He suddenly stops. "If it's too much, I'll stop."

I shake my head like he's crazy. "Your tongue is fucking perfect. Stop and I might die."

He chuckles at me before lowering his mouth back where I want him. "You taste so good, rebel, I could come just by eating you."

He devours me until my legs shake. One hand pinches my nipple while he sucks on my clit and when he adds a finger inside of me, I'm seconds away from falling apart.

A moan slips from my lips as I watch him pull my hips closer to his mouth. "Keep going," I murmur, watching him explore me with his tongue.

I hold on, as long as I can, until his finger inside of me curls, finding that sensitive spot. His tongue circles my clit, and that's all it takes. My orgasm crashes over me in waves and I'm screaming his name. I come hard. Tucker keeps going, doesn't stop, as pleasure rips through me until I'm sitting up and dragging his face to mine.

Our mouths take their time exploring one another as my hands cling to his shoulders. A weird emotion scratches my throat as we're holding one another. This feels safe. Touching Tucker and being intimate with him feels comfortable.

"You look so hot when you come." I kiss him and he kisses me back. "I've never tasted anything better."

He kisses me again, wrapping my thighs around his waist, lifting my sated body back into the pool. One of his hands tangles in my hair while the other palms my ass, squeezing my cheek as his length pushes at my center. His lips devour me as he walks us out of the pool, his possessive hold on me lighting a fire in my soul.

He stops in front of a pool lounger and lowers me down to my tip toes, refusing to break the kiss.

Tucker pulls back suddenly, his eyes searching mine. "Still okay, Dais? I don't want to move too fast."

The concern etched on his face is touching. The Tucker I know has always been a little cocky, a little arrogant. I'm surprised to see a different side of him.

"It's perfect," I tell him. What I really want to say is, *you're perfect, I can't get enough.* Because I want more. I want tonight to never end. I want him to own me. I want him to destroy me then put me back together one piece at a time.

I take his erection in my hand, stroking the length of his smooth, velvety skin slowly but firmly. The motion has him groaning as he somehow grows even harder in my hand. A jolt of lust knocks me square in the chest.

I can't stop stroking him. I'm mesmerized by the way he feels in my hand. Soft. Smooth. Tucker groans and his eyes squeeze shut. I've never seen anything sexier in my life.

For years, I've fantasized about touching him. Just thinking about it was enough to turn me on and oh, how it has. But nothing compares to this moment. With my eyes fastened on his, I sink to my knees.

I look up at him, my hands resting on my thighs, watching his throat flex as he swallows.

"Fucking hell, Dais. I'm going to come any second like some inexperienced teenager if you don't touch it."

I smile back at him watching his entire body shudder when I wrap my hand around his thick shaft and press a kiss to the tip.

Tucker sucks in a deep breath, every muscle in his body tightening when I begin to stroke him from base to crown.

"Feel good?"

"You know it feels good," he groans, pushing a lock of my hair behind my ear. "I'm harder than fucking granite for you and I know you can feel it."

I chuckle, not able to help that I want this to be just as good for him as it already has been for me. "Tell me what else you like. What else makes you feel good?"

"Do you want to taste it?"

His perfect lips curve up, his eyes glazed, and I realize I'm about to cross another fantasy off my list.

"I don't need you to," he says. "Your hand feels pretty fucking perfect, but I bet your mouth would feel like heaven too."

My answer is an easy one. I want to taste him. I want to know what Tucker's cock feels like in my mouth, because I have no idea how long we can keep this arrangement going.

So, I nod my head, lick my bottom lip and remind myself this is just a pact.

FOURTEEN

DID WE REALLY JUST DO THAT?

Tucker

"Open."

She is stunning, her wet hair long and dripping down her tits, her knees slightly spread and planted on the ground —for me.

I lose the ability to think as Daisy stares up at me with big blue eyes. I can't help the hitch in my breath when her lips part and she opens her mouth and her perfect, wet tongue waits eagerly for my dick.

"That's it... such a good girl for me." I grip the base of my leaking cock and run the tip over her tongue.

"Dais..." I swallow, running my hand through her hair as she gazes up at me. I've pictured her a thousand times like this—naked, sucking my cock into her mouth—but nothing compares to what's happening right now. Just the sight of her with my dick between her lips is enough to make me come.

I groan when her pretty pink lips suck on just the tip, and then she wraps her hand around the base and takes me further into her warm, wet mouth. Over and over, she slurps and sucks, hollowing her cheeks, taking me further each time with my hard-as-stone cock in her hand.

Fuck. I'm drowning in the feel of her mouth, the way her nipples have hardened, the little noises she makes like she's enjoying this just as much as I am.

My eyes roll to the back of my head when her wet, warm tongue licks a stripe from the base of me to my tip before swirling it around my crown. She works me with her hands, stroking my length. I'm impossibly hard, my breathing is labored, and I know I'm fucking close to blowing my load when my balls tighten. And as much as I would love to come in her mouth… tonight I want more.

So, I pop her off my dick, hauling her up to her feet. "You have no idea how badly I want to finish down your throat. You look so fucking hot on your knees for me." My voice is tortured. Chills erupt over my damp skin. "But Dais…fuck… what you do to me."

I need to finally know what it would feel like to sink inside of Daisy.

"I want you."

"I want you too," she says, and I swear my cock grows harder.

"You sure?"

"I'm positive."

"I don't have a condom, and I've never been with anyone without one, but fuck, do I want to with you."

Her gaze is steady as sexual tension crackles in the air between us. This wasn't my intention when I picked Daisy up at her apartment tonight, but from the moment I watched her strip out of every piece of clothing on her body, all I've been able to think about is how much I want her.

"I've never done it either, but I'm protected. I'm good without one."

My heart stops. *Fuck*. When will it stop doing that? I have never considered going without one with anyone else I've ever been with, but Daisy is different. She's my best friend. If she's okay with it, then so am I.

"I would never do anything to harm you, you gotta know that, right? You trust me?"

"Of course."

I scoop her into my arms and lie her down on the pool lounger under a heat lamp. Every cell in my body, every fiber of my being, sparks to life just from looking at her soft, creamy skin under mine as I decide how I want to take her. I've imagined it a million different ways— Daisy on her hands and knees as I take her from behind. Daisy up against a wall with her thighs wrapped around my waist riding my cock while I pump into her. But tonight, I decide I want her on her back so I can look at her. The beautiful girl who I've never been able to take my eyes off.

"Fuck, look at you. You are beautiful," I whisper into her neck. I press a kiss below her ear, her jaw and her chin before nudging her legs open with my knee, settling between her parted thighs. I'm an inch away from sinking inside her; my cock teasing her entrance, not penetrating, just toying with the wet folds between her thighs. I know that if we do this, everything changes. Our friendship. Our future. If we do this and have regrets, there will be no coming back from this.

Is it worth it?

Yes. My pulse speeds. Being with Daisy is worth the risk.

My heart beats wildly in my chest. I've wanted this— wanted *her*—for almost half of my life. This isn't just fucking. This is claiming Daisy.

My mouth moves down Daisy's body, sucking a nipple into my mouth. She writhes, back arched, her pelvis rocking into mine. Her legs wrap around my hips, sealing my body to hers as I trail kisses across her ribcage to her other nipple, sucking the stiff peak between my teeth.

"Tucker," she breathes.

My dick twitches at the sound of my name in her voice. "What do you need, Dais?"

"You."

Her entire body trembles under mine, her breaths shallow as I keep flicking my tongue against her nipple. "I'm going to fuck you, I promise."

But first I need to play with her tits. I need to take my time, two perfect handfuls that have been driving me insane all night. I lick and suck, flick and nip at the blush-colored peaks as her hands dive into my hair, gripping the short strands and tugging.

"That feels so good," she murmurs. "Your mouth, Tuck, is so good."

God, she is so fucking perfect.

Her thick hair is fanned out over the cushion, her eyes hooded, cheeks the prettiest shade of pink.

My cock is aching, begging, leaking at the tip. And I wrap my hand around the head, coating it in my precum before stroking myself until I'm slick. Then I'm notching my cock at her entrance, holding her gaze as I slowly work myself inside her.

Holy hell, she feels so good. She's tight but Daisy stretches around me to take me until she fits me perfectly. Pure ecstasy fires through my veins to my core, somehow intensifying the deeper I bury myself into her. "You feel incredible like this."

Her lips are parted, and I watch her eyes flutter closed. She makes a groaning sound that I feel straight to my cock. I close my eyes as I rock back and forth into her warm, wet heat before pressing in even deeper until my balls rub against her opening.

She makes another one of the sounds that I'm already addicted to, as her fingernails claw into my ass. I'm so fucking turned on from seeing her on her knees for me with my dick in her mouth, that I'm teetering on the edge ready to spill right now.

But I will myself to hold off my release. She writhes beneath me as I pump in and out of her in rhythmic strokes. Again and again, I glide my cock into her, every stroke taking us higher, until I can feel a warmth build at the base of my spine. It's a sign that I'm close, but I'll hold off until I can get her there first. Besides she feels too good for this to end.

My cock swollen and bare inside Daisy is better than anything I've ever felt.

I try not to think about what this means for us, about how it was crazy to think we can go through with this without crashing and burning at the end. Instead, I push the thoughts to the back of mind and allow myself to drown in the depths of Daisy Carter.

We're fucking slowly, her hand wrapped around my neck, my eyes pinned to hers. And *damn*, if this doesn't feel better than anything I've ever experienced. I shouldn't be surprised. Everything with Daisy is better than with anyone else. It always has been.

"I'm so close," she whimpers, as her breathing changes from short to fast.

"Come for me, Daisy." I beg. "Come for my cock like the good girl I know you are."

She clenches hard around my dick, mouth parted before she shatters underneath me, crying out my name. I watch her body tremble, the fluttering of her eyelashes as she struggles to keep her gaze on mine. I feel her thighs come together, squeezing my sides. I'm infatuated with it all.

Her nails dig into the flesh of my arms as she pulls my body down to hers, needing my mouth. Without hesitation, I lean into her, pressing my lips to hers, breathing in every whimper and whine that leaves her pretty mouth. Then I'm rocking back into her, rolling my hips into her warmth, fucking her in short, deep thrusts as I hold us even tighter together.

"Fuck, yes, Daisy. You take me so good." Her legs shake around me, the little noises she's making spurring me on.

And then I'm coming, spilling inside of her when I feel her walls pulsing around me. I come undone on a growl, telling her how good she feels, how perfect she fits me, until my ears start to ring, and my vision goes black.

I hold her body as close to mine as I can, my chest contracting as I press a kiss to her forehead, closing my eyes before dropping my forehead to rest against hers. When I open them, I'm jolted out of my post-sex haze. This feels intimate as fuck. I see every emotion, every desire staring back at me and every reason why this is just an arrangement. But she's the one who makes a move to separate us first.

On a sigh, I pull myself out of her body, remembering rule number one, then I collapse on the pool lounger next to her.

I remind myself this is sex only. This isn't a relationship and never will be one. I can handle this. I will not fall in love.

I breathe out a shaky exhale. Then Daisy is covering her face with her hands. "Did we really just do that?"

She peeks at me through her fingers, and I want to die at

how cute she is. "We did and it was fucking amazing. I can't wait to do it again."

"I'm glad you liked it."

"Are you kidding me, Dais? How could I not? You are incredible." I smile, reaching for her hair, pushing a few strands from her face.

"I can't believe I came twice."

"Is that a first?"

"In my life."

But the moment she catches her breath, Daisy flies from the lounger, hurrying to get her clothes. *Fuck.* I know what we're doing is supposed to be just fooling around, but damn if it doesn't sting. Does she really need to be in such a hurry to get up and get dressed? We just had sex for the first time.

My eyebrows pull together and I run my palms over my face. All sorts of fucked up emotions run through my mind as I watch her slip into her dress. How I want to hold her. Keep her close. Be the last man on this planet to ever see her naked again.

But I can't. That isn't what this is. It isn't what I truly want. I'm not a relationship kinda guy. This is just a pact. So, instead I tell her, "Those other guys didn't deserve you. And remember, rebel. No one else touches what's mine."

Daisy lips tip up in a small smile that makes my chest burn so intensely, I cover the space over my heart to try to stop it. But it's my heart that is on fire that is the problem. And I have no idea what happens next.

This is just supposed to be sex. I'm sure I'll be able to handle it.

Then why am I wondering how the fuck I'm going to keep this arrangement going without falling for my best friend?

FIFTEEN

THE POST-SEX HUG

Daisy

I need to get out of the house and out of my head. Every time I think back to last night, my stomach erupts in what feels like a million little butterflies. I had sex with Tucker. Repeat... I had sex with Tucker! And it is all I've been able to think about. I feel like I'm going insane.

It's been less than 24 hours since Tucker's hands were on me, and I'm already wondering when we can do it again. Being with him was better than any fantasy I've ever imagined; the gentle way his hands touched me, the possessiveness in the way he fucked me, and the two orgasms he gave me? They were the best orgasms of my life.

And the way his eyes locked with mine after he finished inside of me, as if I was the most beautiful thing he had ever seen—I will never forget it. Waves of heat prickle my skin. Now that I've felt him inside of me, I know once won't be enough. One night with Tucker Collins, and I'm addicted.

When it was over and he had rolled onto his side, I got up and got dressed and told him I would call an Uber to get back home. It would have been so easy to stay, but the rules are in place for a reason. No cuddling. No sleeping over.

Tucker insisted on driving me back to my apartment and he seemed disappointed when I jumped out of his truck as soon as he pulled up in front of my building. I'm sure he was hoping for a round two, but I felt like I needed some space to come to terms with what had just happened between us. I also knew I wouldn't survive the post-sex hug goodbye. The only way this is going to work is if we keep that line drawn in the sand. There's no other way.

I grab my water bottle and shove my phone into my belt bag. I'm hoping that a walk will help me clear my head. I pull my hair back into a quick ponytail and lace up my runners, then I'm heading for the door. Briar is on the couch in the living room, feet up with a bowl of pasta on her lap.

"You sure you're not hungry?" she asks. "I put the leftovers in the fridge if you want them."

"Thanks, I'll probably eat later," I say, the constant, nervous flutter in my belly leaving me with zero appetite. I haven't told her about last night yet. When she asked me about it, I told her I just needed some time.

"Okay. Well, enjoy your walk. It looks like you could use it. We'll talk when you get back?"

"Promise." I nod.

"Taking anyone with you?"

"If that's your sneaky way of asking if Tucker is coming, you'll be happy to know that he's not."

She shrugs. "I'm actually kind of invested in this whole frienemies-to-lovers story you guys have going."

I shake my head, rolling my eyes. "You read too many of those smut books, Briar."

"Got that right. All the cool girls do," she says with a snort as I open our front door. "I'll be right here on this couch when you get back and I want to hear every dirty detail."

"I can't wait," I say with an eyeroll before shutting the door behind me and heading in the direction of the beach. My walk takes me past the cafés and shops of First Street, past Bloom, my favorite flower shop, and Buttercup Bakery a little further down—their signature lemon cupcakes are to die for. Briar and I stop in there at least a couple of times a month.

Soon, I've reached the boardwalk of White Harbor Beach, the largest and busiest beach in town. White Harbor is where you'll find the crowds of tourists who flock to Reed Point each summer. Locals know to stay away, choosing quieter spots like Haven Harbor, where Tucker and Holden have their place. I will be staying far away from there tonight though, not wanting to risk running into Tucker.

I breathe in the salt from the ocean, my runners echoing off the warm concrete in the late afternoon sun. I look down the sand to the bluff a mile or so down the beach and it reminds me of him. As kids, Tucker and I would hike the bluff trails to the lighthouse at the top. We would race up the steps to see who could get up to the viewpoint the fastest, then we'd sit up there and watch the sun go down. I would rest my head on Tuck's shoulder, staring out at the purples, reds and pinks that danced along the horizon.

I haven't been back there for 10 years, but my feet take me there tonight. Before I know it, I'm at the mouth of the trail, my mind flooded with memories. I'm an only child, but I've never felt like one. Growing up, Tucker was the sibling I never had. The big brother who would have done anything for me. And he did. He watched over me, protected me. I guess that's why the loss of our friendship was so painful. It had always felt like there was an invisible tether that joined us together, but then one day it just snapped. As the years went by, I had to accept the fact that Tucker would never be part of my life again, not really. We'd see each other at family dinners, we'd be pleasant enough for our parents' sake, but we'd never be close again. But now here he is, and I feel whole again. I feel happy. And I want more.

I pick up my pace on the trail, willing myself to stop these constant thoughts of Tucker. I look around at the tall grass, the pink and purple ombre sky, the glimmering ocean below. This view will never get old. Eventually I reach the lighthouse and start climbing the stairs. When I reach the top, my heart is pounding and my head is clear.

I sit down on the stone gallery deck, my back propped up against the wall, and pull my knees into my chest. The night is unseasonably warm for the middle of fall, high sunlit clouds blanketing the coastline like an overprotective mother, waves crashing into the jagged coastline.

I'm lost in my thoughts, staring at the sailboats dotting the turquoise sea below, when a noise startles me. My gaze slices to the stairs just in time to see Tucker reach the top of the lighthouse.

"Daisy... What are you doing here?"

My eyes stay glued to Tucker as he closes the distance between us. I swallow the nervous urge to laugh. I came all the way up here to try to get Tucker out of my head, and now here he is, standing right in front of me. The universe seems to be conspiring to put this man in my path at every opportunity.

"I felt like going for a walk after work, and I guess I lost track of time." I try to appear unaffected by his presence, but even I can hear that I sound nervous and a little out of breath. Seeing him makes me want to be back in his arms, back with his warm body against mine. "What are *you* doing here?"

"Needed to clear my mind, and this place, um…I haven't been here in a long time. It's always felt special. The last time I was here I was with you."

His response throws me for a loop, and my lips tip up at the corners in a half-smile. "Wanna sit?"

"Love to."

Tucker sits down next to me, folding his long legs in front of him. Energy crackles between us, my body hyper-aware of his. The urge to nuzzle into his side like old times vibrates through me. Instead, I wrap my arms tighter around my knees, forcing myself to resist.

"How was your day?" he asks, flicking a glance my way. "Anything exciting?"

"Nope, not unless you consider a peanut M&M lodged up the nose of a 12-year-old boy exciting."

Tucker snorts. "Does that really happen?"

"Are you serious?" I look at him with raised eyebrows. "I have seen *way* worse than that. You don't wanna know."

"Do you remember that time you went face first over your handlebars? You had a goose egg on your forehead the size of a grapefruit. I thought you were going to die."

I drop my head into my knees, shaking my head. "That hurt so bad. And then you dumped your bottle of lemonade on a Kleenex and stuck it against my forehead. So, I was in pain *and* sticky."

"In my defence, the lemonade was ice-cold, and I thought it might help. I never said I was a doctor, Daisy." Tucker laughs at the memory. "You refused to cry, though."

"I didn't want you to think I was a baby. I was scared you wouldn't bike ride with me anymore if I did."

"But you had a concussion. It was a big deal. Your parents took you to the hospital."

"And you came with me," I remember with a soft smile. "You refused to stay at home."

Out of my peripheral vision I notice his eyes move from me to the view. He shifts, crossing his legs at the ankle. "I was so worried about you."

"It was just a lump."

"It looked like your brain had exploded."

We both begin to laugh, the sound bouncing off the lighthouse wall behind us. I would know the sound of Tucker's low, rumbling laugh anywhere, and hearing it tonight makes me realize how much I've missed him. He was my entire world for 16 years, and then, one day, he was gone.

"Come on, I'm starving, let's get something to eat." He nudges me gently with his elbow.

"We can't."

"Why?"

"We'd be breaking a rule."

Tucker huffs out a breath. "I'm hungry. I bet you skipped dinner and you're hungry too. It's not a date, it's just food. Last I checked, two friends eating burgers together is not against the rules."

As if to bring his argument home, my belly lets out a low grumble.

"See? You're starving." Tucker playfully slaps his hand against my knee. "Plus, I haven't had anything to eat since lunch. I'm going to get hangry any moment and then you'll be wishing you let me eat."

"Fine." I can't believe I am agreeing to this, but if Tucker isn't considering it a date, then why should I?

We hike back down the trail to the beach and then into town, making easy conversation. Tucker talks about the team and the upcoming games and then I tell him about Italy and all the places I want to see when I'm there. He's quiet after that, and I chalk it up to him being hungry. I can't help but wonder if he might miss me when I'm away. A month ago, he probably would barely have noticed. There'd be one less person at family dinner, but other than that I doubt it would have really crossed his mind. Now, though, I'm not sure how he feels about it. Things between us have changed so much.

We turn into Delila's Diner, an all-night spot that has been around forever. The place is iconic in Reed Point, popular with hungover students who come here on Sunday mornings for their six-dollar trucker special breakfast.

Tucker and I are seated near the back of the restaurant, where we slip into an avocado-green leather booth. We're lucky that we don't have to wait; Delila's is busy as always, just about every table in the 50s-inspired space is occupied.

I look at Tuck, who is sitting across from me with his ink-covered arms resting on the shiny red table. He's wearing an athletic shirt with the Outlaws logo on the chest and a backwards baseball cap. Immediately, I feel fireworks deep in my belly just from glancing at him. He's beautiful. I force myself to tear my eyes off him and focus on the menu.

"What are you going to get?" I ask, my voice shaky, trying to act like being here alone with him isn't a big fucking deal. Tucker and I have dinner with our parents every week, but I've never actually been out to a restaurant with him, just the two of us. I know it's not a date, he made that clear—but right now, it feels a lot like one.

"Probably whatever you're having," Tucker says with a grin.

"You haven't changed a bit in 10 years, have you?"

"Nope," he says with a shrug. "Why would I change now?"

I wouldn't want you to, I think to myself. It feels good being here with him like this. It feels familiar. When we were kids, Tucker and I would celebrate our birthdays together and he would always just go along with whatever birthday cake or dinner I chose. His response was always, *Whatever Daisy wants.*

I'm thankful when our waitress, a cute blonde, appears at our table to take our drink order, jolting me from my memories. "Oh, hey, Coach Collins. Big game coming up. I can't wait, the team is looking so good."

"Thanks, I appreciate that."

"The Outlaws are having quite the year thanks to you," she smiles, her green eyes drinking him in. "So, what can I get you?"

She turns to me when Tucker nods in my direction. "I'll have a cheeseburger, extra pickles, no tomato with fries and a glass of water."

"Make that two. And we'll share a chocolate milkshake." The smile that spreads across his face makes his eyes crinkle, and the effect it has is palpable.

Tucker is painfully good looking. He's built like an athlete with his lean frame, flat stomach and broad shoulders. Add to that his steel-blue eyes, his collection of tattoos and the fact that he's famous in our small town for coaching the Outlaws, and he's arguably the hottest guy in Reed Point. Our waitress certainly seems to think so.

"I'll get everything out to you right away. Your dinner won't be long." She takes our menus, brushing her shoulder against his. She's beautiful, and I'm annoyed by the wave of jealousy that roils in my belly. Tucker seems completely unaware, keeping his eyes on mine.

"Don't let our pact stop you from getting her number." It's a catty thing to say, but I can't help it. Women practically throwing themselves at Tucker brings out the spiteful side of me.

He flashes me a smart-ass smirk that heats my cheeks. The way he's looking at me is enough to flare to life the pulse that has been lingering in my core since last night. An image of Tucker, naked, flashes through my mind. I have never been with a man like him before. It was like we were the only two people left on this earth. Feral. Consuming.

"Someone's jealous," he says, reclining in his seat. Tucker knows me better than anyone. I shift on the leather seat, feeling as if he can read my mind. As if he knows every one of my secrets.

"Am not."

"Are too."

I huff out a breath, crossing my arms over my chest. I take note of the way Tucker's eyes drop to my chest. It's impossible not to think about the fact that he now knows what I look like underneath my clothes. He knows my body intimately. I move my hand to my throat, feeling suddenly like there is not enough air in this booth, in this entire diner. Tucker's eyes follow the movement, landing on the hollow at the base of my neck. It's like he notices every little thing about me. Every movement, every breath, no matter how small it is. He cocks his head, his eyes returning to mine with that sexy-as-hell smirk still on his face. "Tell me how you feel about last night."

Heat slams into my cheeks. The question throws me off guard. I'm tempted to change the subject or beeline it to the restrooms, but it's a conversation I know we should probably have. "I still can't believe we did that."

"Me neither. It was better than I ever imagined."

My eyes go wide at his words, at how forthright he is. I feel my stomach drop to the black and white checkerboard floor.

"So, you've thought about having sex with me?"

He cocks his head while I force myself to hold eye contact as I wait for his answer. He leans in closer, his voice low so that only I can hear him. "Of course I have, Dais. I've fantasized about it since we were 15 years old."

My jaw falls open, my brain running in circles at the weight of his words. Tucker Collins just admitted to wanting me. I've wondered for years if the attraction was mutual, and now I know it was.

"Is that so hard to believe?"

"A little."

His expression softens. "Why?"

"I don't know," I answer, feeling a little embarrassed. "Besides that kiss..." I pause, noticing the way his Adam's Apple bobs in his throat. "You never really looked at me like you wanted me."

"Two burgers, fries, and extra pickles," our waitress announces as she appears out of nowhere with our orders. "And I'll be right back with that milkshake."

Tucker flashes her a smile that could melt icecaps, and she bats her eyelashes in response. "Thanks very much."

When she leaves, I glance at Tucker, who's already busy dipping a French fry in ketchup. The moment between us is forgotten, so I move on as well.

"You really like ketchup."

"I do."

"What else do you like?"

"Pickles," he says, scooping one from his plate.

"I hope not together."

"My god, never."

I grin, reaching for a fry.

"How about you, Dais? What do you like?"

I tuck a lock of hair behind my ear and dip my fry into the ketchup on his plate. "Chocolate, obviously. Chocolate covered almonds, to be specific."

"No, I mean, what makes you happy?"

"Oh." I pause, thinking for a moment. "I like sunsets, *Gilmore Girls*, 90s movies, fuzzy socks. The lemon cupcakes from Buttercup Bakery—literally perfect. And anything with a daisy on it, of course." I hold up my wrist, showing him the beaded bracelet Briar gave me for my last birthday, a string of tiny white and yellow daisies.

"It doesn't take much, huh?" Tucker's eyes meet mine as he leans in for a sip of our milkshake that our waitress just slid into the middle of the table and my heart pounds just a little harder. "What else?"

He takes a bite of his burger, quiet, as he waits for me to answer.

"I like rainy days in bed watching movies. And I love it when someone plays with my hair."

"That's weird."

"That's *not* weird. It feels good. It's totally relaxing when it's done right, you feel all tingly and boneless."

He looks skeptical. "'Boneless?' You're not convincing me."

"Your loss," I say with a shrug.

He laughs as he picks up his burger. We eat in silence for a few minutes, and I can't help but think back to Tucker's admission: *I've fantasized about it since we were 15 years old.*

I tell myself to not read too much into it, but it's hard not to let my mind wander to how different everything could have been for us. What if Tucker hadn't pushed me away? What if we had let that kiss be the start of something? It could have been something great.

But so much time has passed, and now we'll never know. I look out the diner window, trying not to think about what might have been.

SIXTEEN

WHY ARE YOU GIVING ME THAT LOOK?

Tucker

Daisy is a lot of things— sweet, adventurous, easy on the eyes—but the girl is also as stubborn as they come. And trying to get her to bend against her will is just never going to happen. Which is why, after we finished dinner, I said goodnight to her at Delila's.

First, she wouldn't allow me to buy her dinner, and then she wouldn't allow me to walk her home. I argued— man, did I put up a fight—but I knew there would be no changing her mind. My guess is that she thought it would make tonight feel too much like a date if I paid for the meal or escorted her back home. God knows, she's made it clear that we need to stick to the rules. I get that she wants to stick to the pact, but does she really need to act like dating me would be worse than getting poked in the eye with a hot stick?

That's Daisy, though. The girl has always been so damn independent. She'd probably have my head if she knew the lengths I went to in high school to keep guys away from her.

She thinks I've interfered too much in her personal life over the years, but she doesn't know the half of it. I made sure every guy at Heritage High knew that Daisy Carter was off limits. And if some idiot was stupid enough to go near her, I made sure he knew I wasn't fucking around.

I always had her best interests at heart. There just wasn't a single guy worthy of dating Daisy, so why bother wasting her time?

I'm walking up the driveway to my house when Jake pulls his F-150 into his driveway next door. He parks, and Everly slowly slips out of the passenger seat before opening the rear door for her daughter Birdie. Ev waves to me, her other hand rubbing her pregnant belly, as Jake rounds the car and presses a kiss to her temple. I have never seen Jake this happy, and it is all because of Everly and Birdie.

I love the guy, but Jake has always been a bit grumpy. When us guys would get together, he'd be the one sitting in the corner complaining about the noise. Or the food. Or the company. But that all changed when he met Ev. She had moved to Reed Point after leaving her ex-husband. She's seven years older than Jake, but their age gap never seemed to matter. He fell fast and hard for her.

None of us saw it coming, but Jake knew what he wanted and went after it. Everly hadn't been looking to get into another relationship, especially because she had her daughter to think about, but she slowly let her walls down and the rest is history. Now they're engaged, have a baby on the way, and are living their own happily ever after.

I'm happy for Jake. I don't know if I can see it for myself—marriage, kids, the whole package. But if I were to force myself to try to imagine it, I would only ever see Daisy. God knows I've compared every woman I've ever dated to her, only to have them all come up short. But the white picket fence, two and half kids and a minivan—nope, not for me. Would I feel differently if I thought a life with Daisy was a possibility? Sometimes I wonder. A part of me thinks that my heart has decided that if it can't have her, it doesn't want anyone else.

"Where are you coming from?" Jake asks shutting the truck door as Birdie skips toward me.

"Hey, cutie pop!" I ignore Jake as she crashes into me and wraps her little arms around me in a hug. "Why do you look extra cute today, huh? I might need to call the cute police on you."

I ruffle her blonde curls, careful not to knock the pink cat ears headband she has on every time I see her. "We went to see Aunt Sierra at the bakery. She's trying out a new cupcake flavour, pink lemonade, and she said I could taste test."

"And...?" I ask her.

Her little brows pinch together. "And what?"

"And how was it?"

"It was soooo good," she beams, stretching out the *o* sound. "But everything Aunt Sierra makes is delicious."

"I agree, Birdie," I say, bopping her on her nose.

"Hey, Dad, can I go play on the swing set?"

"Of course you can, Birdie-girl. We'll meet you back there in a few minutes," Jake answers, crossing the lawn to where I'm standing as Birdie takes off for the gate at the side of their house hollering, "Bye Uncle Tuck!" It's fucking cool to hear Birdie call my big brute of a friend "Dad." I know how much that little girl means to him, and he is her dad in every sense of the word, even if she doesn't have his DNA.

"I'll see ya later, Tuck," Everly says with a wave. "I'm going inside. My feet are killing me."

"I hear you were out with Daisy?" Jake asks. "You're finally manning up. It's about fucking time."

I shake my head. Living on the same street in the same small town with your best friends is the dream, but it also makes having a private life basically impossible. "It wasn't like that. We sort of ran into each other on a hike, and we were both hungry, so we went to Delila's. That's all."

"If you think for a second, I'm buying your bullshit, you're fooling yourself. Anyone with two eyes can tell that you have a thing for her. Hell, you've had a thing for her for years. What the hell are you waiting for?"

I stare at Jake for a second, weighing my options. I haven't admitted my feelings for Daisy to anyone. Not ever. Jake has always been easy to talk to. He's also the human version of a vault. So, I know that whatever I say to him will stay between us.

"I slept with her." I exhale, feeling some of the weight lift from my shoulders.

With a nod, he drags his hand over his beard. "Okay, and..."

"It's complicated. She's not into me like that. We're not dating, we're not together. We're just friends with benefits for the next few months, until she leaves on her trip."

"Why the fuck would you agree to that?"

"It was my idea." I wince.

Jake lets out a slow whistle, shaking his head. "And now you've caught feelings for the girl."

"Yeah," I force out, running my fingers through my hair.

"You realize this isn't going to end well, right? Someone's getting their heart broken and I have a feeling it's going to be you."

Jake isn't telling me anything I don't already know. It was clear to me after the kiss in my father's office that this wasn't just a pact for me. Daisy has always been it for me. She's always been the one.

"You could tell her how you feel. Let the chips fall where they fall."

"Not that easy, man. One, I told you she isn't into me like that. And two, my parents would have a huge issue with it. Three, I finally have her back in my life, and I don't want to lose her."

"You think your parents will get caught up on the god-sister thing?"

"It's my dad. He can barely tolerate me, but he's always thought of Daisy as a daughter. I'm sure he thinks I'm not good enough for her. Fuck, if he so much as knew I was sleeping with her, he would bury my body."

"Well, then I guess you have your fun on the down-low, hopefully fuck her out of your system and move on with your life."

"That's your advice? I watched you put it all on the line to get Ev, and you're telling me to fuck the girl I've wanted for my entire life and then just *move on*? Is that what you would do?"

"Fuck, no. There's no way I could have said goodbye to Ev, and just friends was never going to be enough. I would have done anything I had to do, and I wouldn't have stopped until she was mine."

I chew on my lip, thinking about what Jake just said. In another world, maybe I could be with Daisy. Our families would adjust, my father would get over it, and everything would just be... okay. But there's no reasoning with my dad. And he doesn't bark out threats without backing them up with consequences. He would never understand what Daisy means to me. He's so convinced I'm a fuck-up, of course he'd assume that I'd screw up her life, too—tire of her or break her heart, and shatter our family's bond with the Carters in the process.

"So, what are you going to do?"

"I wish like hell I knew."

Jake shakes his head with that smug look that he gets when he thinks he knows everything.

"What? Why are you giving me that look?"

He shrugs. "I'm not giving you any kind of look."

"You are too. It's that thing you do when you push your lips together, raise your eyebrows, and do that thing with your eyes."

He busts out laughing. "I think you have it worse for Daisy than you're willing to admit. Look at me, Tuck—did you ever think you'd see me married with kids? And happy as hell about it? You could be next, buddy."

"The fuck? Good for you, man, but that's not for me. I care about Daisy, sure, but you're way off track."

"You literally can't stop smiling when you're talking about her."

"That's because she's my best friend." I raise my voice at him.

"And you have a serious crush on her."

"For the love of everything, you need to listen to my husband," a voice shouts from behind Jake. "You're crazy about the girl, Tucker, it's so obvious."

Everly is standing in their front door, a hand on her belly.

"You good, baby?"

"I have a craving for a McDonalds's sundae. Will you, pretty-please, go get me one?"

"You know I will. I'll go right now."

Jake starts to walk to his truck, grinning at Everly, who blows him a kiss before going back inside. Without turning around, Jake shouts at me from his driveway.

"Good luck, my man. Don't fuck it up."

I snort. Knowing me, that's exactly what I'll do.

SEVENTEEN

I'M JUST EXPECTING TO USE HIS DICK

Daisy

When I get back to the condo after work, Briar is already cooking dinner, and just the aroma of whatever it is she has on the stove has me salivating. I need a shower, a nap, and then possibly an entire pot of coffee, but that will all have to take a back seat to dinner because I am starved.

"Hey, girl." Briar calls to me over her shoulder as I join her in the kitchen.

"Hey. Whatever you're cooking smells so good."

"Thai chicken and rice."

"Amazing. What can I do?"

"Just grab us some plates. Let's eat on the couch. You have some talking to do."

I sigh, putting my bag and car keys on a kitchen chair. "Yeah, I guess I've left you hanging."

"That's putting it mildly."

A few minutes later, we've taken our plates to the living room, where I take the armchair and Briar flops down on the couch.

"Okay, Daisy. Get to talking. I wanna know if he was worth it."

"He was."

Briar's eyes go wide, and her eyebrows shoot to the sky. "Oh my god, you slept with him. Tell me everything."

"You really want to know the details?"

"Hello? *Of course* I want the details. Start from the beginning. Don't leave anything out."

I fill her in on everything that happened in Tucker's parents' backyard. From stripping in front of him to being spread wide open on the edge of the pool to sucking him on my knees. I didn't get into *too* much detail but gave her just enough to get the gist of what happened between us.

"Sex outside in his parents' yard. Scandalous. How was it?"

"His parents weren't home, I'm not that insane. But it was good."

"Good?"

"Okay, it was great. Incredible. So great that I want to do it again soon."

"That's more like it!" She smiles, pulling her legs underneath her on the couch. "Is he still on board with all of it? The pact? He wants to sleep with you again?"

"The pact stands. We are keeping it a secret." I give Briar a pointed look as she brings a forkful of rice to her mouth. "That means you have to keep the secret too."

"Bible." She holds one palm up as if she's taking an oath. "So, when are you getting it on again?"

"I don't know, but I hope soon.

"You're already so into him."

"No, I'm not."

"Dais, I love you, but you know you're playing with fire, right?"

"It'll be fine. I know what I'm doing."

"You really believe that, don't you?"

I nod, but deep down I'm not sure I'm buying it either.

"The longer you keep hooking up with him, the stronger your feelings are going to be. And Tucker isn't the type who's looking for a relationship."

"Neither am I."

"Right. I know you tell yourself that, but I'm not so sure it's the truth."

"I mean it, Bri. I'm not expecting this to turn into anything. I'm just expecting to use his dick for the next two months."

"For fuck's sake, Dais. I almost spit out my chicken. Warn me next time before you say shit like that."

I laugh. "Are you getting excited for your trip?"

Briar is quiet for a moment before she sighs. "I still need to pack, so I guess I'm not ready, but I'm really looking forward to seeing my mom and brother for Christmas. I really miss them."

"Hard not to miss them when you're as close as you three are."

"Yeah, I guess so," she says, nodding. "Dais, you know I just worry about you, right?"

"I know. And I appreciate it. Love you, Briar."

"I love you, too."

Briar smiles and then gets up from the couch to take her empty plate to the kitchen. I follow her, rinsing off my plate and depositing it in the dishwasher. I'm desperate for a shower and a nap, but more than anything I am missing Tucker. I know I can't have all of him, but I'm willing to settle for what I can get.

Briar's right, though, I need to be careful and remember what this really is: just a silly pact where no one gets hurt.

EIGHTEEN

BE A GOOD GIRL FOR ME, REBEL

Tucker

The two weeks leading up to Christmas are some of the best days of my life

Holden has been spending most nights at Aubrey's, so I have Daisy in my bed for a few hours before she eventually goes back to her place. We've promised one another that we're going to stick to the rules and so far, we have... for the most part. Even when everything in me has wanted to pull her back into my bed and go to sleep with her warm body against mine, I've stayed strong. When I wake up in the morning, Daisy is still the first person I want to talk to.

The only thing that has stopped me from breaking our rules is knowing that Daisy is mine—at least until she leaves. And god, do I love having all her attention on me.

Daisy and I have been inseparable, spending all our free time together. We hide away at one of our houses and snuggle on the couch and watch movies when we have a place to ourselves. We take drives to the next town over where we won't be seen, and we go for early morning walks along the beach. It still annoys me to no end that she spends her days with Dr. Dick at the clinic, but she's made it pretty clear that there was never an attraction there for her. It doesn't mean I don't wish that he would pack up and start a new practice in North Dakota.

When I'm not with Daisy, I'm with the team. I watch an hour or two of tapes every day with Jesse, and after the guys are finished in the weight room, I go in and workout in peace and quiet. I'll slip on my headphones and try to focus on weights, but the championship game is always on my mind. In three weeks, we'll play our final game of the season.

Tonight is Christmas Eve, which means Daisy and I are at my parents' place for dinner. It's been a tradition for as long as I can remember. Of course, our families have no idea that anything's going on between us, so we are keeping our distance. It's so fucking hard to be in the same room as Daisy and not be able to touch her. Whenever it feels like nobody is watching, I try to catch her eye, and we exchange a private look that is meant for only us. Just that one look is enough to keep me going, even though it feels like being this far away from her might kill me. I've kept my hands to myself all night, my willpower being put to the test.

"Is it time to open our presents yet?" my sister asks, nodding to the 9-foot Christmas tree in the corner of the room as she flops down onto the couch next to Daisy. The entire house is decorated, stockings hung, and my mom's favorite Michael Bublé Christmas CD drifts through the built-in speakers.

"You're like a giant 5-year-old, Addy," I tell her, shaking my head.

"I just like Christmas."

"You just like presents," I counter.

She grins. "You may have a point."

Every year we do a Secret Santa and this year I drew Jonathan's name. Easy as pie. The guy likes to golf, so I splurged and bought him a range finder and a box of Pro V1 golf balls.

"Let's do it, who wants to go first?" my mom asks, setting her glass of eggnog on the coffee table. We're all in the living room: Mom and Dad, Uncle Randy and Aunt Victoria, Daisy, Addy, Jonathan and me.

"I think we should let Addy open her gift," Jonathan says as he takes a box from underneath the tree and hands it to my sister. "Before she implodes."

Addy hugs the shoebox-sized package to her chest, then motions for Jonathan to sit next to her on the couch as she slips the bow from the gift. She looks excitedly at her husband when she finds a smaller box hidden inside the larger one, then opens it to reveal a pair of diamond earrings. "Jonathan! These are beautiful," she says with her hand over her heart. He gazes back at her like he knew she was going to love them.

It makes me wish I could put a smile on Daisy's face like the one on Addy's. The thought surprises me. Daisy and I aren't even dating, but lately I often catch myself thinking about her as if we are in a relationship.

We go around our little circle, everyone taking their turn to open a present, until the only person who hasn't given their gift to someone is Daisy. She stands in front of me with a box tied with a green ribbon, her eyes twinkling as she hands it to me. I meet her eyes, conscious of the fact that everyone in the room is now looking at us.

"Merry Christmas, Tuck. I couldn't resist!" Daisy sits back down on the couch as I unwrap the present.

I laugh as I unwrap the tissue paper to reveal a pair of pajamas with my face printed all over them. "Wow. I know

I'm pretty popular around Reed Point, but I had no clue they make jammies with my face on them."

"Who knew?" Daisy shrugs, indulging me as I stand and hold up the set for the others to see.

"These are the best. I'm never taking them off."

"Not a good look," Addy teases. "Daisy, he's full of himself as it is, do we really need to encourage him?"

"Hey, Dais, what did you pay for those?" Jonathan jokes. "I may need to get myself a pair."

"Not if you ever want to sleep with me again." Addy gets up, collecting the wrapping paper from the floor while I walk over to Daisy and wrap her in a big hug. Then I remember we have an audience and back away quickly.

After the gift exchange, the eight of us play a game of Rummikub before calling it a night. It's eleven o'clock when Daisy's parents head home. Addy and Jonathan don't last much longer, saying goodnight and going upstairs to my sister's old bedroom after helping my mom tidy up. My sister and I are staying at my parents' house like we do every Christmas Eve and Daisy is staying next door with her family.

My parents are busy in the kitchen, so I slip out and quietly sneak up behind Daisy as she looks for her jacket in the closet. I run my fingers softly through her hair because every time I do, she makes this moaning sound that my dick loves to hear. With my lips at the shell of her ear, I whisper, "Can I kiss you goodnight?"

She spins around to face me, her cheeks flush. "Don't you dare," she says, unconvincingly.

"Just one kiss." I grab her by her hips and grind my cock against her center. She's fighting a smile as her arms move to my chest, playfully pushing me away.

"Behave," she warns.

"What if I don't want to?"

She shakes her head, linking her pinky finger softly with mine. Quietly, so only I can hear, she whispers against my cheek, "Make it quick, Tuck."

Her eyes settle on mine, and I stare into them before taking her cheek in my hand leaning in to kiss her. I groan against her mouth as I'm backing away. "Night, rebel."

"Night, coach."

I watch her walk across the lawn making sure she gets home, then I walk upstairs to my bedroom. For a minute, it feels a lot like it did when we were kids.

I strip out of my clothes, brush my teeth, and climb into my old bed, lying under the blue and black buffalo plaid comforter and staring up at the ceiling in the dark. Everything in the room seems to remind me of Daisy. Leaning against the wall is the surfboard I taught her how to surf on. In a frame next to a few of my high school trophies is a picture of a sunset I took in Hawaii; Daisy was sitting on the beach next to me when I pulled out my phone and focused on the orange and red sky. And then there's the window where I used to sneak out and meet her by the pool.

Looking around, I'm reminded that so many of my memories involve Daisy. So much of my life belongs to her. So does my heart. How did I ever last 10 years without talking to her? It seems impossible.

I sit up in bed, my heart jackhammering beneath my ribcage as I reach for my phone.

I need to see Daisy.

> Me: Are you still up?
>
> Daisy: Can't sleep either?
>
> Me: Nah. What are you doing?

> Daisy: Staring at the clock on the wall. It's forty-three seconds to Christmas.

I look at the time on the screen of my phone and wait until the numbers change to 12 o'clock.

> Me: Merry Christmas, beautiful. Meet me by the pool.

I smile when she messages me back within seconds.

> Daisy: Merry Christmas!

> Daisy: We can't be seen together, and it's freezing out.

I know she's right, and I hate it. I hate that it feels like Daisy is some sort of filthy secret, but I have to be honest: I like having her as only mine. What we have is all ours.

> Me: Be a good girl for me, rebel. Put a jacket on and meet me at the side of the pool house. 5 minutes.

When she doesn't respond, I know she'll be there, so I throw on my new pajama pants and a sweatshirt and my jacket. I step into my slides and grab my baseball hat from my dresser. Before I quietly leave my bedroom, I stuff the gift I bought Daisy last week inside of my jacket, then I slip out the back door and wait for her like old times.

DAISY

. . .

Tucker is standing outside in a black puffer jacket and the pajama pants I bought him, his hands stuffed into the front pockets of his coat to keep them warm. It's freezing outside, the concrete patio sparkling like diamonds under a layer of frost that is illumined by the string of Edison lights his parents left on. It's beautiful. The night feels magical. When he notices me, his blue eyes sparkle and a small smile curves at his lips.

My eyes flicker to the pool, a place that holds so many memories for me as I cross the yard. When I stop in front of him, my heart takes flight, but I try not to let it show. When he leans in, brushing his lips over the corner of my mouth, I think I may spontaneously combust. Never in my wildest dreams would I have imagined I would be standing here being kissed by Tucker Collins at midnight on Christmas morning. Tingles run up my spine.

But then I remember none of this real. It's just a pact. Nothing more.

"Hi. Nice pajama pants."

"I told you I'm never taking them off." Tucker smirks. "I'm going to need you to order me three more pairs, so I have a rotation."

"Oh my God." I roll my eyes, but inwardly I'm a mess for this man.

"Come here." He crooks a finger. "You look cold," he whispers, reaching for me and pulling me closer. His arms wrap around me as if he's eager to hold me, his lips are against my temple. "I'll warm you up."

Our bodies are so close, but it's not enough. Somehow, I've become addicted to him. I wish we could shed every layer of clothing separating us, but I know this is just a quick hello. That's all it can be, with our families nearby.

"So, I have something for you."

I pull back, tilting my head to one side. "You do?"

"It's just something small, but I hope you'll like it."

"Tucker, you didn't need to—"

"Daisy," he stops me. "I know I didn't need to, but I wanted to."

He releases his hold on me and bends down to pick up a box with a black ribbon that is leaning against the pool house. I was so focused on him that I guess I missed it.

"For you," he says, a look of anticipation on his face. "Open it."

I slip the bow from the box and unwrap it, then pull out a green and gold Outlaws jersey, a white number 20 and his last name, Collins, outlined in gold on the back.

"Tucker," I stammer as my fingers glide over the material. "The number 20, for my birthday—"

"Our birthday," he says. "I know it's kinda silly, but I wasn't sure what other number to put on there. Is it okay?"

I swallow down the emotion lodged in my throat. The gift feels very personal and unexpected, but what's more unexpected is the realization in this moment that what I told myself I wouldn't do is actually happening.

I'm falling for him.

It's overwhelming, and scary, and I immediately remind myself that these feelings are probably one-sided. But I can unpack all of these emotions and worries later. For now, I want to allow myself to just be here in this moment with Tucker.

"I love it. And I love that you chose our birthday. It means a lot to me. So, thank you."

"You're welcome."

He beams, and my heart beats out of my chest, reminding me that it belongs to him.

I'm in so much trouble.

Whatever this is between us, there is a deadline on it and the clock is ticking. What will I do when our pact ends? I'll be left to clean up what's left of a broken heart. I'll be ruined for good.

But it still doesn't make me want to stop.

When it feels like we're beginning to press our luck being out here alone, I tell him I need to go. Before I leave, I stand on my toes to press a kiss on his mouth. Tucker deepens it, stroking his tongue against mine. I practically melt into the kiss, savoring the feel of his lips against mine. I inhale his scent that is so uniquely him, the smell of pine like an addiction to me now. Reluctantly, I tear myself away from him and walk across the darkened backyard back to my parents' house before I allow myself to fall any harder.

These feelings for Tucker snuck up on me, but there's no avoiding them now. I am way too far gone to pretend that he's a friend and nothing more. Everything about the two of us is temporary, but for some reason, I can't keep from holding on for dear life.

NINETEEN

NOT JUST A BOOTY CALL

Tucker

I've never been so keyed-up in my life.

The next few weeks were a blur for me— a whirlwind of early morning drills, watching tape in the afternoons, and gruelling practices that nearly broke my players. When they weren't running sprints or special teams drills, they were going through position drills, all of that then followed by nights in the gym. We have been preparing mentally and physically for the massive challenge that is coming our way tomorrow night. The Division 2 national championship. It isn't enough to practice hard on the field. My players then had to spend hours upon hours in a darkened room stretching their minds to the absolute limit watching tape. But it hasn't been just a few weeks of hard work, it has taken a year's worth of blood, sweat, and tears to get us to tomorrow's game and I refuse to let us back off now. The level of competition and intensity I have demanded from the team this week puts everything these guys have ever done to this point to shame. The only way to achieve success is to outwork and out-prepare the competition, and that's exactly what we've been doing. It's been all-consuming, which has left me little time for Daisy.

Any chance I've had, I've sent her a text—usually something I know will push her buttons. I've always loved getting a rise out of her, and I know exactly how to do it. I picture her reading them, a cute blush creeping up her cheeks.

But with the game coming up, the text exchanges have been few and far between and it hasn't been nearly enough.

I've craved her.

It's been impossible not to think about Daisy, wishing my cock was buried inside her velvety softness. Finally, last night, I couldn't take it anymore. I snuck into her apartment and into her bed, careful not to wake Briar. I worshipped every inch of her body for hours under her sheets, and after I came, I got dressed and left, sticking to our rules like the chickenshit I am. Every cell in my being wanted to curl into her, my front to her back, and fall asleep with her in my arms—a fact that scares the living hell out of me. But I left, full of regret, because walking out her door after fucking her felt all wrong.

Daisy is not just a booty call. She deserves so much more than that.

I pour myself a cup of coffee then sit on the small couch in my office, flicking on game tape. My phone buzzes as soon as it starts to play. I smile when I see Daisy's name on my screen.

> Daisy: You ready for the game tomorrow night, coach?
>
> Me: Never been more.
>
> Daisy: Of course you are. You were born ready.

> Me: Are you going to celebrate with me after we win?
>
> Daisy: I like your confidence. What did you have in mind?
>
> Me: You, ass up on my bed while I fuck you from behind.
>
> Daisy: That can probably be arranged.

My cock hardens behind the zipper of my pants.

> Daisy: I hate to ruin a good time, but you're going for dinner after the game, right?

I sigh, flopping back into the couch. Bringing up my dad is the ultimate boner killer. My parents have always liked throwing parties—any excuse to get dressed up and talk about themselves with their friends. My mom decided that the last Outlaws football game of the season is the perfect excuse, and while I doubt my dad gives a shit about the game, he agreed to the party. They've booked the back half of Catch 21, Reed Point's swankiest restaurant, after tomorrow night's game. I told them I would go, but my plan is to eat and run.

> Me: I am, but only if you're coming with me.
>
> Daisy: I'll be there. You know I always have your back.
>
> Me: I know, and I appreciate it.
>
> Daisy: Good luck, coach. Go get 'em.
>
> Me: Night, rebel.

I toss my phone to the side and return to watching tapes,

trying hard to shake off the distraction of the many filthy ways I plan on celebrating after the game with Daisy.

I WOKE UP THIS MORNING WITH A PIT IN MY STOMACH THE SIZE of a golf ball. It was 6 a.m. when I finally jumped out of bed after tossing and turning all night. I went for a run then hit the weight room at the university. After a quick shower, I went to class and it was clear that the students were as checked out as I was, already buzzing with anticipation for the Division 2 national championship tonight. I couldn't blame them. The Outlaws are the hometown team, and this is the biggest event of the year. By the time classes were over, students were running out the door to get ready to watch the boys take home the title.

If it's up to me, that's exactly what we're going to do.

"You look like you could use a stiff drink with that sandwich," Jesse says as he lowers himself into the chair across from my desk, nodding to the turkey clubhouse in my hands.

"I probably could. Slept like shit. I guess you know what that's all about."

He nods as if to prove my point. "I love Noah more than anything on this planet, but the kid hates to sleep."

"You only have another 20 years until you get a good night's rest," I say, grinning at him. "And don't they say those years fly by or some shit like that?"

Jesse chuckles, sipping from a coffee mug that reads, *This is what an awesome dad looks like* with an arrow pointing up.

"Are you done making fun of me?" he asks with a bored stare.

"For now."

"You laugh now, but one day it's going to be you."

"I doubt that very much."

A strange feeling sparks to life behind my ribcage. Not long ago, I could have said that without a second thought. Now, though, I *can* imagine a life like the one Jesse has. With Daisy. Married, a house, a dog, a baby. All of it.

Have I lost it? Every day that passes has me questioning my sanity. It wasn't that long ago that I looked at a woman and saw nothing but a hook-up, a good time. And now? The only thing I want to do when I'm not coaching football is hang with Daisy. Now that I have her back in my life, I'm scared to let her go.

Jesse rolls his eyes, then raps his knuckles on my desk before pushing to stand. "If you need me, I'm going to run down and check in on Austin. He's having his shoulder taped. Otherwise, I'll see you at warmup."

"I'll head down once I'm finished here."

Austin Davies is our QB1. He tore his rotator cuff last season and now, one year later, he's back on the field. He sat on the sidelines for the first half of the year before being given the okay to get back into the game just as we were entering the mid-way point of the season. We beat SFU that night thanks mostly to Austin, and we've been looking strong as a team ever since.

When I reach the locker room, it's alive with a buzz that is invigorating, the guys chanting in a circle, the volume of their voices growing louder. My eyes rest on Austin, who is leading the hype-up in the middle of the room with players clapping shoulders and bouncing up and down all around him. I nod and listen from where I'm standing along the outside of the room with Jesse next to me, but as much as I try to feel it too, inside it feels like I'm drowning in a pool of anxious thoughts. Nerves or not, when it's time to hit the field for warmup, I will swallow down the fear, becoming the calm and pragmatic coach my players need me to be.

That is my job. It's what I get paid to do. More than that, being on the field in front of stands full of Outlaws fans lights a fire in me.

It's cold but sunny when our warmup gets underway. I'd woken up to frost on my truck this morning, which is normal for the middle of January, but you would think it was the beginning of spring with the way the sun is shining over Reed Point as I jog onto the field.

I look up into the stands and see hundreds of RPU Outlaws fans holding handmade signs and cheering for our boys in green and gold. I allow myself a moment to take it in. We are one win away, and we've worked too hard to let anyone take it away from us now.

Thirty minutes later, the place is going wild as the game is set to start. I am as focused as I've ever been when I huddle our players around me for a brief meeting, yelling to be heard above the deafening roar of the crowd. I meet the eyes of every single player and see the confidence and determination in them. They hit the field vibrating with a raw, nervous energy.

"Hut!"

My eyes are on Austin as the game ball finds his hands for the first time. He's moved back into the pocket looking for a receiver and when he finds one, I watch his arm snap the ball high through the air. I've seen him throw the ball more times than I can count this season, but I still worry about his arm every time. He rubs his shoulder after the play, but I know with just one glance that his rotator cuff is stable. You would never know he's rehabbing an injury. I need it to stay that way for the next four quarters.

The first two quarters pass in the blink of an eye and then the team is back in the dressing room, huddled around Austin and me. We're down 14 points thanks to a 47-yard touchdown by the Vikings' leading receiver early in the second quarter and a fumble on our end that they were able to capitalize on. We've had to come back from worse deficits, but we have a long road ahead if we're going to win this.

We are a few minutes away from starting the second half, so I whistle to get everyone's attention and then let Austin take it from there. Most of the guys take a knee, quieting down as they listen to their QB.

"This is it," Austin's voice echoes off the walls, and I feel the weight of his words in my chest. Every player in the room feels it too. "We have two quarters to get this done. The Vikings are good. They're tough and they've shown us that they want this W just as much as we do." He looks around the room, making sure everyone is listening. "But we're the better team and we're going to prove that tonight, boys! I want to see your blood, sweat and tears out on that field! Let's fucking go!" A roar rips through the team in response.

"Outlaws in three!"

In one booming voice, the players count to three, then yell "Outlaws!" The guys bounce up to their feet, clapping each other's backs, the energy in the room turning explosive. We spill into the tunnel and out onto the field like a pack of hungry lions stalking our prey.

I slow my pace as I approach the sidelines, stopping just a few feet from where I know Daisy is sitting in the stands. My heart rate kicks up when I spot her looking more beautiful than I've ever seen her. She's wearing the Outlaws jersey I gave her under a jacket that she's left open, a green and gold ribbon in her hair. The setting sun casts a golden hour glow over her, her chestnut brown hair shimmering in the fading light.

Her eyes meet mine and I stand rooted in place for a beat, game playbook in hand. For a split second, it's just me and her in the stadium while everything else fades away. She nods at me, and I pinch the brim of my ball cap and then turn and jog over to where Jesse stands, putting on my game face.

I have a game to win. Let's fucking go, Outlaws.

TWENTY

BRACE YOURSELF, DAISY. THIS IS GOING TO BE ROUGH

Daisy

I'm a mess for Tucker. It feels like the entire town has come out to watch tonight's Division 2 national championship game. Tucker has his own cheering squad here: Me, Briar, Addy and Jonathan, my parents, and Aunt Daisy and Uncle Mark.

I'm thankful that Uncle Mark showed up, even if he seems to be slightly annoyed with almost everything. The line-up to get in was too long, the tailgating too loud, and the weather too cold. But he's here, and that's what matters. I know it will mean something to Tucker, and the truth is it means something to me too. I hate it when my uncle isn't supportive of Tucker, but tonight I hope he'll be proud. God, I hope he will see what everyone else does when they watch Tucker coach.

I'm wearing the jersey Tucker gave me, hoping it will bring some luck. I'm not sure what I'll say if anyone asks me where I got it, but I'm hoping if I keep my jacket on all night, no one will see the number 20 and his name on the back.

The boys could use some luck right now. At halftime, the

Outlaws are down by 14. We're being outplayed and the Vikings look steady. My attention hasn't swayed far from Tucker all night. He looks more focused than I have ever seen him. I notice the tight set of his jaw, the tension in his stance.

He also looks ridiculously handsome in his game gear: an Outlaws jacket over a black polo, the sleeves pushed up just enough to reveal a hint of his tattoos, and his team ball cap pulled low on his head. I can't tear my eyes away from the intoxicating mixture of confidence and intense male energy. His jaw ticks, his blue eyes are laser focused. It's enough to make my pulse race watching him do what he does best.

Tucker Collins, head coach for the Reed Point University Outlaws and the man I have secretly wanted for half of my life.

By the time the teams return to the field for the third quarter, my heart is in my stomach. I watch him with his head down make his way to the sidelines but as he gets there he stops suddenly and looks up, searching the crowd until his eyes lock on mine for a moment. I resist the urge to wave, but I hope he can see in my eyes how completely I believe in him. Tucker has worked so hard to get here today. I suck in a breath and silently pray for things to go his way tonight.

My prayer seems to be answered, because by some sort of a miracle, a quick pick six gets us back in the game and after a field goal conversion we've narrowed the Vikings' lead to 7.

The Outlaws have come to life in the second part of this game, and the crowd senses it. I can barely hear myself think through the thunderous cheering and stomping of feet when with minutes left in the game, the Outlaws back up the Vikings to their own two-yard line. Our star defensive end blows by the left tackle and sacks their quarterback, Ubels, in the Vikings end zone.

Safety! The stadium goes wild. The Vikings look stunned.

The Outlaws get the ball back, and we're down five with a little over one minute to go.

"We can't lose." I reach for Addy's hand, holding it in mine.

"It's not over yet," she says, her eyes glued to the field. "We still have time."

When my eyes flicker up to the scoreboard, my heart slams against my chest. We are losing. Tuck is losing. I'm not sure how I'm going to survive these next few minutes.

My gaze drifts to Tucker, who pulls his headset down around the back of his neck as Jesse whispers something in his ear before Austin Davies takes his position, hands ready to receive the ball. Our center snaps the football into Davies' hands, and he takes three steps back, searching the field for a receiver.

Davies launches the ball up high and it spirals perfectly until it lands safely into the hands of number 68.

The crowd erupts. There isn't anyone in their seat.

Dallas, the Outlaws' star wide receiver, bolts down the field, his arm hugging the ball close to his side as he weaves through players looking to take him down. He keeps going, every step taking him closer to the end zone, until he's finally brutally tackled to the turf.

My gaze rips to the scoreboard. It's first and ten, the ball is at the 19-yard line.

I watch Tucker huddle with Jesse. Then he calls a timeout with only six seconds left to go, the Outlaws still down by five.

Addy holds my hand a little tighter. I look down our row and see the anxiety I feel reflected in everyone's faces. My mom rubs her palms together like she can barely stand it. Even Uncle Mark is on his feet, hands on his hips, completely dialed in.

"They've got this. I know they do," Briar says, her hands on either side of her face.

I hope she's right. I can barely breathe, silently saying a prayer for Tucker. I'm not sure I've ever wanted anything more in my life.

"This is too much," I say quietly, my hands covering my face. "Shit. Come on. You've got this. Let's go."

As soon as the timeout runs out, all eyes are on Davies who is lined up in the shotgun but my eyes are glued to Tucker. My heart rate spikes. The man stands on the sideline, a look of steely confidence on his face. He's here to win whatever the cost.

The Outlaws aren't giving up. The ball is snapped into Davies' hands. The crowd erupts. Time ticks down, second by second, and then his right arm rips back looking for a pocket. When he sees a window, he fires the rock with precision, sending it high toward the end zone where number 48 catches it before being tackled to the ground. And as hard as he was taken down, he gets right back up with the ball in his hands.

Touchdown.

I scream, jumping up and down with Addy and Briar, who wrap their arms around me in a bruising hug. My parents and Tucker's family are jumping up and down as confetti rains down over us. Even Uncle Mark is cheering now, the look of pride on his face unmistakable.

Tucker throws his fist in the air in victory before being bear hugged by Jesse, then they're both swarmed by coaching staff and players. The entire stadium goes haywire as fireworks go off in the sky, streamers shooting from cannons onto the field.

The Outlaws win.

Tucker did it.

He won the Division 2 national championship game.

I watch on with a smile as a giant container of Gatorade is lifted and poured over Tucker's head. He must be cold as hell, but he doesn't show it. He just smiles and laughs, taking it like the champion he is.

Through the celebrating, Tucker's eyes scan the crowd until they find mine, and the smile on his face says it all. He lifts his chin just a notch, dragging his hand through his wet hair before putting his hat on backwards, and my breath catches in my throat. Every cell in my body vibrates and there are tears in my eyes as I mouth the words, *you did it.*

I did it, he mouths back, nodding. And even though it's now freezing out, warmth blooms through my body. He grins this boyish grin, and if anyone were to look at the two of us right now, they would probably think we were in a real relationship, but I remind myself that isn't the case. That's where it gets confusing because even though I'm not sure what the look means, I know it feels good; specifically, the way it has my knees turning weak.

And even though our families are right here next to me, we don't look away from each other. I stand here, breaking one of the rules I'd insisted on in the very beginning.

I flirt with him anyways.

TUCKER

. . .

LILY MILLER

I peel my Gatorade-soaked clothes from my skin and step under the hot spray of water. The moment the water hits my skin, the tension in my muscles from the stress of tonight's game begins to loosen. The knot that had taken up permanent residence between my shoulder blades over the last week starts to untangle. I sigh, stretching my neck from left to right, replaying the game in my mind. We won the motherfucking national championship! We fucking did it.

It feels amazing, like an out of body experience. We played our hearts out and took the win that we rightfully deserved.

I was so focused on the game, that I forgot my dad was in the stands. When I spotted him on his feet with a smile on his face after we were declared the champs, I was surprised. It still doesn't mean I'm looking forward to seeing him at dinner tonight. I'm sure he'll refuse to acknowledge the win, or he'll find some way to make the night about him like he usually does. The saving grace, though, is that Daisy will be there and maybe, if I'm lucky, I can celebrate the win with her *after* dinner... in my bed.

I take another five minutes to wash the sticky blue drink out of my hair and off my skin, enjoying the quiet of the locker room around me. The guys and the rest of the coaching staff have left, off to celebrate the big win with their friends and families.

Only when the water begins to run cool do I turn the water off and reach for my towel. I step out of the shower stall, towelling off my hair, when I stop in my tracks. Daisy. I wipe my eyes with the towel, wondering if I'm seeing things, but when she comes back into focus, I know I'm not dreaming.

"Congratulations."

A smile spreads across her face, and like it's contagious,

my lips tip up too. She's taken off her coat, so I get to see her in the jersey I bought her—the one with my name and birth date on it. *Fuck*, why is that so hot? There is a green and gold ribbon in her hair, and I can think of 10 different ways I could tie her up with that thing if she'd only let me. Something inside me tells me she would. It instantly turns me on seeing her in Outlaws gear, and my dick twitches behind the towel that is carelessly draped down the center of me.

God, she is so fucking sexy.

I stalk closer to her, bringing the towel behind my hips and giving her a full view of my body before wrapping it around my waist. Even though she remains rooted in place, her eyes have catalogued my every movement. I can tell by the heat in them and the way she rolls her lips together that she likes what she sees.

"Is there anyone waiting on us in the hallway?"

She slowly shakes her head. "No. They all left."

"Good."

The way her eyes hold mine is enough to make me crazy. It sends a rush of heat barreling down my spine. I haven't stopped thinking about when and where I could taste her again. When I'm a foot away from her, she takes two steps backwards until her back presses up against a locker.

Two heartbeats later and I'm caging her in against the metal, her face tipped up as she watches me. She's waiting for me to make the first move. Happy to.

I lean in closer until I can feel her breath drift over my lips. I watch as her tongue darts out to moisten her lips, then I suck her bottom lip into my mouth. Her eyes close on a moan like the kiss means something to her.

"What if someone walks in?"

"They won't," I assure her.

"And if they do?"

"Daisy, I said goodbye to every player and every member of my coaching staff. No one is walking in here."

When the tension is so thick I can't stand it anymore, I slant my head and swipe my tongue over her lips. Daisy goes up on her toes, winds her arms around my neck and fuses her lips to mine. I deepen the kiss further, ready to take every scrap of clothing from this woman's body and carry her to the first bench I can find.

Pushing my body flush against hers, I know she can feel every thick, hard inch of me pressed against her abdomen. That thought is confirmed when she gasps.

"Dais," I breathe into her hair, hitching her leg up over my hip as I roll my hips into her core. Every cell in my body sparks to life as I nestle my now full-blown erection between the V of her thighs. "Need you."

My hand slips down between her legs, putting pressure on her clit where she needs it most. Her head lolls to the side, mouth parted, eyes closed with breaths coming in short, even pants.

"Did you like watching me on the field, Dais?"

She reaches for the towel around my waist. It drops to the floor. "I wasn't watching you. Don't flatter yourself. This is just sex, remember?" Another gasp escapes her lungs when I grind my cock between her legs.

I don't know why her defiant attitude turns me on so much, but it does. Unable to wait a second longer, my hands frantically undo the button on her jeans, then the zipper, before I tear her pants down her legs, taking her lace thong with them.

My cock is so hard that it's aching, the tip swollen a purplish red hue. I suck in a breath, kissing her hard as my hand dips down to the apex of her thighs, groaning when I dip a finger inside her, feeling how wet she is.

"You are soaked. Were you this wet when you were watching me tonight?"

"Shut up, Tuck, and fuck me before someone sees us. That is what you want, isn't it?"

I chuckle at my little rebel, grinning against her neck, pushing inside her even deeper this time with two fingers. She whimpers in response, so I keep going, in and out, fucking her with my fingers.

She rides my hand, her body responding with the most perfect sounds.

"Goddamn, you look so pretty when you're needy and desperate for it." I keep her back pinned to the locker. "I know what will feel even better. I'll give you my tongue before I give you my cock," I say, dropping to my knees, one hand shuttling my length, the other hoisting her leg up over my shoulder. Then I eat her like I'm a starved man, until she's shaking, unable to stand. When I apply pressure to the bundle of nerves where she needs me, she cries out my name, looking for the relief that I know she needs. I feel her core spasm around my tongue, and I feel a shock of electricity shoot straight to my dick.

"That's my fucking rebel," I praise her. "Such a good girl for my cock."

Then I'm sucking my fingers into my mouth, sucking herself off me. I lick them clean before immediately standing, hauling her sated body up into my arms. She wraps her legs around my waist, locking her heels behind my back, as I pin her against the cold, hard metal of the locker. "Brace yourself, Dais. This is going to be rough."

Her hands grip my neck, her eyes pinned to mine, as I grab her ass in two handfuls, flexing my hips and sinking home. I fill her to the hilt. I'm balls deep. I rock my hips in and out in a punishing rhythm.

"Do you know how good you feel, Daisy?" I ask, wishing I had removed her T-shirt so I could suck on her perfect tits. "God, Dais, I'm the luckiest guy in the world."

Daisy lets out a moan, gripping my neck, as I fuck her hard and relentlessly. And when she falls apart in my arms, finding her second release, her entire body shudders, tightening around my cock.

I keep rocking my hips into her, until my balls tighten with the need to release. My cock pulses inside her warmth as I bury myself as deep as I can, her name falling from my lips. "You're such a good girl for me. The best."

Sparks burst behind my eyelids. I'm a live wire splintering apart. I ride out the most intense orgasm of my life, pouring myself into her, never wanting it to end. I continue to slowly pump into her heat until my cock is too sensitive, and I'm forced to pull out. When I do, my release leaks down her thigh and the caveman inside my brain wants to push it all back in with my fingers.

But then I remember where we are.

I help clean her up with a towel and then we both get dressed. Every bit of me feeling the urge to pull her into my chest, kiss her mouth, stroke her hair, but I don't. It doesn't mean my chest doesn't ache from wanting to.

TWENTY-ONE

LET ME WORSHIP WHAT'S MINE

Tucker

Less than 30 minutes later, Daisy and I are walking through the doors of Catch 21.

I have prepared myself for the icy greeting I expect to get from my father and an awkward night with my parents and their social circle. I covertly sneak a glance at Daisy to get a read on how she's doing after what just happened in the locker room. I could tell her wheels were turning the entire car ride here. Hell, my mind was spinning too. Getting dressed immediately and pretending like the hottest sex of my life meant nothing to me felt all wrong. And I worry how she's feeling about all of it. As soon as we get through dinner tonight, I plan on checking in with her.

Daisy's dad is the first to notice us arrive, walking toward us and clapping me on the shoulder.

"The man of the hour is here! Coach Collins! What a game, son. Man, you made us all proud tonight."

The rest of room cheers and claps, and soon I'm surrounded by a small crowd of people wanting to congratulate me.

My Aunt Victoria slips a glass of champagne in my hand. "How does it feel to be a conference champion? You're a legend!"

"I don't know about legend, Aunt Vic, but it feels good."

"Oh sweetheart, don't be modest. You're amazing." My mom smiles brightly, wrapping her arms around me. "Come say hi to your dad, honey. He is so proud of you."

I narrow my eyes at Daisy, and she tilts her head with a shrug. In what fucking universe would my dad ever be proud of me? Not this one, but to keep my mom happy, I follow her through the crowd of people who are mingling with drinks in their hands.

"Bill, that's exactly what I was just saying—"

My dad is cut off mid-sentence when my mom stops beside him. "Sweetheart, Tucker is here."

I see his expression change when he notices me. His back stiffens and his grin falters, but he reaches his hand in my direction and cautiously I receive it.

"Great game, son. Congratulations on your win."

"Thanks, Dad. I appreciate it."

"Bill, you know my son, Tucker," he says to the man standing next to him. I'm pretty sure I've seen him at the country club my parents belong to.

"I'm not sure we've met, but it's my pleasure," he says, shaking my hand enthusiastically. "Great game today, kid. I've followed the team all year and you are one hell of a coach. It's just a matter of time before the NFL is calling you."

My dad seems to puff his chest at the compliment, like maybe the idea of an NFL coach for a son is something to be proud of.

"Thank you, sir. I can't imagine that would happen

anytime soon, but if and when the day comes, I for damn sure wouldn't say no."

I wait for my dad to come up with some sort of dick response like, *He has a better chance of becoming president*, but he doesn't say a word. I'm not sure how to react, this isn't what I'm used to from my father. Part of me is waiting for the other shoe to drop, and I look around to see if Daisy is witnessing this strange shift in my dad's attitude.

I spot her several feet away, standing next to a guy about my height who's wearing nicely tailored gray suit pants and a crisp, white collared shirt. At first, I don't recognize him, but when Daisy moves to the side, I get a better view of him and realize that he looks familiar. I can't remember his name, but he went to high school with Daisy and me. He was a year or two younger, so we never really hung out. It's been years since I've seen him. Daisy seems to know him better, because when he wraps an arm around her, pulling her into him for a hug, she smiles widely and leans into him. She has obviously kept in touch with him, *closely*. Jealousy burns a hole in my chest. The guy obviously thinks she's hot, and while I know we agreed to be exclusive until she leaves on her trip, we never said anything about flirting. A huge fucking mistake on my part, I realize now. I watch the two of them, biting the side of my cheek in irritation, wondering how much more of this I can stand.

They continue to talk as I'm dragged around the room by people who want to congratulate me, eventually ending up talking to Jake and Holden. There are 80 or so people here tonight, a mix of family, my friends, influential people from the social circles my parents run in and a few guys from the Outlaws coaching staff.

I quickly find out from Jake that the guy I want to murder is Nathan Boyd, a physiotherapist and all-around nice guy from a well-respected family. Apparently, he has had a thing for Daisy for years. From the looks of it, that may be mutual. She hasn't taken her eyes off the guy, and she's putting her hand on his arm way too fucking much for my liking. If they're so into each other, then why haven't they gotten together? Or maybe they have? The thought makes me sick.

Nathan leans in closer, his hand at her waist as he whispers something in her ear. I grip the stem of my champagne glass so tightly I half-expect it to shatter.

"Tuck, do yourself a favor, and go get your girl before Nathan gets her first," Jake says in a voice only loud enough for me to hear. I sip from my champagne trying to keep my frustration under control.

As if she knows we are talking about her, Daisy looks over her shoulder at me. She must see the infuriation written all over my face because she says something to Nathan, smiles and then walks in my direction.

"Holdey, let's get another drink," Jake says, tugging his arm and making a quick exit for the bar, leaving me standing at the high-top table alone.

Daisy stops in front of me, a mischievous look in her eyes. She leans in, going up on her tiptoes to whisper in my ear. "Everything okay? If I didn't know better, I might think you're jealous of my friend Nathan."

"Why would I be jealous? He isn't the one who had his dick inside of you less than an hour ago."

"Which is exactly why you are jealous. You've never liked it when I pay attention to any guy who isn't you."

"Well, now you're mine, so Nathan should find someone else to flirt with."

"Is that what I am? Yours?"

"Yes." I give her my cockiest grin and I notice that it

seems to set her off balance. "For the next eight weeks you belong to me."

Daisy

"Meet me on the patio in five minutes, Daisy. Be a good girl for me."

A shiver dances up my spine as I watch Tucker walk away, slipping out of the restaurant door and onto the dark patio. My mind spins. Tucker is always unpredictable. Slipping my phone from my purse, I check the screen for the time. I'm stuffing the device back inside my bag when Jake appears at my side.

"Oh, hey, Jake. It's good to see you." I smile at him. "How's Everly? Is she here?"

"She is not. She's home with Birdie. The game was enough for the two of them so she's sitting tonight out. I'm only here for a drink to support Tuck, then I'm heading home too."

I like Jake, so I'm trying to make small talk, but the buzz in my veins and the fluttering in my stomach is not making it easy. "It was nice of you to come. I know it means a lot to Tucker."

"Anything for him," he says. "He's one of the best." Then he adds, "Often misunderstood, but the guy's got a huge heart."

Something about the remark has me feeling like it was meant just for me. Was he trying to tell me something?

"Anyways, I better say hello to Mr. and Mrs. Collins before I head out. It was nice seeing you, Daisy."

"Good to see you too."

I say goodbye, then take a quick glance around the room before surreptitiously walking to the patio doors. When the door shuts behind me, I'm gripped by my arm and pressed up against the cold wall.

Tucker and I are all alone in the dark, the only lights casting a glow over the secluded area are coming from two fire lanterns perched on the corners of the glass railing. The muted sound of laughter drifts out from the restaurant, met by the crash of the ocean waves on the shore 50 feet away.

Holding eye contact, he stares at me with hungry blue eyes. "You can flirt all you want with every guy in Reed Point, but no one touches what is mine. Not even a finger. Only my hands will touch you until this pact is over. Got it?"

Tucker presses the length of his body against mine and I feel his warm breath against my forehead. The possessive grip he has on my wrist and the feel of his hard chest against my body has me melting with lust.

Standing firm, I hold his eye contact. "You're cute when you're jealous."

"I never said I was jealous."

"But you are. Why won't you just admit it?"

Goosebumps erupt over my skin when he sucks my earlobe into his mouth. I moan softly at the feeling, closing my eyes, my head tilting to one side, encouraging him to keep going.

"I shouldn't have to watch another man touch what is mine," he growls, slipping his hand up my shirt and yanking the cup of my bra below my breast before he pinches my nipple. "Admit it, rebel... you like getting a rise out of me. You can be such a brat."

"You're one to talk. You know exactly how to push my buttons," I whisper as he keeps twisting the stiff peak. "Just like you're doing now."

My breathing is shallow. The feeling of his fingers plucking my nipple shoots straight between my legs until he suddenly stops, leaving me wanting more.

But it gets better when the same hand slips down between my legs, under the band of my pants and carefully slides my underwear to the side before pushing a finger inside of me. When I moan, he growls against my neck. "Someone likes it when I push their buttons. You're drenched for me."

"Maybe I do like it."

"You love it. And damn, if that doesn't make my dick hard."

"Tucker—" I release a breath, as his finger moves in and out of me, before he adds a second. "That feels so good."

"Spread your legs a little wider for me, baby. I'm going to remind you who you belong to." I do what he says as his fingers push deeper inside me. "Now I want you to keep your eyes closed and don't open them until I tell you to. Understand?"

"Tuck... what if someone comes out here?"

"Trust me, rebel. Now do what I say and close your eyes."

My eyes flutter closed as he gently slides two fingers slowly inside me, adding his thumb to my clit where I ache for him the most.

"Kiss me, Daisy," is his next command, and with parted lips and my eyes closed, I slowly lean forward to where I think his mouth his, my breathing shallow, my lips searching for his. When I finally find them, he gently kisses me as if he's never kissed me before.

A slow, sensual lingering kiss. It's almost too tender like it means more than a silly pact. When he breaks the kiss, a whimper escapes me.

His fingers continue to pump inside of me, while his thumb draws tiny circles over my clit. I'm squirming and whimpering, riding a potent cocktail of multiple sensations.

Tucker Collins knows how to touch a woman.

I exhale a tiny breath when his fingers inside of me slow to a stop. "Kiss me again, rebel. Keep those pretty eyes closed." With parted lips, and my eyes still shut, I lean forward, again seeking him out, slowly searching for what I want. My mouth opens, desperate to get a taste of him, and then I feel the tip of his tongue draw a long-wet line over the length of my bottom lip. The sensual way his tongue wets my lip, the careful way he's taunting me with his mouth while my eyes are closed has my body lit up. My tongue flicks at his before he kisses me again.

I gasp against his mouth when his fingers start to move again, faster this time, in a perfect rhythm. He picks up the pace, his fingers curling inside of me as I rock against his hand.

"That's it, rebel. Fuck my fingers. Show me how desperate you are to have my cock inside of you." His fingers find my G-spot, his thumb stroking my sensitive bundle of nerves, while he holds my mouth to his like he needs my breath to breathe.

"Now, open your eyes and keep them open until you come. If your eyes are anywhere else but on mine, I will stop."

This is reckless. Anyone could walk by and see us, but I push those thoughts down, not giving a damn. I slowly open my eyes, riding his fingers as he pumps inside my slick center.

"My god, Tucker. You know how to make me feel so—"

I come hard on Tucker's hand, biting my bottom lip to stop myself from screaming. An intense wave of pleasure spreads through my body leaving me lifeless as my heartbeat slows and I ride out wave after wave of my release. I cling to him as my body falls limp against the wall when he slips his fingers from me, and he wraps an arm tightly around my waist to keep me from toppling over.

Tucker's mouth slants over mine in a bruising kiss. The hand he used to fuck me is pressed against the wall, and his other hand cups the side of my face. I can feel his erection when his hips hold mine in place, making me desperate to want to get him off too. My hand palms his length over his pants, but before I can undo the zipper, he moves it away.

"That was for you, Daisy, to remind you who you belong to. You are mine. And I don't want you to forget it."

Goddamn this man, he knows how to send a shiver up my spine. Three orgasms in two hours is just asking for trouble. If I had any sense in me, I'd cut this thing off right now. But I can't. It feels too good to be drowning in the depths of Tucker Collins.

"But what about you? You're hard. I felt it."

"Go back inside, Daisy." His hands straighten my hair. "I told you this wasn't about me."

Without another word, I turn and walk back into the restaurant, still sated, my hand clutched to my heart.

I return to the party and do everything I can to not think about what just happened. Or how much I like the idea of being *his*.

Somewhere along the way this has become more than just friends with benefits. Somehow, I've developed a deep connection that is about so much more than just great sex. But what if Tucker doesn't feel the same? I ache to know how he's really feeling but I worry that if I force that conversation, I'll scare him away.

It's a risk, I decide, I'm not willing to take.

TWENTY-TWO

GOOD THING WE'VE HAD ALL THAT PRACTICE

Daisy

By the time Tucker and I get into his truck after the party at Catch 21, I'm desperate to get my hands on him. I barely made it through dinner and out to his car. Half of me wants a repeat of what happened in the locker room, and the other half wants to pump the breaks on all the mind-bending sex we've been having. I know I need to get him out of my system, but I've never been interested in being with anyone else. It has always been Tucker.

His eyes meet mine as he turns out of the parking lot, and he gives me a look that makes it clear he knows exactly how badly I want him. I feel like I'm 15 years old again and madly in love with Tucker. The more time I spend with him, the easier it is to blur the lines of our friendship. It has started to feel like Tucker and I have something real building between us, and as much as I like the feeling, I also find it confusing.

He moves his arm to the back of my seat and threads his fingers through my hair. I close my eyes and lean into the touch as he twirls a lock of my hair around one of his fingers then pulls it free. Goosebumps dot my arms. Tucker is a quick study; he has learned exactly how I like my hair played with.

"Tired?" he asks, glancing over at me again.

"A little. It's been a big day. How 'bout you, you must be exhausted."

"Strangely, I'm not. I must be still running on the adrenaline from the win." The hand that is in my hair tickles my neck.

"I've never been prouder of you."

"Thanks, rebel."

"Hey, was it just me or was your dad in a strangely good mood tonight?"

"Wasn't just you. My mom must have read him the riot act before the game this morning."

"You think that's what it was? Maybe he's coming around."

"Maybe." His hand slides up and down my hair, feather soft. I sigh, focusing on how good it feels. How good it feels to be close to Tucker again.

"Daisy... I'm not ready to say good night. Come back to my house?"

"What about Holden?"

"We've been sneaking in and out of our houses since we were 12 years old. I think we've got this."

I laugh, realizing he has a point. "Good thing we've had all that practice."

"Good thing."

With my grip on the door handle, I push the door open and step outside. I freeze right there when Tucker appears out of nowhere next to me, his hand replacing mine on the handle.

"What's wrong?" I quickly ask. "Are you okay?"

"You don't ever need to open your car door around me again." His blue eyes cement me in place.

My stomach dips at his words, with the way he's looking at me with pure want in his eyes. A shiver prickles my skin. "And why is that? I've been perfectly capable for years."

"I know." He swings the truck door shut, intertwining his hand with mine. "But when you're with me... you're going to have to get used to being treated the way you deserve."

And then he smiles. That ridiculously charming, earth-shattering smile that steals my breath away every time, and I forget that he can be a caveman. I almost forget that I'm only *his* temporarily.

Ten minutes later, we quietly make our way down the hall to his bedroom, where he shuts the door behind us, and I hear the lock click. Holden's truck was in the driveway when we pulled in, but the lights in the house were all off, so he must be already in bed.

As soon as we're inside Tuck's bedroom, his hands are on my hips, my legs, anywhere he can get them. It feels like he wants to remind me again that I belong to him. His lips find mine, and he's kissing me as if he's starved, as if the two times already today that he's had me in his arms weren't nearly enough.

When we finally pull apart for air, he rests his forehead against mine as his fingers run the length of my body to the hem of my jersey.

"As much as I love you wearing my colors, I also love the idea of this on my bedroom floor," he says as he slips the Outlaws jersey over my head.

His shirt goes next as he drags it over his head and tosses it onto his dresser where my gaze catches on a framed photo sitting on a shelf next to a collection of three or four trophies. It's a picture of me and Tucker on our prom day.

He's wearing a dark gray suit, and I'm standing next to him in my fuchsia pink dress. Neither of us wanted to take the photo—at the time we were barely speaking— but our moms practically pushed us together so they could snap the shot. We both couldn't help but laugh at how over-the-top excited they were and the photo my aunt took capturing our smiles in that moment.

I stare at the photo as my heart spasms in my chest.

"I've had that photo on the shelf since the day I moved in here." Tucker's voice surprises me, and my breath hitches. I cross the room, taking the frame from the shelf to get a better look at the photo. I trace my fingers over the glass, remembering that day.

"Why?"

"Why do I have it on the shelf?"

"Yes." My voice is quiet, just above a whisper.

"You were the most important person in my life for a very long time, Daisy. You still are."

I stare at the photo wide-eyed, barely able to believe that he's had a picture of me in his room this entire time. My heart is sliced wide open; it's bleeding all over his floor.

"Does that freak you out?" he asks, looking at me with curiosity.

"That you have a photo of me in your bedroom?" I pause. "Not at all. I like it. I'm just a little surprised. I assumed I didn't mean much to you."

"You have always meant everything to me," he says softly, moving to stand behind me, and pulling my body back into his. "You've always been my person, and you will always be my best friend."

"We used to be so close." I pause, lost in memories. "Did you know that when you asked Ruby to prom, I was devastated? It broke my heart. I know it sounds silly, but I always pictured us going together. I only said yes to Josh because I knew I couldn't go with you, and I always felt guilty about that... like it wasn't fair to Josh that he was some sort of consolation prize."

"I wanted to ask you," Tucker tells me. "But I was too scared. I thought you'd say no and then knee me in the balls." He laughs softly into my hair.

"The thought did cross my mind a time or two."

"I'm really sorry I never asked you, Daisy."

"It's okay. I forgive you."

Tucker grips my shoulders and spins me around to face him. There's an intensity in his eyes, and as much as I know he wants to strip me naked, like it always is with us, it feels like he wants to take his time with me tonight. Something between has changed.

My fingertips trace the tattoos that cover his chest, up to his shoulders and then down his arms. "I've always wondered about these."

I'm mesmerized by the patterns, the pictures. There are so many of them, and this is the first chance I've gotten to really look at them. The other times Tuck has been naked in front of me it's either been in the dark, or we've been too frantic, too feral for each other, for me to admire them. So tonight, I want to catalogue every one of them.

The tattoos that wrap around his arms like vines. The ink on his ribs. I want to know the story behind every single one. Tucker swallows hard when my finger reaches a small yellow daisy in the space over his heart. My heart is in my throat when I see my initials etched in the center of the flower.

"You tattooed my initials on your body."

"One of the first tattoos I ever got."

A wave of intense emotions crashes over me, tears stinging the back of my eyes. "When?"

I trace my fingers over each petal, swallowing the lump in my throat. My vision blurs with the tears that I'm trying not to shed. For so many years I have wondered why he pushed me away. I've never really understood it. Now, hearing him say that I've always mattered to him—so much that he has my initials tattooed on his chest—just adds to my confusion.

"I was 18. The summer after we graduated, that's when I got the flower on my chest. Then on your birthday—our birthday—I added the initials. You've always been close to my heart, Daisy, even when you couldn't stand me."

I press my fingertips to my cheek to stop the tears that have spilled over. "We weren't even talking then, Tuck. I thought I had done something wrong." I swallow. "Why would you ink my initials into your skin after you did everything you could to push me away?"

His thumb swipes a tear from my cheek. "Daisy—"

I look into his eyes, trying to figure out what he's thinking. None of this makes sense to me. I honestly think Tucker is oblivious to the fact that he cracked my heart in two. Ten years later, it still hasn't fully healed. After everything that has happened between us, I need answers. "Tucker, what did you mean when you told me you didn't have a choice? I need to know."

My voice cracks, but I force myself to hold his gaze. Tucker sighs, wiping a hand across his forehead.

"Please," I beg, heart clenching. "I need you to tell me everything."

He motions for us to sit on the bed and when we do, he looks down at his hands and then blows out a breath before he starts talking. "After you left that day, the day that I kissed you in the living room, my dad asked to speak to me in his office." He swallows. "He saw us kiss... and as I'm sure you can imagine, he wasn't happy."

Tucker casts a sideways look at me, and I nod for him to keep going.

"He told me that it never should have happened. He said that we were too young to know what we were doing. He was upset, saying that you trusted me, and I shouldn't have taken advantage of you."

"You told him he was wrong, right? We both wanted that kiss."

"I couldn't," he says through a lump in his throat. "I know I should have, but I... just couldn't. You know how he is, Daisy."

"So, you thought you would just stop talking to me?" I ask, struggling to understand. "Why didn't you just tell me what he said?"

"Because of the ultimatum."

"What are you talking about?" I ask, shaking my head as my stomach turns. I know that Uncle Mark can be tough, be he loves me. He would never do anything to hurt me. He loves Tuck too, even though their relationship isn't easy.

"Dais," he croaks. "He forbade it. He told me that if I didn't stay away from you, he would send me away to some stupid boarding school until I graduated. I didn't know what to do. I was chasing a football scholarship and worried what leaving the team would mean for my future. And if I left Reed Point, I would never see you. At least if I was here, even if I couldn't be with you, I could be *around* you. I could still look out for you."

"He made you stay away from me." My entire body tenses as an unrestrained anger rips through me.

I never knew what to think. It ate at me for months. All I

could guess was that Tucker just didn't want me. I was sick when I saw him at school in the weeks following our kiss. The first time I had to see him with a girl, it just about killed me. Reliving that pain is not something I want to do, but I know we need to finally work through this.

I'm overwhelmed, so angry, but the sadness I feel outweighs everything else in this moment. I shake my head and try to move away from him, but Tucker puts his hand on my thigh, keeping me next to him.

"I didn't have a choice, Dais. He told me we were family. He was your godfather; we *were* practically family. He said I would only hurt you, and honestly, I thought maybe he was right. I was a kid, I was fucking up left, right and center back then, doing stupid shit. He said it could never work between us, but it would destroy things between our families. That your mom and dad would never forgive me if you got hurt. It wouldn't be worth it. I know that I was an idiot to listen to him, but at the time, I was really scared. But I know now how hard it was for you, and I'm so sorry for that."

"You could have just told me," I say through the pain in my throat. "It broke my heart not knowing what I had done for you to stop talking to me. All I wanted was a reason. I felt so lost, and I missed you, and I wanted the chance to fix what I had done wrong."

"You didn't do anything wrong, Daisy. It was never you. Do you understand me?" he says, reaching for my hands.

"You broke my heart, Tucker." My voice trembles. "That kiss meant everything to me, and for *years* you let me believe that it meant nothing to you."

I think back to every message I sent that went unanswered, every time he looked the other way when he saw me at school. The way my heart broke again and again.

"Daisy—"

"No, I need to get this out," I says in a choked whisper, cracking my heart wide open for him. "You knew me. You knew how much our friendship meant to me. And you knew what pushing me away would do to me. How could you do it? How could you hurt me like that?"

"You think I wanted to hurt you?" he shouts. "You think it didn't kill me?"

"Then why did you do it? Why didn't you just tell me what your dad was doing? We could have at least figured it out together."

"I was 16. My dad is a powerful man. He never issues threats that he doesn't back up." Tucker shakes his head as if he's reliving the memory. "I wanted to stay at Heritage. I was scared to go away. And worst of all... if I did leave... who was going to be there to look out for you?"

He hangs his head, and even though I know I'm treading in dangerous waters, I stay here with his hands in mine.

His glassy eyes meet mine. "I knew I couldn't have you, but if I left here and never saw you, that would have killed me, Daisy."

"Why, Tucker? Am I missing something here? Because I've watched you date practically every girl in Reed Point, all while keeping any guy who showed even an ounce of interest away from me."

"Daisy, none of those girls really mattered to me because none of them were you. And I know it's not fair, but if I couldn't have you, then I couldn't stand to see anyone else with you."

My pulse beats like a drum as I try to understand what Tucker has just said. I've spent the past 10 years believing that I meant nothing to him.

"But you didn't want me." It comes out a whisper.

His eyes find mine, and now he's the one who looks

confused. "I said I *couldn't* have you. I've *wanted* you every day since that kiss. I wanted you before that kiss. There isn't a time in my life I can remember my world not revolving around you."

My eyes well until two tears fall down my cheeks. My head spins. And then I remember to breathe again.

"I spent so long trying to understand... and then I just convinced myself that you didn't want me," I sob. "You were just gone after that day."

He pulls me into his chest, his hand sweeping through my hair as I try to stop the tears that keep falling. "Daisy, I'm so sorry. I'm so sorry I never talked to you. I should have said something. I know now how badly I handled the situation."

"You were scared," I say through my tears. "It wasn't all your fault."

He pulls back, removing his fingers from my hair, framing my neck with his big, strong hands. "Can you forgive me? What do you need from me? Anything. I'll do it."

I search his gaze, not sure what I expect to see; I find pain in his deep blue eyes, but I also see the concern, the care he has for me. He looks so sure, so confident, and it has me wondering how I never saw it before. If over the years, I refused to see the want behind his eyes for fear of being wrong.

"I am so angry at your dad. I'm not sure how I'm going to forgive him, but of course, I forgive you, Tuck. You were just a kid."

Tucker leans in, pressing his forehead to mine, his beautiful blue eyes clear and honest. I wish he hadn't kept this from me, but the truth is I'm only mad at my uncle for putting Tucker in that impossible situation.

"I never forgot that kiss," he whispers. "I couldn't if I tried."

I close my eyes as more tears fall. "It changed me forever. It has been imprinted on my heart, permanently tattooed there."

I want to tell him that I've loved him since we were kids, that I've never been in love with anyone but him, but I don't. Instead, I keep going, asking him where we go from here.

"What do you want, Tuck? What comes next?"

"I want you. I want all of you. No hiding. No sneaking around. I'm done with the secrets," he whispers, his eyes blurry and red. "Be with me, Daisy. All in with me. I don't want you going anywhere... because I won't survive losing you again. My heart can't take it."

His words hit me straight in the chest. I am jarred by his vulnerability. "I want a say in us, Tuck. I need you to be honest with me from here on out. This is about what I want too. And I want... you."

Tucker cradles my face in his hands. "If you'll have me, Daisy, I'll do anything to be with you."

"I have waited my entire life for you to say that." I run my finger along the side of his jaw. "Please tell me I'm not dreaming this?"

Tucker laughs, dropping his head on my shoulder. Then he reaches for my hands, placing them on either side of his face as he looks into my eyes. "Real. This is real. I'm here in front of you telling you I want you. And I'm praying like hell you want me too."

"I've never wanted anything more." I nod, my bottom lip trembling.

"It's you and me, Daisy. From now on, we will figure things out together." His lips brush over mine. "I'm not letting you go. Never again, Dais. No more stupid rules.

You're mine, do you understand? I don't give a shit what my dad has to say. I am done letting anyone get in between us. It's you and me, Dais—"

I silence him with my mouth, my hands gripping both sides of his jaw. Tucker's mouth clings to mine as if he's afraid to let me go, deepening the kiss before his tongue licks the inside of my mouth.

And I melt into him, swearing to myself that I'll never let him go. That I'll never again allow anyone to come in between us. It will be Tucker and me against the world.

He pulls me by my hips until I'm straddling him, and I lower myself onto his lap. He kisses a trail down my neck. "Tucker... I've missed you a lot."

"I'm here, baby. I'm not going anywhere. Let me worship what's mine."

TWENTY-THREE

I THINK I FELL IN LOVE TODAY

Tucker
More.

I want more of Daisy's mouth, the nip of her teeth when she drags them over my bottom lip. More of Daisy's hands, the scrape of her nails, clawing at my shoulders, keeping me where she wants me. More of the perfect little sounds she makes when I grind my swollen cock into her, knowing she's just as turned on as I am. The need to fuck her into oblivion, over and over until she doesn't know up from down or left from right.

I want more.

I want Daisy.

I want what's mine.

My mouth descends on hers as my hands grip the thick strands of her hair. I am wild at the feel of her lips claiming mine, her softness pressed against my hard. I've thought about this day for a very long time. The day I can say with certainty that Daisy is mine. I can barely take how fucking happy I am to know that Daisy's heart belongs to me.

Desire has replaced the pain in her eyes from earlier.

They now blaze with lust, and my body vibrates with the need to be inside of her. I know when I take her this time, it will be different from all the rest. This time I'll be making love to her. I want to cry at that realization.

I hold her right where I want her, and she doesn't stop kissing me. God, her mouth is perfect. Soft too, and with her hands in my hair, Daisy allows me to control the kiss. The way her mouth surrenders to mine and her body nestles in close. She likes it when I take control.

I unclasp her lace bra, peeling the straps slowly over her shoulders as I suck on her neck. I toss the scrap of lace to the floor and move to her pants, tugging them slowly over her hips and carefully down her legs. Once they're on the floor with the rest of her clothes, I lean back to look at her. She runs her hands over my pecs, down to my abs, my skin tingling at the feel of her fingertips. She stares for a moment at my bare chest and the daisy with her initials.

"Baby, you're mine," I whisper, watching her pupils flare. "Always have been."

"I love hearing you say that."

"You better get used to it, rebel. I plan on reminding you every day."

She smiles the sweetest smile, her cheeks still damp from crying, and then crashes her mouth to mine. The kiss tastes salty from her tears— my girlfriend's tears. Daisy who I have waited my whole life for. I had no idea how badly I've needed her. Wanted her. Dreamed of her.

She moans softly into my mouth when my hands slide lower to her ass cheeks, massaging them with my palms. The way she grinds onto my erection when she feels my cock nestled between us makes me harden even more.

"Fuck, baby. Keep grinding on my cock like that. It's going to feel so good when I'm deep inside of you." I use the grip I have on her ass to help her ride me, spreading my legs wide until I can't take another second, and I need to get my jeans off.

My hands move to my belt, but she swats them away, crawling backwards until she's kneeling on the floor between my parted thighs. "I can do that."

I push her long hair back from her face so I can watch the way her tongue darts out over her bottom lip as she unbuckles me. "Lift," she commands, and I raise my ass off the bed so she can remove my pants, leaving me in my boxer briefs.

Daisy palms my cock over the fabric, earning a moan from me, rubbing the length of me as I pump my hips into her grasp.

"Take me out. Please, Dais. I'm going out of my mind."

She just smirks as she teases the waistband of my briefs with her fingers, the other hand massaging my balls. My hips rock forward when her hand dips inside the fabric, wrapping her hand around my shaft. I look down to where her hand is massaging my dick and see the tip of my red and throbbing cock poking out of my boxers.

"Fucking hell, Dais." My hands reach behind me on the mattress as an anchor, holding myself up. "Don't stop. Your hand feels so fucking good."

She continues to work my cock. Her nipples are hard, and the space between her breasts has me imagining how good it would feel to fuck them. But I'll save that thought for another night. Tonight, I want to connect with Daisy on a deeper level. I want her to know how much I've missed her. I want her to feel how much I need her.

"So beautiful." I caress her jaw. "You want it, don't you, beautiful girl?"

"Yes," she breathes, giving my shaft a squeeze.

"Then take me out and suck me to the back of your throat."

She pulls my briefs down my legs so that we're both completely naked before she picks my dick up from where it's lying hard on my stomach and wraps her lips around me. I see stars when she begins to lick and suck me, doing everything I like until my body begins to tense. She must feel that I'm close because she pops off my dick and uses just the tip of her tongue to lick the sensitive spot on the underside of my cock, absolutely fucking torturing me.

It doesn't take long before I can feel the edge of my orgasm starting to build so I reach for her, hauling her up into my arms and flipping her on to the mattress. She locks eyes with me as she crawls backwards into the center of the bed, and I swear I can hear the beating of our hearts. For the years we lost. The mistakes I made and the hurt and pain that we've both endured.

Everything vanishes.

Time stands still.

I settle into the V of her thighs, lining up at her entrance, and with a slow thrust of my hips I slide inside her.

"Oh, Tuck," she cries as her body stretches around my cock.

I bite my lip, squeezing my eyes shut as the pleasure zips up my spine. I sink in as deep as I can and stay there until my pelvis is touching hers and Daisy's hips rock up into mine, encouraging me on.

"Always so wet for me. That's my girl." I pump my hips, changing the angle until I find the one that sparks her orgasm.

"I really want to come," she moans, her eyes still wide open and locked on mine. Eye contact while I'm inside her is the hottest fucking thing.

"I know, baby. I'll get you there." My voice is strained, my finger sliding between us to her clit where I run my finger in tiny circles. Her back arches and her mouth falls open and the image alone almost sends me over the edge.

"Come for me, Dais." My voice is strained, the hold I have on my control fading away.

Daisy loses control, clenching hard around my dick, as I continue to rock my hips into her wetness. "You were made for me," I growl. "God, Daisy, do you feel that? It just gets better with you every time."

She's drenched my cock with her arousal, the sound alone something I will never forget. I pin her leg to the bed with my hand, keeping her spread wide open, until pleasure pools at the base of spine and white light steals my vision.

"Daisy." I come on a groan, pouring inside her as her walls flutter around my cock, milking every drop of me. I tell her how perfect she feels, how perfect she is for me, how much I want her as I draw out the orgasm as long as I can, losing all control and concept of time. My heart thunders in my chest and I allow myself to fall deep into the abyss of my release, until I finally surface for air.

Heart beating, I collapse onto her chest, regaining my focus slowly as my breathing returns to normal. She whimpers as I pull out of her before I turn over to my back, taking her with me. I hold my breath, waiting for Daisy to get up and collect her clothes. To run for the door like she always has. But she cuddles into me instead. Her long hair tickling my arm, her palm flat on the center of my chest.

We have never slept in the same bed together. I have never spent the night with anyone. But I want Daisy to stay more than anything. I want to wake up to her. I want it to be Daisy who is the first person I see when I open my eyes.

Softly, I kiss the top of her head before sliding out of

bed. "I'm just going to turn off the light," I say, reaching for the corner of my duvet and yanking it back. "Get in, Dais. I want you to stay."

I hold my breath, worried this might be too good to be true. My heart is in my throat as I pray that she won't second guess herself and find an excuse to leave.

And while I do everything in my power to will her to stay, she climbs underneath the covers and curls up with her head on my pillow.

I flick the switch on the light and climb back into bed beside her and a few minutes later, she's asleep in my arms.

Well... fuck.

I think I fell in love today.

TWENTY-FOUR

WE BROKE ANOTHER ONE OF YOUR RULES

Daisy

I wake up the next morning with Tucker's arm draped over me.

I am in Tucker's bed.

For the first time, instead of making a beeline for the door, I stayed. All through the night.

My heart pounds behind my ribs when I remember last night and everything that happened. Tucker has a photo of me in his bedroom, and he has my name tattooed on his body. He said that he wants me, that he's never stopped wanting me. The confession is enough to make my heart stop. I've always dreamt of hearing him say those words, but never actually believed I would.

I stay in the warmth of his arms for a stolen moment before carefully slipping out from underneath him to stand. Then I tiptoe to his ensuite bathroom, thankful that I don't have to chance an awkward run-in with Holden.

I quietly shut the door, then run the tap until the water turns hot, splashing my face. My hair is wild, and my lips are pink and swollen from Tucker's kisses. I look like a mess, but

I don't care. It was one of the best nights of my life. Tucker is mine.

I'm drying my face when I hear a soft knock on the door. I wrap my body in a bath towel before opening the door to see a half-awake Tucker standing there. He's put on a pair of boxer briefs and he's leaning against the doorframe with the sweetest grin. He's so beautiful it hurts.

"Morning, Dais."

My cheeks flame. "Morning."

"I was worried you left me."

I smile. "I'm here."

"We broke another one of your rules."

"I'm pretty certain we've broke them all."

Including the last one, I think to myself, but I don't dare tell him that. It's way too soon to admit that I'm in love with him.

"Just in case I didn't make it clear last night... I'm done with the rules, Dais," he answers, kissing the side of my temple as he walks past me toward the shower. "But I should warn you that I've never done this before. Being in a relationship, I mean; it's new for me. But I want you. I want us. I'll do what it takes to make this work."

"I want that too." I go up on my toes and press a kiss to his mouth then I check my pulse and make sure it's still beating. My God. Am I okay? How is this man mine? I can't be okay. I'm distracted by how gorgeous he looks in the morning. He gives me his most charming grin as he slides his briefs off onto the floor. "Have a shower with me, yeah?"

Tucker reaches for my hand, and I slip my fingers into his as the towel wrapped around me falls to the floor. His eyes roam my body before he kisses me softly on the mouth. He turns on the shower and then pulls me under the spray with him, his big arms wrapping around my waist as his lips brush the shell of my ear.

"I'm going to fuck you the way you deserve and then we're going to get dressed and after that I'm going to feed you breakfast. And when Holden asks what's going on, I'm going to tell him that you're mine because I refuse to keep you and I a secret anymore. Good?"

He pops a chaste kiss on my lips before I give him my answer. And of course, my answer is...

"Good."

The next few weeks fly by in a blur. Tucker and I are both busy with work. The clinic has been crazy—I'm still trying to get Hazel up to speed, and Tucker has been busy traveling out of state to visit potential recruits and their families in preparation of next season. When he is in town, he's been prepping for training camp. Whatever free time we manage to find, we spend it together, and most nights I fall asleep with Tucker's arms nestled around me.

We haven't told our parents yet that we're together—neither of us have felt ready for that discussion. It's meant we've skipped Sunday dinners for the past few weeks, so I haven't had to see Tucker's dad. Finding out what he did to keep us apart all those years ago felt like a sledgehammer to my heart and sometimes I wonder if I will ever be ready to see the man I once thought of as a second dad.

Tucker and I won't be able to avoid them for much longer, though. Our birthdays are coming up, and our parents are insisting on throwing us a party this Sunday, so it potentially could be a very awkward evening.

We have, however, shared the news with our friends. For

the most part, it was met with a chorus of *what took you so long* and *it's about time* and I admit that has made me hopeful that my parents might feel the same way.

Despite the nervousness we both feel about having to confront his dad, things between Tucker and I have been incredible. We have been making up for lost time, getting to know each other again, and even though I know Tucker almost as well as I know myself, it has still been fun learning all the little details of his life that I've missed out on. Things like what he likes to eat for breakfast, and what side of the bed he sleeps on, whether he snores (I was happy to find out that he doesn't) and what shows he binges on Netflix (currently, sports biographies, but I'm determined to get him into true crime).

There is one thing we seem to steer clear of: The fact that I leave for Italy in just a few weeks. It's sort of the elephant in the room with us. It's like we can both hear the clock ticking, but neither of us wants to bring it up and risk bursting this little bubble we're in. After what we've been through over the past 10 years, I feel confident that we will be able to get through three months apart. But I'm going to miss him so much.

Today, though, I'm spending the day shopping with my mom before I meet up with Tucker and a few of his friends later for dinner to celebrate our birthdays. When we walk into Nordstrom, I feel my phone vibrate in my back pocket.

> Tucker: What time are you finished shopping with your mom?
>
> Me: Why? Is everything okay?
>
> Tucker: I miss you. I haven't seen you in ten and a half hours. I shouldn't have to be without you for this long.

A smile stretches across my face, and I have to remind myself to play it cool.

> Me: Will you survive?
>
> Tucker: I'm not sure.
>
> Me: I'll be home around four, pick me up at six?
>
> Tucker: If I can wait that long *sad face emoji*

I shove my phone in my pocket, noticing that my mom is staring at me with a curious expression.

"Why are you looking at me like that?" I ask.

"Just wondering who it is who has you smiling like that."

I chance a glance at her. Her eyes are on me, and it's obvious that she can read me like a book.

"Well…" My mom grins, then her eyebrows raise as if she's waiting for me to spill the beans. "Whoever he is, he must be special for you to light up like that. It's nice to see. You deserve to be happy, honey, and from the look on your face, it seems like you are."

I can feel a smile spreading across my face, and I hope it's not as obvious as it feels. I swallow, looking down at my feet, then I decide to rip off the Band-Aid. "It's Tucker."

I steel myself for her response, for the disappointment in her eyes. So, for a full 20 seconds I keep walking, looking straight ahead while I wait for her to tell me that it would be ridiculous to date the man who was practically a brother to me growing up. We keep walking, the silence stretching out between us.

But when my mom stops and looks at me, there is no judgment in her eyes.

"Are you and Tucker together?"

"It's new, but yes."

She exhales, considering this. "I can't say that I'm surprised. I've seen the way the two of you look at each other."

I laugh, releasing the breath I've been holding. "I've been so afraid to tell you. I didn't know how you would react."

"How did you think I would react? You know I love Tucker like he's my own."

"That's part of the problem. We've always been so close; I think sometimes people forget that Tucker and I are not actually related."

"Who would think that?"

"Uncle Mark."

I fill her in on everything, starting with the kiss when we were 16 years old. I tell her about Uncle Mark making Tucker agree to stay away from me, I tell her about Tuck's tattoo, the photo, and almost everything that has happened over the past few months.

I obviously leave out our pact.

By the time I've finished filling her in, the expression on her face has softened. "Oh, Daisy," my mom says, pulling me into a hug. "You have been smiling a lot lately. I am so happy you and Tucker found your way back to each other. But I would like to have a word with Mark."

"No, please don't," I shake my head. "Tucker and I plan on handling it, but I appreciate it."

"He needs to learn. It's not right how he treats Tucker. He's grown up to be a good man who has done very well for himself, despite his dad's constant criticism."

"That's what I don't understand, Mom. Tucker can't seem to ever do anything right in Uncle Mark's eyes, but to everyone else in Reed Point he's practically a legend." I inhale a sharp breath. "When will Uncle Mark see him for the man that he really is?"

"Your dad and I have always wanted to give him a piece of our mind for that. He has never gotten over the fact that Tucker didn't follow in his footsteps. But... *my god,* that boy was born to coach football."

She looks at me with an abundance of love in her eyes–it's the same way she's looked at me since I was a little girl, and I feel incredibly lucky to have two parents who have always loved and supported me and my decisions.

"So, are things serious between you and Tucker?"

"I think so," I shrug. "It feels like he could be ready for a relationship, he told me he wants to try. But it's funny how life works considering I'm leaving on my trip soon."

"Oh, honey... If he cares about you and you care about him, he'll be here waiting for you when you get home."

"Thank you," I say with a soft smile.

"For what, honey?"

"For always being there for me."

My mom takes me by the shoulders and pulls me into her arms. Her voice is quiet when she squeezes me a little tighter and says, "I love you, baby. Always have, always will."

"I love you, too."

My heart clenches and I'm hopeful that Tucker's parents will be as accepting of our relationship as my mom is.

But I have a feeling deep down in my gut that won't be the case.

TWENTY-FIVE

ENJOY WHAT'S MINE

Tucker

"How's it going with Daisy?" Jake and I are sitting at the bar, waiting for the others while Daisy, Briar, and Everly are in the restroom.

"She's perfect."

Jake makes a big show of looking shocked. Head tilted backwards, a smile on his face like he's just witnessed the birth of Jesus Christ himself.

"You act like a moron sometimes," I say before taking a sip of my scotch.

"I just never thought I'd see the day. Can it be real? Tucker Collins is finally settling down?"

"You're hilarious," I mutter. "But *you* should probably settle down. I'm happy and I'm committed, but it's not like I'm proposing."

"Yet."

I raise my brows with a smirk from behind my rocks glass.

"What's going on with Holden and Aubrey?"

I grimace. "He didn't tell you?"

"I haven't seen him, but I've heard rumblings that things aren't going well."

"They broke up."

Jake throws me a curious look. "I'm not surprised. Seems like things have been bad for a while. How's he taking it?"

"I'm honestly not sure. He's hardly ever home."

"Sounds sus."

Just then, the girls return from the restroom. Daisy comes to stand next to me at the bar and I slip my arm around her waist. We hear a burst of noise at the front of the restaurant and look to see Grayson and Sierra, Beckett and Jules and Holden crowding into the restaurant foyer.

I raise a hand in greeting, and they all come meet us at the bar before we're taken to our table. A waitress soon drops off a round of shots for the group, with mocktails for Everly and Sierra. "Happy birthday!" Grayson yells, raising his shot glass in the air. "To Daisy and Tucker. Can you guys believe these two are finally together? It's about fucking time."

"Cheers to that," Holden agrees, holding up his drink. "You two are cute as fuck!" The table erupts in laughter as we all stand to click our glasses before knocking back the shots. I smile as I look around the table. I fucking love my friends and I'm so excited to have Daisy here tonight to start to get to know them better. When we sit back down, I rest my hand discreetly on Daisy's thigh under the table, and her fingers intertwine with mine. Just being out in public with her with all my friends makes everything feel right in the world.

"Tuck," Grayson says, stealing my attention away from my girlfriend. "I hear that you agreed to cat sit for Jake and Ev. What the fuck is that about? I didn't take you for a cat guy."

"I'm cat-sitting for Birdie," I correct him. "You try saying no to that sweet little face."

Jake is taking Everly and Birdie on a babymoon. I have no idea what the fuck a babymoon is, but the three of them are going to Florida for a week. When they had no one to watch the kitten Jake bought for Birdie, I stepped up, forgetting that I sort of hate cats.

"It means the world to Birdie-girl," Jake says with a slick smile. "She somehow believes Lucy is in good hands over at Uncle Tuck and Uncle Holdey's. You two better not fuck it up."

"Geez, man, have a little faith," Holden says, grinning. "Tucker and I are very responsible, upstanding young men."

"Debatable," Jake scoffs.

"Don't listen to my husband," Everly says, kissing Jake on his cheek. "He just likes to give you guys the gears. Now, back to the two of you." She looks from me to Daisy. "I'm really happy for you guys. I heard a little about your history, that you've been friends since forever."

"Yup," Daisy smiles next to me, squeezing my thigh. "Which has made things amazing but also sort of... complicated. Our families are so close that our parents tend to treat us like we're siblings."

Beckett leans in to join the conversation. "Do your parents know..."

"That we're together? No, but I did tell my mom, and she supports us." When Daisy told me earlier today that she told her mom about us, I wasn't surprised that Aunt Vic was so cool about it. My dad, on the other hand, is going to flip the fuck out.

My expression must reveal my worries about my dad, because Grayson suddenly claps a hand on my shoulder.

"Relax, man. Once your dad sees how happy the two of you are together, he'll change his tune. You'll see."

I nod before taking a sip of my drink. "I hope you're right."

I can't help but notice the way Daisy fits in so effortlessly with my friends. She's been laughing and smiling all night, and of course they all seem to adore her. I love seeing this side of her.

She sets her drink on the table and leans in closer to me. Her piercing blue eyes look at me through dark lashes, her mouth only an inch or so away from mine, and I instantly unravel from the eye contact. I press a kiss to her mouth, but it isn't nearly enough. I'm already wanting more.

"You look so hot. Do you have any idea how bad I want you right now?" I growl, my mouth only an inch from her ear, my hand in her hair.

A small sound escapes her lips. "I think I have an idea, but it's going to have to wait. Think you can hold off for a little while, Coach Collins?"

I should take her up against the wall in the bathroom for sassing me like that, but instead, I murmur into her ear, "You're so sweet around my friends, but if they only knew the filthy things that are running through your mind right now, rebel."

My girl– fuck, I love the sound of that– wraps her pretty pink lips around her straw and sips from her drink with a smile on her face. My dick perks up in my pants.

"I'm going to take my time with you tonight, Dais. Fuck you slow and steady before I fuck you hard and fast. Enjoy what's mine."

She gives me a wicked smirk that sends a bolt of lust straight to my cock. And that's all that needs to be said between us. We both know I will make good on my promise.

When the night ends, we walk toward the beach where I parked my truck. As soon as we reach it, I grab her by the back of her neck and pull her face to mine, erasing the space between us.

We kiss with the urgency of two people who've been waiting all night for this exact moment. Every minute of pent-up desire bursts in a merciless kiss up against the door of my truck. Her tongue searches for mine. My hands grip either side of her neck like I never want to let her go. I groan into her mouth as my cock grows painfully hard behind the zipper of my jeans.

When we finally break the kiss, we're both breathless. And I know without a shadow of a doubt that my obsession with Daisy has turned into a full-blown addiction. How did this happen so quickly?

As I pull away, I whisper, "So, are you going to invite me back to your house?"

A quiet laugh escapes her lips, making my entire body light up. "Tucker, would you like to come back to my house?"

"I would love to."

TWENTY-SIX

MY NAUGHTY FUCKING GIRL

Daisy

The next morning, I wake up to the feel of Tucker's mouth kissing a trail over the curve of my shoulder, the arch of my back nestled into the warmth of his body. The scent of Tucker is the next thing that floods my senses, followed by the realization that it's his birthday. That means it's also mine.

"Happy birthday," he whispers against my shoulder in a raspy morning voice.

Turning in his arms, I stretch my leg over his hip before I plant a soft kiss to his pillowy lips. "Happy Birthday to you too."

He frowns when I untangle myself from his body. Reaching under my bed, I pull out his gift, which I stashed there last night.

I watch him smile as I hold it out to him, flopping back into bed. "I got you something."

He takes the large, wrapped box from me and sits up in bed to unwrap it. He pulls away the layers of green and gold tissue paper to reveal the framed 11 x 14 image of Tucker on the sidelines at the moment he won the Division 2 national championship game. His hands are raised, his smile wide, green and gold confetti in the air. In that moment, he was as beautiful as I've ever seen him.

He looks speechless when he pulls the frame from the box. "Where did you get this?"

"The image?"

He nods, taking in the photo.

"I contacted the team photographer. Might have told him I was your sister so he would share it with me."

"Rebel." He chuckles before pulling my face to his, kissing the life out of me.

I smile, fluttering my eyelashes at him. "Worth it."

"It's amazing, Dais. Thank you." Tucker leans into me pressing a long and lingering kiss to my lips. "I have something for you too," he says before climbing out of bed and reaching into his overnight bag. My eyes sparkle up at him when he hands me a little silver box. Plucking at the white ribbon wrapped around it, I open the box and gasp. I stare at the necklace, a thin gold chain with a diamond pendant attached. A daisy. I told him that I love anything with a daisy on it at the diner months ago, but I never expected him to remember. Does he have any idea how much this gift means to me?

"I don't know what to say. I can't believe you remembered."

"Happy birthday, Daisy." His knuckles brush over my cheek and I lean into the touch. "I remember everything you say. Here, let me help you."

Tucker opens the clasp and then moves behind me, placing the dainty gold chain around my neck. "I want you to wear it on your trip, so you feel close to me," he says before kissing the back of my neck and putting my hair back in place.

My fingers brush over the pendant as emotion clogs my throat. "I love it so much. I'm never taking it off."

"It looks pretty on you." He smiles back at me before hopping out of bed again. "That's not all. Stay here. Don't move, I'll be right back."

"What are you doing?"

"Celebrating my girl's birthday."

"It's your birthday too."

"It'll be my birthday tonight when I tie you to my bed, spread your legs wide and eat you instead of my birthday cake because it's my birthday and having a taste of you is my favorite thing in the world," he says with a wink, before disappearing into the hallway.

Fifteen minutes later, he walks back into the room wearing only the silly pajama pants I bought him for Christmas with his face plastered all over them, and he has a cup of tea and two lemon cupcakes that I recognize from Buttercup Bakery in his hand.

"Breakfast for the birthday girl." He hands me the plate before grabbing the TV remote and opening the blinds.

"Shit, rebel. I couldn't have planned this better if I tried. Do you see this?"

I sit up in bed, following his gaze to the window, where I notice it's raining. I cock my head to the side, wondering how this is a good thing. Tucker starts rifling through my drawer until he finds a pair of my craziest fuzzy socks and one of his RPU T-shirts that I stole.

"What is going on?" I ask him as he slips into bed beside me handing me the T-shirt and socks, looking like he's clearly up to something.

"Put these on. We're doing all your favorite things today,

Daisy." He stacks two pillows against my headboard, leans back and opens his legs wide, patting the spot between them. Once I've slipped the cotton over my head and shoved my feet into the socks, I move so I'm sitting between his legs. "We're going to watch a movie in bed while I play with your hair, and can you believe it... it's raining. Just the way my birthday girl likes it."

I turn to face him, my eyes wide. "Tuck..."

"Is this okay? We can go out for breakfast if you want, or we can head down to White Harbor? Go shopping? Whatever you want, Daisy." He nervously rattles off the list of activities while my heart expands in my chest.

I could just tell him that this is the nicest thing anyone has ever done for me, birthday or not. Instead, I wrap my arms around his neck and pull his mouth to mine.

"I take it I did good," he says through a smile when we break the kiss. "I've never done anything like this before, but I really wanted to make you happy."

Oh. My. God. Okay, I might never recover from that. I take his face in my hands, and tell him, "It's perfect. You've set the bar. I will compare all other birthdays to this one. So yes, Tucker, you have made me very happy."

"I'm glad." He kisses my forehead, followed by my nose then my mouth. "So, it's better than our 13th birthday when I smashed your face into the cake and then told Addy to push you in the pool?"

I laugh into my hands. "Oh my god, remember how mad I was at you? I didn't talk to you for a week."

"When I tried to apologize you called me an assclown," Tucker says, cracking up. "You yelled it, actually, in the hallway at school. I never forgot that."

"I'm sorry. That wasn't very nice of me. Even if you were being an assclown."

"You can apologize to me later. I have ideas."

"Before or after you tie me up and eat me for dessert?"

He presses his lips to mine. "My naughty fucking girl."

Then he's scrolling through Netflix with my head on his chest until he finds *Wedding Crashers* and hits play.

It feels like it did when we were kids, except so much better. I swallow a moan when his hand makes the first run through my hair, and all I can feel is my heartbeat behind my chest, the way my skin erupts in shivers.

Tucker plays with my hair in silence as I listen to the steady beat of his heart, my hand drawing circles on his abs. Tears pool in my eyes, and I swipe them away, grateful that he can't see my face.

"I'm going to do a shitty job of pretending you're not my girlfriend tonight, you know," he murmurs as his hands brush my shoulder. "Apparently, it's obvious how much I like you. That's what the guys tell me anyways."

I prop my chin on my hand, glancing up at him. "We could always just tell them."

"We could, but I think we should we wait until after our birthday. It's been such a good morning; I don't want to ruin our day with a big fight."

Tucker is right. I don't want to ruin our day together either. I sit up, straddling his waist, and then I pull his RPU shirt over my head. I kiss him until we're both breathless before taking off his pajama pants, lining myself up with his already weeping cock and lowering myself onto him. Then I show him with my actions and not my words how madly in love with him I am.

NEVER SAY NEVER

AS WE WALK THE STONE PATHWAY TO MY PARENTS' FRONT door, I'm wondering if I am ready to be here, my anxiety already spiraling. Do I have it in me to be cordial to Tuck's dad? Will his parents suspect that we're together? And when we finally do tell them, how will they react?

"You're nervous," Tucker says, looking concerned.

"I'm not nervous," I quip back.

"Daisy." He frowns. "I've known you all my life. I know when you're nervous."

"It's nothing. I'm fine," I say, tucking my hair behind my ear.

I take a deep breath. It's just Sunday dinner, we've been doing this for over 26 years. Well, sort of. I've never been Tucker's girlfriend before, and I am a freaking stressed. I am also wondering how I'm going to look my Uncle Mark in the eye. I'm still so angry with him.

Tucker's warm hand settles on the base of my spine. And just that little bit of contact is enough to settle my nerves.

"They don't know that we're together now, but we're going to have to tell them soon."

"I know, just not tonight," I remind him. "Let's try to enjoy our birthday."

My heart is racing by the time we walk into the kitchen. The moment I see Tucker's dad, my back stiffens. He is standing at the kitchen island pouring himself a glass of wine. His stance is cocky, as it always is. I used to think it was confidence, now all I see is arrogance.

"Happy Birthday, sweetheart," my mom says, putting her arm around my shoulder and squeezing me tight. "And you too, Tuck." She pulls Tuck into her other side.

My uncle's dress shoes tap against the tile floor as he walks toward us, and I have to force a polite smile onto my face when he stands in front of me. Typically, I would give him a big hug when I see him, but after everything Tucker has told me, I'm finding it difficult to even say hello.

"Happy birthday, Daisy. I can't believe it's been 27 years since the day you and my son were born." My body stiffens when his arms reach for me, and with an uneasy smile, I reluctantly step into his arms. I know how bizarre it must look to everyone else in the room when I greet my uncle so cooly, but it's the best I'm able to do.

Thankfully, the awkward moment passes quickly as my dad and my Aunt Daisy are waiting to give me a birthday hug, followed by Addy and Jonathan.

"Let's get you a glass of wine," Tuck says with his warm hand pressed softly into the small of my back, sensing the tension.

"Good idea," my mom says with a giant smile, clearly excited to see Tucker and I together as a couple for the first time.

Tucker hands me a glass of Riesling and I follow his sister to the living room to sit near the fireplace. I tuck my foot underneath me and curl up on the couch with my wine, enjoying the fire.

"Everything okay?" Addy asks, sitting next to me. Clearly, I'm doing a shitty job of hiding my emotions.

"Yeah, I'm fine. How is everything with you?"

She shifts in her seat, turning toward me. "Are you sure everything is okay? Something seems off with you. My brother is acting strange too."

"I promise you, I'm fine. I'm just tired. I went out for my birthday, and I guess I didn't get enough sleep."

"Did you at least have a good night?"

"I had a great night." *God, if she only knew just how good.* "What did you get up to this weekend?"

I listen to Addy tell me about the new restaurant

Jonathan took her to, the weekend getaway they're planning, the documentary she watched on Netflix. Eventually, we are joined in the living room by my mom and Aunt Daisy. My dad and Uncle Mark are chatting at the bar, mixing drinks.

"Can I make you a special birthday drink, Daisy?" my dad asks over his shoulder.

"That actually sounds nice, Dad," I tell him, thinking it could help to take the edge off. "But not too strong."

"Your dad has no idea how to make a weak drink," my mom says. "Randy, you are an accessory to a bad hangover."

He laughs. "I should make you one of these, Victoria. Might get me lucky tonight."

"In your dreams." My mom laughs, rolling her eyes.

Tucker emerges from the kitchen with Jonathan just as my dad hands me the drink. I try not to let my disappointment show when Tuck sits on the couch next to his sister instead of the empty spot next to me. I'm not ready for our parents to know about our relationship, but my body craves his attention. Even from the other side of the couch, I am hyper-aware of his presence. God, I wish we could just get tonight over with.

I've dated other guys, but no one has ever made me want them like Tucker does. What will I do when I leave for Italy? How will I ever survive the distance when I'm sitting here sulking over not being able to sit next to him?

"So, son, I was talking to Jack Mayers last night," Tucker's dad says, sinking into the high-backed chair across from us. "His daughter just broke up with her fiancé. You remember Julianna. She's a nice girl, you should think about taking her out."

Julianna Mayers is a gorgeous blonde with big, brown eyes and a body that rivals any swimsuit model. She is also the daughter of a very wealthy doctor. I don't know her well, but I've met her at the country club, where my parents are also members. There's no way I can hold a candle to a girl like Julianna. Irritated, I grip my martini glass so tightly that it tips, spilling down my shirt.

"Shit," I mutter, and in a split second, Tucker is up on his feet, handing me a napkin and taking my drink from my hand. His eyes meet mine briefly before he retreats to his spot on the couch, and he looks apologetic. As soon as Tucker sits down, his dad immediately continues where he left off. "She was asking about you, Tucker. Told me to congratulate you when I saw you next on your big win. I told her you'd give her a call."

"I'm not interested in Julianna, Dad," Tucker says in a frustrated tone.

"I don't see why you wouldn't be. She's a gorgeous girl."

"I told you, *I'm not interested*."

Relief floods through me, but I'm still wound tight at the thought of a girl like Julianna Mayers being interested in Tucker. *My Tucker*. I take a deep breath, careful to keep the façade in place.

"I'm going to check on dinner," my mom announces, breaking the awkward silence.

"Let me help you," Aunt Daisy says, looking at Uncle Mark and adding, "Honey, can you check the wine fridge for a nice bottle to have with dinner?"

As soon as our parents have left the room, Addy relaxes into the couch, looking from me to Tucker. "So, are you two going to make me ask the obvious, or should I just assume?" My eyes widen in surprise. I should have known that Addy wouldn't be easy to fool—she knows me almost as well as her brother does. When Tucker opens his mouth to answer her, I stop him. I don't want to lie to her.

"We're together, Addy, but we're not ready to tell our—"

"For the love of Pete, it took you long enough," she says, interrupting me.

Tucker looks at me, his lips tipping up in amusement. Maybe this will go better than we expected.

"How could you keep this from me?" Addy's voice is a loud whisper.

"It all kinda just happened," Tucker explains. "And we aren't sure how everyone will take it."

"You mean how Dad will take it."

"Mainly." Tucker agrees with his sister.

"Oh, who cares what he thinks? Besides, even if he's not excited about it at first, he'll come around. He might just need a little time."

Tucker looks skeptical. "And if he doesn't, I couldn't give a fuck."

"Well, *I'm* thrilled. And Aunt Victoria and Uncle Randy will be fine," Addy continues. "So will Mom. Dad might throw a fit, but you're used to his shit by now. It's nothing you can't handle."

"Point made. Now, can we change the subject before someone hears us?" I ask. "I want to know all about the hotel Jonathan took you to."

"Oh, it was to die for!" Addy leans forward in her chair, slipping her phone out of her pocket, and scrolling through her camera roll. "Just look at this pool, Daisy."

I look across the couch to Tucker and when our eyes meet, he winks. Maybe this will all work out after all.

AFTER DINNER, TUCKER AND I ARE THE FIRST TO LEAVE. Neither of us can stand to be there another minute, but even more than that, we're both aching to touch one another. My muscles are stiff, my jaw tight from the act I just put on in front of Tucker's dad. It wasn't easy to look him in the eye and not tell him how much he has hurt me. It also wasn't easy to lie to Aunt Daisy and my dad about being in a relationship with Tuck. I get in Tucker's truck and lean back against the headrest, rolling my head from side to side.

"Are you okay?" He doesn't start the truck, instead turning in his seat to face me and reaching for my neck. I groan when he begins to rub the knot that has formed above my left shoulder blade.

"I'm fine. Just a little tense from tonight. How about you?"

"Besides not being able to drag you back into my dad's office and christen his desk, I'm okay," he says, still massaging my neck. "Come here."

Tucker leans across the console and I meet him halfway. When his lips settle over mine, a whimper escapes my mouth and soon our tongues tangle. A shiver skates up my spine; it's a kiss we have both been eager for all night.

"You have no idea how badly I wanted to kiss you in there," he says when he finally pulls away.

"Oh, I think I do," I say, going back for more. This time, Tucker's hand cups my face while his mouth slants over mine.

This is everything I need.

Just as we break the kiss, I see a figure through the windshield. My breath catches in my throat.

Shit. Shit. Shit.

Tucker's dad is standing in the driveway.

I freeze. The air in the truck is stifling, so thick it feels hard to breathe. Tucker's back stiffens when his gaze follows my line of sight.

This can't be happening. My eyes squeeze shut, hoping

that I'm seeing things but when they reopen, I'm staring right into the angry eyes of my Uncle Mark. He crosses his arms over his chest, then we both watch as he turns around and stalks back inside the house.

"Fuuuuck." Tucker stretches the word out, pressing his fingers against his closed eyes.

"That is not how I planned on telling him," I say.

"Me either." He drags his hand through his hair with a sigh. "But it's done."

It was careless of us to kiss like that in the driveway with our families just feet away, but as awkward as this is, I also feel a sense of relief that we no longer need to hide.

"Should we go inside?" I ask quietly.

"Yeah, let's just get this over with."

TWENTY-SEVEN
THIS ISN'T THE END OF US

Tucker

Daisy's hand is in mine as we head inside to face the wrath of my father. We're both pretty positive he's the only one who will have an issue with us dating. I think it will be a shock for my Uncle Randy and my mom, but once we explain that we have real feelings for each other, I'm betting they will understand. My dad, on the other hand, is going to lose his mind.

My hand grips Daisy's a little tighter when we walk through the foyer toward the kitchen. I pause for a second, looking down at her. "Ready?"

"Yes. It's going to be fine, Tuck. We haven't done anything wrong."

We enter the kitchen to find my mom and Aunt Victoria huddled together at the island, talking in hushed tones. When they see us, their expressions soften. I assume Aunt Vic has filled my mom in on everything. I instantly feel guilty that I wasn't the one to tell her I'm dating Daisy, but I refuse to feel bad about being with her. We're adults. If

Daisy and I want to be together that's up to us. Nobody else gets a say in this.

I take a quick glance around the space to see if I can find my dad as I hold Daisy's hand a little tighter, but he isn't around.

"Victoria told me about the two of you after dad stormed into the house in a rage," my mom says, meeting us in the middle of the kitchen. "She said you two are together, which is quite the surprise. She said it's serious."

"It is," I admit. "And I'm not apologizing for it, so please don't try to make me."

My mom holds up a hand to stop me. "I'm not here to make things worse for you, Tucker, but I also want to know what's going on. I hate that you kept this a secret from us."

"I'm sorry, Mom, I really am," I tell her, wishing that Daisy and I had just come clean to our parents weeks ago. "Are you upset?"

"That you kept it from me... yes. But you're not a child, Tuck. And it's not my place to tell you who you're allowed to date. I just hope you both have thought this through."

"We have." Daisy nods. "It's sort of a long story."

"I don't need the details. Daisy, you have always been like a daughter to us. You are our family, blood or not. So, if it takes us a minute to wrap our heads around the news, I hope you'll understand." My mom pauses before looking at me. "I'm your mom, Tucker, and I only want to see you happy, and if Daisy is the one to do that, then how can I stand in your way?"

"Thank you, Mom." I feel the emotions start to bubble up inside of me. My mother usually sides with my father, she rarely goes against him. And even though she doesn't appear to be over the moon happy, her understanding is good enough for me. I know she'll come around.

"I love you both," Aunt Victoria says, resting a hand on my shoulder. "And I just want to see you both happy too."

Her response doesn't surprise me, but I am grateful to her all the same. I have so many happy memories with my aunt. She has always been there for me, but I have never appreciated her more than I do right now.

Swallowing down my nerves, I ask, "Where's Dad?"

"He's outside talking to Uncle Randy. He's pretty upset. Randy is trying to calm him down."

"Did you two get into it out there?" my mom asks.

"No," I reply. "He didn't stick around after he saw us kissing."

My eyes drop to where my fingers are laced with Daisy's as I try to decide how much I should say. "There's more to the story," I admit. "I've been upset with him for a very long time over it. I'm tired of him thinking that he knows what's best for me."

"Maybe you two can finally work this out," Daisy's mom says. "Do you think it's something you can forgive your dad for?"

"I'm not sure."

I look to Daisy, her warm, blue eyes looking up at me, and it takes everything in me not to gather her up in my arms and hold her close to me. But first, I need to deal with my dad. I pull her into me and press a soft kiss to the top of her head, not caring that our moms are watching the display of affection. "I'm going to go talk to my dad," I whisper into her hair.

"Okay."

I leave Daisy in the kitchen and head out to the patio, where I'm greeted by my dad's icy gaze. He's holding a tumbler of scotch, half-full, a look of intense anger on his face. My Uncle Randy stands stiffly beside him.

"What the hell was that, Tucker?" Dad snaps. His brows are pinched together, and his eyes are glued to me.

I cross my arms over my chest, straightening my spine. It's very clear that he's upset, but I'm not backing down. I unclench my jaw and try to keep my voice calm. "I think it's obvious."

My dad shakes his head. "Enlighten me. Why the hell were you kissing Daisy? Are you together?"

"We are," I answer firmly.

I glance at Daisy's dad, trying to figure out where he stands in all of this, but his expression is one I can't read. He seems to be more concerned with calming my dad down, which I appreciate. My dad can scream and yell as loud as he wants, it won't change a thing about my feelings for Daisy. In this moment, she is the only person I care about.

"I'm going to go inside and talk to Daisy." Uncle Randy looks at my dad and then to me before walking inside. He closes the door behind him, and the second he does, my dad turns to me with anger in his eyes.

"I thought I made it clear a long time ago that you are not to mess with Daisy," he fumes.

"*Mess* with her?" If he's trying to piss me off, he's a doing a good fucking job. "When have I ever messed with Daisy? I've spent my entire life looking out for her. I would do anything for that girl, and I think I've proven that."

"Oh, come on, Tucker." He rolls his eyes. "You did all that because she's family. Because I asked you to. Even you must see that this is a terrible idea. You're just going to fuck it up. You'll get tired of her, get bored and break up with her. Stop thinking with your dick and consider the damage it will do to all of us when you break her heart." My dad gestures toward the house where the others are inside.

"Why the hell would I break her heart?"

"Because you don't do relationships, Tucker. I lost track of the number of women you've dated a very long time ago. You'll get bored with Daisy within weeks, and then it will be over. You can't commit to a house plant, you've proven that. Hell, in 27 years you've never even brought a girlfriend home. If that isn't a sign that you have no clue what commitment means, then I don't know what is. So, this is what you are going to do: you are going to leave Daisy alone. And you're going to do it immediately. Let her find someone who actually wants a future with her, not just a good time."

The accusation is like a punch to the gut. Does he really think I'm that much of an asshole? Sure, he's right, I *have* dated my fair share, but I've been up front and honest with the women I've been with. I may not have wanted to commit to them, but that doesn't mean I don't want something serious with Daisy. Everything changed the moment I started seeing her. I've kept my mouth shut for far too long and I am done. I. Am. So. Fucking. Done.

"Let's make one thing clear. I'm not asking you for your permission. If you have a problem with Daisy and I being together, that's on you. I won't stop seeing her this time. I'm not some frightened teenager who will listen to your ultimatums." I pause and then in a clipped tone I add, "There is nothing you can say or do that will get me to change my mind."

Anger flashes across my dad's face and his voice gets louder. "You have no idea what you're doing. End things now before you break her heart and destroy our families in the process. Daisy doesn't deserve this bullshit. The last thing I need is for you to fuck the poor girl up."

"Would it kill you to just have a little faith in me, Dad?" I shake my head, infuriated. "This conversation is over. I'm sorry you had to find out that way, but I will never be sorry for choosing Daisy. I would never hurt her and honestly, I am baffled that you can't understand that. But that's your problem, not mine."

There is so much more I want to say. I want to tell him that she's always been it for me. That I choose her, and that I regret not choosing her all those years ago. But I want Daisy to be the one to hear those words first.

"I've lost her once, Dad, and I won't lose her again."

A look of surprise passes briefly over his face, but he doesn't say a word. Instead, he takes a long drink of his scotch and then turns away from me.

There's nothing more to say. Thank fuck, that's over. We might not see eye to eye on much, including my relationship with Daisy, but if he wants to be a part of my life, he is going to have to figure out how to get over it.

I leave him on the patio outside, returning to the kitchen to find my uncle leaning against the island, as if waiting for me. I can't exactly read his expression, but he doesn't seem angry. He looks pensive, but also open to having a discussion. He proves that when he pulls out a stool for me and motions to it.

"Let's talk, Tucker," he says, taking a seat himself. I can hear the faint voices of Daisy and our moms in the living room and although I want to check on her, I know I need to have this conversation first. We're silent for a moment as I try to decide what I want to say to him. But when I look at him, I can tell he has something to say as well, so I wait and let him go first.

His eyes find mine and I brace myself for what he is about to say. "First off, are you okay?"

Emotion tugs at my chest as I remember all the times I would sit with him and my aunt in their kitchen after I'd had an argument with my dad. "I will be, thanks."

"Good. Your dad will calm down. I'll have a talk with him."

"You don't need to do that."

"I know I don't have to, but I want to." He takes a long, steadying breath.

"I'm really sorry we kept it from you, Uncle Randy. This is not how I wanted you to find out."

"I'm not mad at you, Tuck. You did what you thought was right at the time," he says before clearing his throat. "Your relationship with Daisy is none of my business, but I do want to know if it's serious."

I nod, then I brace myself for what I'm about to say next.

"I'm in love with her." I swallow. "And I realize that may seem strange to you, but I promise you that what I feel for your daughter is real. She means everything to me, and if being with her means losing my relationship with my father, then so be it. I want you to know that I'm not going to stop seeing her. I don't care what he says or what he threatens… it's Daisy and me. I will choose her every time."

"I had to ask," he says, smiling. "Daisy is a smart girl, and I trust her to make her own decisions. But I'm her dad and I can't help but feel protective."

"Of course."

"You really do love her," he says.

"I do. She's it for me."

He nods, looking into his whiskey glass before looking back at me. "Tucker, if you love her like you say you do, I support the two of you."

I exhale, feeling a weight lift off my shoulders. I feel like I'm so close to having everything I've ever wanted. "Thank you, Uncle Randy. I appreciate that."

He claps me on the shoulder, nodding. "You know I'm always here to talk."

"I know," I say.

I still feel like a kid sometimes when Uncle Randy and I have one of our talks. He's still the man I go to when I need advice, and no matter what it's about, I always leave feeling like I am enough.

"I'm glad that you're happy, Tuck."

"Even if it's because of your daughter?"

"Even if."

He knocks back the last of his whiskey before taking his glass over to the kitchen sink. "I think we should all call it a night."

"I think you're right."

"Everything okay in here?" I turn to see Daisy standing in the entrance to the kitchen, looking hesitant but hopeful.

"Everything is just fine, sweetheart. Come here." Uncle Randy holds his arms wide for Daisy and she steps into them. He pulls her into his chest and presses a kiss to her hair. "Love you, Daisy."

"I love you, too, Dad."

Then her gaze shifts to me. "Come on, Tuck, let's get going."

We say our goodbyes and then leave, thankful the night is over. We drive back to my house on Haven Harbor knowing this isn't the end of us.

At least, not yet.

TWENTY-EIGHT
FEELS A LOT LIKE GOODBYE

Tucker

It's our last night together before Daisy leaves, and we're spending it at her apartment. Daisy's flight to Rome is tomorrow afternoon. I'm flying out to New Hampshire the day after that to meet with a potential recruit. We had debated going out tonight with friends, having a little send-off party, but in the end we decided on a quiet night in at her place with some take-out Mexican food from Cocina Caliente.

Since our relationship news blew up at Daisy's parents' house a few weeks ago, things with our families have been as good as we could have expected. Aunt Vic and Uncle Randy have been great. My dad hasn't been in touch, but I'm hardly surprised by that. I've talked to my mom on the phone a couple of times, and she's assured me that she's working on him. I'm not holding my breath and honestly, I couldn't care less. I've had Daisy in my arms every night, and that has been good enough for me. More than good enough.

Being in a relationship—the first one I've had in my life, as crazy as that sounds—feels good and surprisingly natural for us to be a couple. Sometimes I wonder if I was subconsciously just waiting for Daisy all along. I think it's the real reason I never wanted more with any of the girls I hooked up with. They weren't Daisy. No one has ever come close.

It feels like we're getting to know each other again. A long time ago, I knew absolutely everything about Daisy, but it's been years since we've been close, since we've shared secrets with each other. One of my favorite things about being with Daisy, is learning about her all over again—her likes and dislikes, her go-to lunch order, her 10-minute bedtime skin care routine. Well, that and the incredible amount of sex we've been having. She's become an addiction, like a needle straight to my vein, giving me the most incredible high.

We've talked about our dreams for the future—about my hopes to coach in the NFL, and her dream to visit more of the world. There is so much we want to see and do together, but for now I've just been busy counting down the days until Daisy leaves and enjoying every second I have with her in the meantime.

We just finished the last of our tacos, and Daisy is now sitting on her bedroom floor in the middle of a pile of clothes. I watch as she stuffs another shirt in her already very full suitcase.

"Are you going to be able to carry that thing? You realize the buildings in Italy are 108 billion years old and don't have elevators?"

She shoots me a scowl. "I'll be fine. I can always ask for help."

"How? You don't speak Italian."

Pushing up off the floor, she walks to where I'm sitting on the edge of her bed, then softly strokes my cheek. "I can figure it out. I've travelled to foreign countries before."

She has a point. But the closer it gets to Daisy getting on that plane, the worse my mood gets. The thought of her an ocean away with a 6-hour time difference is torture, but I know I need to try harder. I really am happy for her. This is Daisy. She's always been interested in seeing the world and going on new adventures, and I'd be a dick if I didn't support that.

"Are you sure you're okay with me going?" she asks as my hands move to the back of her thighs pulling her between my parted legs.

"Tuck," she says, leaning into my grasp. "Tell me the truth. Are you worried about me going away?"

"A little."

"Why?"

She runs a hand through my hair before tipping my chin up to face her. "What's going on, baby?"

I press my lips to her chest, inhaling her. "I'm worried things will change with us."

"Tucker, you know I'm coming back home to you, right?"

"I'm not sure." *Fuck, do I sound needy.*

Climbing into my lap, she straddles my waist and then takes my face in her hands. "If you think it's not killing me to leave you, you're wrong. This isn't easy for me either, but I know I need to do this. I finally have you and I will not lose you again. I'm going and I will be coming home to you in three months, I promise you."

Daisy kisses me again and that, along with her reassuring words, feels like enough. I haul her mouth to mine, sliding my tongue against hers, showing her how badly I'm going to miss her. I replay the time we've spent together in my mind, every moment that has brought us to where we are today. If you had told me a year ago that I would be in a relationship with Daisy, having the best sex of my life, desperately wishing I could spend every minute of every day with her, I would have said that you were insane.

But I've never been happier, and I have to admit, I like being hers. Now I just need to figure out how to survive the next 90 days.

"Daisy," I breathe against her lips, "I need you."

We crawl into her bed, slipping between the sheets. We don't say a word as I lower myself over her and kiss her with urgency. I miss her so much already. I know it's just for a few months, but I already feel like I can't live without her. Tomorrow, I'm going to have to learn how to, but for now, Daisy is here, and the need to be inside her is so strong that I start stripping her out of her clothes.

There is so much I want to say to her, important words on the tip of my tongue, but they are words I've never said before, and I'm scared. But I do know how to make her feel good, so that's what I do, and I show her with my body how much she means to me.

Daisy rides me, picking up speed as she glides up and down my shaft. Her bottom lip trapped under her teeth, her back arched in bliss, she's the most beautiful thing I've ever seen. She begins to tremble, but she's not there yet, so I give her what she needs until she's crying out my name and her body shudders in total ecstasy. When she relaxes and there's nothing left of her climax, I pull her mouth into mine in a demanding kiss, thrusting my hips deep inside her. I come hard, filling her up, wishing we could stay exactly like this.

"You are so beautiful when you are desperate for me. I am going to miss making you come, Daisy."

"I'm going to miss it too... but most of all, I'm going to miss *you*."

I brush my thumb over her cheek and notice the way her skin erupts in goosebumps. Her gaze drops down to where our bodies are still joined, and I can see the tangle of emotions threatening to undo her. "I bet the three months fly by like lightning," I tell her.

Her eyes are wet when she looks up at me. "I hope so."

My chest tightens.

Daisy is leaving tomorrow, and this feels a lot like a goodbye. I gather her in my arms, holding her body to mine, and I don't let go until the morning.

I LOAD DAISY'S SUITCASE IN THE BACK OF MY TRUCK AS SHE hugs her parents goodbye. I can't remember the last time I've been this anxious about saying goodbye to someone; the pain in my chest is so strong, it feels like it's hard to breathe.

I made her breakfast this morning–pancakes, strawberries and whipped cream–and we ate in bed. Afterwards, we showered together and then took a walk along Haven Harbor before returning to her place so that she could pack the last of her things.

This is it. The day I've been dreading is finally here. When she's finished with her goodbyes, Daisy hops into my truck and her dad closes her door behind her.

At the airport, I park the truck and carry her bags inside for her, accompanying her as far as security will let me.

"You could just come with me, you know," she teases, but I can see in her eyes that she means it.

"I wish, Dais. More than anything."

We talked about this, about me coming to visit her for a few weeks, but my schedule is jam packed. School is in session and even though spring break falls in the middle of her trip, I'll be coaching camps. It's one of the busiest times of the year for me, otherwise I'd be getting on that plane with her today.

"You need to go, Dais."

"I know," she says with her arms still tightly wrapped around my waist. When she lifts her face, I see tears pooling in her eyes.

"Don't cry, baby. You know I can't handle seeing you cry," I say, wiping her cheek with my thumb.

"Okay," she says, taking a deep breath. "I'll call you when I land."

"You better."

I kiss her one last time and when I watch her walk away, my heart sinks. I knew this was going to be hard, but I didn't know it would feel *this* terrible. Before she gets to security, I sprint past the line, needing to scoop her up into my arms one last time.

"Daisy!" I holler.

I'm jogging across the airport to get to her when she turns around. "Tucker," she says, laughing. "Are you trying to make me miss my flight?"

I stand in front of her, out of breath, and take her face in my hands.

"Tucker? Are you okay?" Daisy looks at me with concern in her eyes.

"Yeah. I just.... before you go and get on that plane, I need you to know... I love you."

"Tuck..." She drops her bag at her feet and wraps her arms around my neck.

"Dais, I've never been in love before. But I *am* in love with you," I say, needing to get this out. "I'm pretty sure I've loved you all my life. Daisy... you've always been mine. My heart is yours."

The words that I've been dying to say to her hang in the

air between us. I swear my heart stops beating. Her teeth scrape over her bottom lip as her eyes once again fill with tears. She rises to her tiptoes and pulls my mouth to hers.

"I love you too," Daisy says with tears in her eyes. "I was born to love you."

I kiss her one last time, then bend to pick her bag up off the ground and hitch it on to her shoulder.

Daisy's lips purse together in a smirk. "I could have gotten that."

"Are you sure about that?" I ask, eyebrows raised. "You packed your entire closet into this thing."

She puts her palms against my chest and gives me a playful push. "Such a guy," she says, rolling her eyes. "I need every single one of those outfits."

I smile, the lump still in my throat. "You better go."

"I know."

Daisy turns, and I watch her walk away, looking back at me with a soft smile. When I get to my truck, my body crumbles into the seat like all the air has been knocked from my lungs. I don't know how long I sit there, with my forehead against the steering wheel, wondering if there's a limit to how much a person can wallow. Then I start up the engine and drive home.

TWENTY-NINE

I'LL FUCK IT OUT OF YOU

Daisy

It's been a little over a month since I've been in Italy, and the constant, nagging feeling of missing Tucker still consumes me. I miss the scent of him. I miss the way he drags his fingertips over my arms in the morning to wake me up. I miss the way he plays with my hair. I miss seeing him walk through the door at the end of the day wearing his RPU gear. I just miss *him*.

We've spoken every day, long telephone conversations and explicit text messages. Tucker listens to my travel stories with genuine interest and I love him even more for supporting me. But what I look forward to most is listening to him talk about Haven Harbor and the team. I love hearing him talk about his day, his thoughts, his new ideas for the Outlaws.

Tucker doesn't talk much about his dad, and I don't push it. I know that they haven't been in touch since that night at my parents' place, and that Tucker has skipped every Sunday dinner since I left town.

When Tucker and I can find a time that works with

our schedules and the time difference, we FaceTime. Our chats have become progressively steamier. Watching Tucker take off his clothes and touch himself for me is a level of hot I never knew existed, and it didn't take long before I found myself craving it. The whole thing made me nervous at first—it was so vulnerable, letting Tucker watch me touch myself over a camera. But it didn't take long for my inhibitions to fade away. Now, I love the way it makes me feel. Knowing I can make him hard even though we're an ocean apart makes me feel powerful. And watching him come in a video is the hottest thing I've ever seen.

I've thought about our future more times than I can count. What will it be like when I come home? Will he want us to move in together? And down the road, are marriage and babies even something that he wants? Where does he see us in five years?

When I lie in bed at the end of the day, these are the questions that cycle through my head. I know with certainty that I want it all with Tucker, and that excites me. But I also know that being in a relationship is a big step for him. Anything beyond that—marriage, kids, a white picket fence—might scare him.

I'm about five minutes from my quaint bed and breakfast in Sorrento when my phone rings. It's Tucker, calling a lot earlier than usual. It's almost 2 a.m. in Reed Point.

"Hi," I say, answering his call as soon as humanly possible.

"Hey, baby," he says, his voice raspy. "What are you up to?"

"I just picked up a coffee and a pastry from a cute café. What about you? Why are you up?"

A low groan comes through the phone. "I couldn't sleep.

Had beers on the porch with Holden, talking him through some shit. I went to bed late."

"Is everything okay?"

"With Holden? Yeah, he'll be fine. Just worried if he made the right decision breaking up with Aubrey."

"And what did you tell him?"

I hear him rustling against his pillow. "I told him if it was meant to be, it would have been. Cliché, I guess, but I think it's true. She obviously wasn't the right girl for him if he was able to walk away. Then we drank beers. A lot of beers. And then he felt better."

"Of course you did," I laugh. "I don't have to imagine what that looked like. I've seen it with my own two eyes more times than I can count."

It's quiet on the line for a full 10 seconds, and I wonder if he's fallen asleep.

"Tucker?"

"Yeah, I'm here." He pauses. "You know that I'm not like that anymore, yeah?"

"I know, but... it's okay if you are. I'm not asking you not to go out and have fun."

"I know. I just wanted you to know."

There's another pause

"Have you talked to your dad?"

"Nope, not at all." I try to decipher his tone, to figure out how he feels about it, but I come up blank. My good mood evaporates wishing I was there with him.

Unfortunately, that has been a theme of this trip. One minute I'm enjoying the rich history of Italy, the next I'm missing Tucker so badly it hurts. But I'm doing my best to try to change that. I've looked forward to this trip for so long, and now I'm here. I don't want to let what's going on at home change that. I feel so grateful to be on this trip, but I also know what Tucker is dealing with back home. He says he doesn't care about what his dad thinks, but I know it has to hurt. If Uncle Mark can't support us, I hope he can at least be civil. For everyone's sake. As expected, Tucker and I being together has caused tension between our families. My mom told me she hasn't spoken to my Uncle Mark much, and besides a short visit a couple of days before I left, I haven't talked to Aunt Daisy. Things feel awkward and tense. Would it always be like this? I really hope not. But for now, this is what we have to deal with—except I'm hundreds of miles away, which leaves Tucker to deal with it on his own. He's told me over and over that he's fine, that he can handle it, but I can't help but feel bad.

"It's okay, Dais. You don't need to worry about it."

"I know, but I still hate it."

"Let's talk about something else. Like that picture you sent me yesterday of you in your bikini."

"My bikini *bottoms*, you mean."

"So fucking hot."

"I'll send you another when I get back to my hotel."

Tucker's groan is so loud I'm sure it woke up Holden. "Tell me what you're doing today," he says.

"You should go to sleep."

"I want to keep listening to your voice. It's my favorite part of my day."

"Mine too."

I smile. I love seeing this side of Tucker—where he is vulnerable and tells me exactly what he is thinking so I don't have to guess. My Tuck, who is sweet and thoughtful and opens his heart for me. It's such a turn on.

"Will you send me a picture before you fall asleep?"

He mumbles something into the phone. He's either asleep or seconds away from it. "Good night, Tuck."

"No... I heard you," he yawns. "I'll send you a pic..."

His voice trails off and I bite my bottom lip to keep from laughing. He is obviously very tired and maybe a little drunk, and the effect is ridiculously cute. "I'm going to hang up now, Tuck," I say quietly. "I love you."

"Love you," he murmurs, then adds, "Daisy? Go enjoy your day, okay?"

The line goes silent before I end the call. Smiling, I stuff my phone in my pocket. Then I do exactly what he said and go enjoy my day.

THE TREVI FOUNTAIN IS MAYHEM, AND THERE'S A HUGE crowd of people blocking my view. Thankfully, I am tiny and determined, so I politely push my way through the rows of people until I get to the edge of the travertine, finding a spot to sit down. I arrived back in Rome last night on a train from Sorrento, and the first thing on my list of sights to see was the most famous fountain in the world. I made sure to remember to bring three pennies to make a wish.

Legend has it that if you throw three coins in the fountain, the first guarantees a visit back to Rome, the second a love affair, and the third means a wedding.

Turning so that my back is facing the fountain, I toss the first coin over my left shoulder, followed by the second coin. I dig out my phone and record a short video of myself throwing the third coin and upload it to my stories on Instagram. I caption the photo *throwing coins and making wishes* and then post it.

In awe, I take one last look at the fountain before making my way back through the crowd. There's a store I walked past on my way here that I want to peek in, so I head back in the direction I came. As I'm window shopping, my phone chimes in my pocket. It's an Instagram notification from Tucker. It's going on 8 a.m. in Reed Point, so he's probably drinking his coffee and scrolling his phone. I open the app and go into my DMs, reading the two new messages from Tucker.

> Tucker: You look damn beautiful.
>
> Tucker: Tell me what you wished for.

I smile, taking a moment to enjoy a welcome breeze. Rome is undeniably beautiful, and undeniably *hot*. I read Tucker's messages again, feeling an ache in my chest at how much I miss him. Leaning against the stone wall of the shop, I type out a response.

> Me: Thank you ;) And my lips are sealed. I actually want my wishes to come true.

A bead of sweat drips from under my hat and down the side of my face. If it's this hot in mid-March, what is it like here in the summer? I'd love to come back with Tucker one day and I imagine the two of us here in Rome, holding hands, walking the cobblestone streets together, sharing a gelato. I shake my head, knowing that I'm getting ahead of myself. The heat must be getting to me. I step into the shop to get out of the sun, looking at the pastel hued Italian coffee presses lining the shelves. I run my fingertips along an aquamarine one, the color reminding me of Tucker's eyes. My phone buzzes again with another message from Tuck.

> Tucker: Don't worry. I'll fuck it out of you when I see you.
>
> Me: Jesus, Tucker.

> Tucker: You miss my dick, don't you? Admit it, rebel.
>
> Me: I miss your dick
>
> Me: But I miss you more

I squeeze my eyes shut, holding my phone to my chest. I wish he was here with me.

> Tucker: You know I'd be there if I could.
>
> Me: I know. I watched a video of you and the guys at camp online this morning. It felt good to see you where you're happiest.
>
> Tucker: You keeping track of me, Dais?
>
> Me: Maybe... You still get that same look on your face when you're focused, just like you did when you were eight.
>
> Tucker: I do?
>
> Me: You narrow your eyes and chew on your bottom lip. It's cute.
>
> Tucker: As long as it's cute. Oh, and you're wrong btw.
>
> Me: Wrong about what?
>
> Tucker: You are what makes me the happiest.
>
> Me: Cheeseball... but you made me smile.
>
> Tucker: Your cheeseball. I love you. Now I'm gonna go take nudes and send them to you later.

I'm smiling like a lunatic in a coffee press store. People are going to think I'm crazy.

THIRTY

SHE'S YOUR END GAME

Tucker

"Collins." Holden snaps a finger in front of my face.

I rip my attention from my screen and the photo Daisy sent me a few days ago. "What do you want?"

"Geez," Holden says. "You okay?"

I don't even know why I just snapped at him. I am clearly not okay.

"Sorry. What were you saying?"

"I asked you if you wanted to get burgers tonight."

He gets up from the kitchen table and rinses off his plate before putting it in the dishwasher. "You've been in a shit mood for days, man. What the fuck is wrong with you?"

No one bothered to tell me that being in a long-distance relationship is fucking hard. I'm only six weeks into this and I'm not sure if I'm going to make it. I'm tired of counting down days on a calendar. I'm tired of missing Daisy. Holden is right. I've been in a shit mood and even I can't stand myself.

"I don't feel like talking about it."

"Well, too bad, because you're going to," he says, taking the chair beside me. "You sat me down not too long ago to get me through my shit. So now it's your turn to talk."

I groan, pulling my baseball cap a little lower over my eyes. "You're not going to go away, are you?"

"Nope." Holden crosses his arms over his chest and raises his eyebrows. "Is it Daisy or your dad?"

"Fine," I say, accepting the fact that I am not going to win this battle. "It's Daisy."

The last time we talked was three days ago, before she boarded a sailboat to cruise the Tyrrhenian Sea for four days. It wasn't a great call. She sensed something was wrong when I was quieter than usual, but I didn't have it in me to tell her I had run into my dad, and he was a total dick. It happened at Dream Bean when I was picking up my morning coffee, so thankfully he couldn't make a scene. But he didn't have to blow up at me to get under my skin. Telling me that I was the reason his relationship with Daisy's parents was strained was enough to piss me off. But I didn't want to rehash it with Daisy, not when I knew it would put a damper on her trip.

"So, the common denominator here is your dad," Holden says after I finish telling him everything.

"Yeah, I guess it is."

"And you're a softie for your girl."

"That too."

"First things first... work it out with him. I know it sucks, but you're going to have to talk again," Holden says. "You're the better man. I say you go over there and see if you can hash it out."

I know Holden's heart is in the right place, but what could I say to my dad at this point that would make him see that I'm not the guy he thinks I am? Besides, do I even care what he thinks? I've always been a disappointment in his eyes. I doubt that will ever change.

I know for damn sure when I have a child of my own— and for some fucked up reason the idea of that with Daisy keeps crossing my mind— I will love that kid unconditionally. And they will love me back. I will earn that love every day of their life.

"I hate seeing you sulk like this. This isn't you, man."

Holden is right. This isn't me. But this long-distance thing is bullshit.

"She's your end game, isn't she?"

"Yeah, I'm pretty sure she is."

"Aw, Collins. My boy here is in love," Holden teases, ruffling my hair. "So sweet."

"Idiot," I groan. "Are you done with your pep talk now?"

Holden laughs, sliding off his bar stool. "Yeah, I'm done. Wanna run?"

"Yeah, that sounds good."

I change into shorts and an old T-shirt and meet Holden by the front door. After I've laced up my tennis shoes, I check my phone for a message from Daisy. *Nothing.* Instead, I stare at the lock screen photo on my iPhone: a selfie Daisy and I took on one of our beach walks. I'm standing behind her with my arms wrapped around her, and I'm kissing her cheek. She looks so beautiful it makes my chest hurt.

Maybe if my dad understood that Daisy really is it for me, that she's the girl I want to spend the rest of my life with, he'd realize why I'm not backing down.

Holden and I head out for our run, and I pour all of my frustration and anger into the pavement. Back at our place, I have a shower and change into a sweatshirt and jeans, and then man up and do what I need to do. I drive to my parents' house and knock on their front door.

NEVER SAY NEVER

My mom opens the door and immediately pulls me into her arms. "Tucker, you have no idea how good it is to see you. How's my baby?"

"It's good to see you too, Mom," I say, kissing the top of her head. "I'm okay."

"How's training camp?"

"It's fine. How are you doing?"

"I'm okay, honey. I've missed seeing you around here." I hear the hurt in her voice. "I wish things weren't the way they are."

My jaw clenches. I wish that too.

"Is Dad here?"

"In his office. Do you want me to—"

"No, Mom, I'll be fine."

"I'll make a pot of tea then. I'll be in the kitchen if you need me." I walk down the hall toward my dad's office. Memories of kissing Daisy up against the door months ago flash through my mind. Our first kiss after a decade of barely talking. At the time, it was just a kiss—an unbelievable kiss, but nothing more than that. The beginning of our pact. It wasn't supposed to mean anything. But here we are, together. What we have is real, and I need my father to know that I intend on keeping it that way.

I tense up as soon as I see him. When I open the door, my dad looks up from his computer but looks away again when he sees that it's me. He isn't going to make this easy, but this time I'm not going to run away.

Neither of us move or say a word, and the silence is deafening. I walk further into the room, sinking into the chair opposite his desk. The confidence I felt driving over here starts to fade.

Man up, Tucker. Tell him how you feel.

I'm going to marry her one day. I'm not sure what my future exactly looks like, but I know it includes her. He needs to get used to us being together.

"I'm sorry I lied to you, Dad," I start, jutting my chin out. "But I won't apologize for loving Daisy."

His focus doesn't leave his computer screen, but I do catch the subtle way his fingers grip the pen in his hand a little tighter.

"We need to talk, Dad. I love her. I've never loved anything or anyone as much as I love her. She's it for me."

My dad drops the pen to the desk before he leans back in his leather chair. Finally, his eyes meet mine.

"Are you sure?" he asks.

"Yes." This is the first time I've been able to tell him that I'm in love with Daisy, because I had wanted her to hear it from me first.

"That's... surprising. You've never loved anything but football."

"And that's always been a problem for you," I counter. His expression doesn't change, but I see the tension in his jaw. "You've never been able to accept me for who I am, Dad. You wanted your son to take over your firm, but that was your dream, not mine."

Something breaks in my chest. I've never said those words out loud to him, but there they are, hanging in the air between us. They are the reason my dad and I have never got along. The reason my dad can hardly stand me.

"You're right. I was disappointed. I built that firm with my own two hands, my blood, sweat and tears. I wanted you to love it just as much as I do."

"But I never wanted that, and I never made that a secret."

"No, you didn't."

"Are you ever going to get over that? Because you should."

I don't ever want to have this conversation again so I'm leaving everything I need to on the table, hoping maybe we can come to some sort of truce.

"You weren't an easy kid, Tucker. If I came down hard on you it was only to teach you a lesson. I did what I thought was best for you."

I grind my molars together. What had I ever done to disappoint him so much? I was a kid. I skipped class. I stayed out past curfew. I back-talked from time to time. But I followed my own path, and I have built a good life for myself: A career that I love, great friends, and a girl that I'm crazy about. Why does he refuse to see it?

"But maybe I was too harsh." He stares at me for a long moment. "I'm sorry. I think it's time I told you that, Tuck."

The enormity of his words almost knocks me off my chair. I swallow hard. This is the first time he has ever apologized to me. I wait to see if he has anything more to say, but the fact of the matter is that is all I've ever needed to hear.

"I watched you win the championship game," he says, scrubbing his jaw. "You made me proud. I'm damn proud of you, Tucker."

I'm almost rendered speechless, but I manage to get out a response. "Thank you." I exhale. "Can you also accept that I am in love with Daisy?"

He nods. "I can. It just caught me off guard. It'll take some getting used to, but... if the two of you are happy and it's serious, that's all that matters. But, Tucker, I will always think of her as my own. That won't change."

"I wouldn't want it to."

I reach for his hand. "We're good?"

"We're good," he responds, taking my hand in his, pulling me in for an awkward hug over his desk.

I move toward the door but stop before leaving the room. "I never thanked you for coming to my game," I tell him.

"Not necessary, son. It was my pleasure."

I swallow the knot in my throat. "Thanks."

I leave wanting to tell Daisy everything that just happened, so as soon as I get into my truck, I dig out my phone and click on her name. I type out a message, then delete it all. Fuck, I hate texting. She's on a boat without cell service and she won't see the damn message for another day anyways. And I want to tell her in person, in a face-to-face conversation, which is hard when she's a million fucking miles away.

I am so done with the distance between us.

So, instead of sending her a text, I open my browser and search flights to Italy.

Fifteen minutes later, I'm heading home to pack.

THIRTY-ONE

WOULD IT HELP IF I SAT ON YOUR FACE?

Tucker

Daisy isn't in her room when I arrive in Florence the next afternoon. The lady at the desk speaks mostly Italian, but we manage to communicate enough for her to let me know that she will call her. The phone just rings and rings, so I have no choice but to sit in the tiny lobby and wait for her. I have no clue how long I'll be waiting. Hours? Days? I'll sit here as long as I need to. I check her Instagram page to see if she posted recently, but there is nothing. It doesn't matter. I am finally going to get to see her.

Knowing that we're so close sends my heart racing. My knee bounces in a steady rhythm as I keep my eyes fixed on the hotel door. Finally, it swings open, and I jump out of my seat when Daisy walks into the tiny lobby looking down at her phone. She smiles at the woman at the front desk as she passes her.

"Ciao, Anna."

"Ciao, bella."

Anna nods in my direction with a mischievous expression, and Daisy turns then freezes on the spot as a look of shock transforms her face.

She does a double take when she sees me, as if she can't quite believe I'm real. Then she is running in my direction. I catch her when she jumps into my arms, wrapping her arms around my neck and her legs around my waist. My mouth crashes into hers with a desperate need and a wild energy as my hands grip her ass tight, and my tongue plunges inside her mouth. I want her in the worst way possible. I remember where we are, but I can't bring myself to stop. Anna will just have to enjoy the show.

When Daisy unclasps her heels from behind my back and drops down to her tiptoes, I take her in. She looks beautiful in a pair of faded jean shorts and a tank top. Her long hair is tied back in a high ponytail accentuating her cheekbones. She smells like suntan lotion and lemons. Her skin is a perfect golden bronze. She isn't wearing any makeup and while she always looks incredible when she's all done up, this is the way I love her best. My entire body shivers as she drags her hands up my chest, circling her arms around my neck again.

"I can't believe this. What are you doing here?"

"I missed you."

She gives me a sweet smile before going up on her toes to kiss me again.

"I thought I'd be able to do it," I say, watching her eyes soften. "I tried my best. I had a plan to focus on spring training. Work hard. Look after my players. FaceTime you every night. The three months without you were going to fly by and before I knew it, you'd be back home... with me."

"But you missed me."

"Like fuck."

She giggles as I hold her tighter.

"I had to see you, so here I am. I hope it's okay."

Italy was her trip. Her dream. I didn't think to ask her if it was okay that I come, I just booked the first flight I could find and got on the plane as fast as I could. Now I'm standing in front of her realizing that maybe I should have checked in with her first. My heart pounds in my chest.

"I realized halfway through the first day that I didn't want to be here without you. Do you have any idea how much I've missed you?" She fists my shirt in her hands, tugging my face down to hers and the room falls away. "So, yes, Tuck... it's more than okay."

"Good."

She smiles, tugging my face even further until her lips are on mine. I seal my mouth over hers. Goddamn, she tastes so good. Like lemons and sugar. My tongue searches for hers, and then we're kissing again without caring who's watching.

The kiss is full of longing and lust. Bold and special. Everything Daisy. And it's over too soon. I growl, and Daisy laughs and shakes her head.

"Wait," she says, her expression turning serious. "How are you here? What about spring training?"

"I need to be back in Reed Point by Monday. Do you think five days is long enough to remind you how fucking good we are together?"

"I haven't forgotten, but I'd still like you to remind me."

She goes up on her toes and nips at my bottom lip with her teeth.

"Dais, *please* invite me up to your room."

"Would you like to see my room?"

"I thought you'd never ask."

I reach for my suitcase and Daisy leads the way. We jog up a marble staircase and two more narrow flights of stairs, tripping over ourselves to get to her hotel room. We are a hysteria of entwined tongues and scraping teeth, her hands in my hair as I push open the door to her place. I have never been so lost in a kiss before. The space between us feels electric. I taste her, realizing I've never experienced this kind of need before. The desire feels like it's burning me alive. Like I've waited for Daisy forever.

I'm grinding my aching cock into her ass as soon as the door shuts behind us. It's already leaking at the tip at the thought of finally getting her naked. When I tear her shirt over her head, my dick starts to throb. By the time she's bare standing in front of me, I'm so hard it hurts.

She's as eager as I am, and it shows when her hands fumble with my belt. And because I can't take another second of my dick being confined to my pants, I help her with the buckle then get to work on the button and the zipper.

Fuck, I need her. Finally, we're both naked and I'm walking her backwards to the small kitchen table—the closest surface I can see—where I hoist her up, so she's perched on the edge. I cage her in as her legs spread wide for me, my swollen cock trapped between us.

I plan on making up for lost time.

"Fuck, baby, I missed you." The smooth skin of her body presses against mine, and I melt into her, letting the warmth of her seep into me.

"Do you feel better now, or would it help if I sat on your face?"

Fuck. That sounds so fucking hot.

"Tucker!" She squeals when I hoist her off the table. "What are you doing?"

Her legs wrap around me as I carry her to the bed, dropping her onto the mattress before flipping her so she's straddling my waist. "Hands on the headboard and sit on my face, Dais."

I help her shimmy over my chest with my hands on her hips until she's straddling my face, and I have her two ass cheeks in my hands. "Spread your legs wider, baby." I groan when I pull her center over my face, licking her mercilessly and sucking on her clit.

"Tuck... my God... your mouth," she moans in desperation as she writhes on top of me. It only spurs me on. I use my fingers to spread her wide open, then I'm feasting on her, licking her up and down.

I have fantasized about this for weeks, and the reality that I am finally tasting her is enough to drive me out of my mind. I try to read her cues, sucking her harder if she groans or her legs begin to shake, and I find the perfect rhythm when I slide one finger into her, and she begins to ride my face like a wild horse.

She doesn't stop, and neither do I, until she's cursing my name and coming on my face, riding every last wave of her orgasm. "Tuck," she breathes after she collapses over top of me. I catch her, rolling her onto her back beside me before I'm sprawling my body over hers, kissing the life out of her. I know she can taste herself on my lips. That thought alone is enough to make every drop of blood in my body flow to my already aching hard-on.

I kiss her tenderly before the need to have her is like a freight train barreling down the tracks, and I can't take it any longer. I rise to my knees between her parted thighs, staring at my girl lying naked on the bed for me. The sunshine seeps through the window, casting a warm glow over her skin. My gaze roves over every inch of Daisy, her flat stomach, ample tits. Her wavy hair fans across the pillow, a mess from my hands flying through it.

Mine. She is mine.

I've never felt luckier in my life.

"Tuck." Her legs fall open ever further. "I need you."

I think that this is when it's over for me. My heart feels like wild horses in my chest. She's perfect. We're finally together. She isn't going anywhere.

She whimpers when I tease her with the head of my cock, sliding over her slick entrance. She's soaked. *Fuck me.*

"Please, Tuck." She goes up on her elbows as she watches me tease her clit, her thighs beginning to tremble. Her hips rock up and down, needing more. I lean forward capturing her mouth then I line myself up with her entrance and sink inside.

"Yes." She lets out a sated moan, her fingers digging into the flesh of my thighs.

I start slow, my cock so sensitive, I know there's no way I'm going to last. I play with her nipples, tugging hard on one and then the other. I reach my hand between her legs and thrust into her harder and faster.

"You feel so good. You're perfect, Daisy. Nobody will ever see you like this again. Only me. I'm the only one who gets to fuck this body. Say it, Dais. Tell me I'm the only one."

"Tuck." She moans and gasps, arching her back, gripping the sheets.

"Say it, rebel. Say it now. I need to hear you say it."

"Only you," she manages to get out. "Only you will ever fuck me like this."

"Good girl. That's my good fucking girl."

And then I'm picking up the pace, driving myself deeper with every thrust.

"Right there, Tuck. Please. Don't stop."

My name on Daisy's lips is all it takes to come hard, my limbs shaking, emptying inside her until my body is spent and lifeless. I want to end every day like this, hearing my name on her lips as she's coming undone, for the rest of my life. This girl is everything I want. Everything I need.

I kiss her hard as she clings to me, one hand on her jaw, the other in her hair. I can't get close enough to her if I try.

"I think it's obvious how much I missed you." I kiss her again, slowly pulling out of her before climbing out of bed. I walk to the bathroom to find a washcloth then I crawl back into bed and clean up the mess that I made.

"Should we wander around Italy?" she asks, sitting up in bed, pulling the bedsheet over her chest. I shrug, then I climb into bed next to her, wrapping her up in my arms.

"I think I'd rather stay here naked in bed with you."

"I think I'd like that too."

I can't think of anywhere else I'd rather be.

THIRTY-TWO

IS THIS REAL? AM I HALLUCINATING?

Daisy

The piazza is relatively quiet at this time of day, with only a few people wandering the streets. We're still sitting outside a little café where we bought pastries and cappuccinos, the morning sun already warming our skin, and the scent of coffee beans and sugar tempting our noses.

We should get going with our day–there is so much I want to show Tucker–but neither of us seems able to summon the energy.

There was so much making up for lost time to do yesterday. How long had we been in bed? The sky darkened and my tiny hotel room went black until we were silhouettes, but it didn't stop us. We finally fell asleep, sated and spent, around three in the morning.

We're exhausted today, but it doesn't matter. I needed him just as much as he needed me.

But this morning there were things Tucker wanted to say. He told me all about the talk he had with his dad, how Uncle Mark had apologized then told him he was proud of him.

Tucker's dad must have realized that his son wasn't going to back down, not this time. I'm sure he knew I wasn't going to either. So, if he wanted to have a relationship with his only son and the goddaughter that he's always considered his own, he'd have to admit he was wrong. I know how hard it must have been for Tucker to take the first step, and I'm relieved my Uncle Mark received him so well.

But most of all, I am proud of my boyfriend. Tucker, with his big, beautiful heart, forgave his dad whether he deserved it or not. Even if he has been unnecessarily hard on him for most of his life, Tucker found a way to forgive him.

It makes me love him even more, if that's possible.

"I think he's changed," Tucker murmurs, picking at his pastry.

I hope it's true. For Tucker's sake.

"And what if he hasn't?"

Tucker reaches across the small iron table to push a lock of hair from my face. "It doesn't matter. Nothing else matters. Nothing but you and me."

I grin, feeling myself melt a little inside. Tucker is sweet and wonderful and so different than I thought he'd be. It feels like we're getting a second chance, like we're starting over. Everything in this moment feels almost too good to be true.

Tuck's gaze shifts toward the piazza, to where a mother is carrying a cloth bag full of groceries as a little boy around 4 years old skips beside her.

"Do you see yourself having kids?" he asks, watching the little boy chatter away to his mom in Italian as he eats his cream-filled maritozzi.

"That came out of nowhere." I laugh.

"I'm curious. It's something we've never talked about."

"No, I guess we haven't."

"So... do you?"

"I do. At least two. I've always wished I had a brother or sister."

It never dawned on me until right this second that maybe that was one of the reasons our parents always treated us like siblings. Because I didn't have any of my own.

"What about you? Do you see yourself having kids?"

I sit perfectly still waiting on his answer. Tucker would make a great dad. I'm not sure how I will react or what it will mean if he says he doesn't want children.

"I didn't, until recently," he says. "I've only ever had one dream for myself, and that is the NFL. When my chances of making it to the league as a player disappeared, I shifted my focus to coaching there. It's always been the goal, but I think I'd probably be happy living on Haven Harbor for the rest of my life coaching the Outlaws too."

Tucker is meant for the NFL, and I know it's only a matter of time before they come calling. I'll have to deal with that when it comes. Would I be able to leave Reed Point and follow him to a new city? Would he want me to come? Neither of those questions need to be answered today, but if the time comes, I'll make the decision that feels right for me. But deep down, I know I'd follow Tucker to the ends of the earth.

I rest my elbows on the table watching him take a bite of his pastry. "Technically, you didn't answer the question."

"Whether I want kids?"

"Yes." I wait, trying to keep my heart in check.

"With the right girl." Tucker licks the cream from his finger then leans over the table toward me to press a lingering kiss to my mouth. He chuckles when he sits back down.

I really hope he means me, but maybe I'm getting ahead of myself. Yes, we're very much in love, but in the big picture we haven't been together very long.

I look out at the piazza, which is slowly starting to fill with locals running errands and tourists setting out on their days. The mother and her son have stopped at a small market across from us. She's sorting through a pile of lemons, passing the good ones to her little boy to carry. He says something to her, and she smiles at him, ruffling his hair. The moment so sweet, I can't help but smile.

"You'd make a great mom, you know."

I turn to face Tucker. "How do you know?"

He laughs like it's obvious. I'm not sure that it is. "Because I know you. I know every little detail about you. You're caring. You're good. You accept people for who they are. You are the best person I know."

Something tugs at my chest. I'm pretty sure it's my heart expanding two sizes.

"You say the sweetest things," I murmur. This is the side of Tucker that I never expected. He is a man who is comfortable wearing his heart on his sleeve. Open, vulnerable.

I blink before the tears can start. I'm not going to cry.

"Come on." Tucker shifts in his seat. "I only have four days, and I want to see as much of Italy as I can."

I want that too, so I toss my napkin on the table and grab my things. The air is already growing hot, the morning temperature spiking to a record high for this time of year.

When he stands and holds out his hand, I notice the way his T-shirt stretches across his chest and his hard stomach. Tucker Collins rivals any of the stone statues I've seen on my trip. He's a sight to be seen. He smirks like he caught me staring, then he clasps my hand and leads me through the piazza, toward the train station.

"Wait." I stop, tugging on Tuck's hand, dragging him toward the monument in the center of the little town. "Let's take a selfie."

"In front of that guy? Tucker motions to the stone statue of a man on a horse. "Do we even know who he is?"

"It doesn't matter who he is. I want a photo to remember my first morning in Italy with you. You can replace that old grad photo of the two of us in your bedroom."

There are endless photos of Tucker and me, there are albums full of them that our moms have been hoarding for years. But we do have 10 years to make up for.

"I happen to like that photo." His arms snake around my waist, holding me tight as I hold up my phone. "That dress was fucking hot. The fuchsia pink. The way it hugged your ass. I couldn't stop staring all night."

"Your poor date. What was her name again? Rachel? Ronnie?"

"Not Daisy, so who gives a fuck."

I laugh when he smashes his lips to my cheek as I'm taking the photo. "One more," I plead. Tucker moves around me and takes my phone from my hand, holding it at arm's-length.

"I can't even see the screen," I giggle.

"Perfect. Now, kiss me."

Going up on my toes, I meet him halfway. "I love you," I say before kissing his mouth. He snaps a few pictures before sweeping me into his arms.

"I have loved you all my life."

"Say it again," I tell him, burying my face against his chest.

"I have loved you all of my life, Daisy Carter."

My mouth meets his again as his fingers thread into my hair. I cling to him, eyes closed. *Oh, god. Here I go again. Don't cry, Daisy!* Why does he do this to me? No other man has ever stood a chance with my heart. It has belonged to Tucker since the day I was born.

Tucker breaks the kiss, a blinding smile stretched across his face.

"You are it for me, Dais. You know that, right? We're together for good when you get back home. I'm not leaving you at the airport ever again."

Four perfect days later, Tucker and I roll our suitcases into the arrivals terminal at Reed Point's airport, exhausted from the 10-hour flight. We weren't ready to leave Rome—I think we could have stayed in our tiny apartment forever, just the two of us. But Tucker needed to get back to training camp and I decided I didn't want to be in Italy without him. Luckily, there was a seat on his flight.

We walk through the terminal hand in hand and as we exit the baggage claim area, a chorus of familiar voices makes me stop in my tracks.

"Daisy! Tucker!" My eyes go wide when I see all four of our parents standing just inside the entrance. Tucker looks just as surprised as me.

"What are they all doing here?" I mumble under my breath.

"Do they ever do anything without each other?" is Tucker's smart-ass response.

"Welcome home!" My mom bellows as she descends on me first then pulls Tucker into her arms.

"Mom, what are you doing here?"

"Saving you an Uber ride. We couldn't wait to see you."

Tucker looks at his parents. "And you two? I've been gone less than a week so I know you can't miss me already."

"It was your mom's idea," Tucker's dad says.

"Oh, he didn't take much convincing," Aunt Daisy interjects, swatting his arm. "He was practically in the car as soon as I suggested it."

Uncle Mark smiles sheepishly then turns to face me. "Welcome home, Daisy. I've been wanting to talk to you."

Had Tucker not already filled me in on their discussion, I might have had my guard up. But when Uncle Mark motions to two chairs a few feet away, I nod and follow him. His expression turns apologetic as soon as we sit down.

"I need to apologize to you, Daisy," he says, shifting in his seat uncomfortably. "I never should have interfered in your relationship with Tucker. It wasn't my place. I allowed my fears to cloud my judgement when I shouldn't have. It's clear that he loves you." He pauses, his gaze shifting to his son still chatting with the rest of the family. "Tucker is a good man. You're both amazing kids. You're lucky to have each other."

"Thank you," I tell him. "That means a lot."

"I mean it. I'm happy for you two. I hope you can forgive me."

"It's forgotten, Uncle Mark."

He smiles and then we stand and share a brief hug. A second later, Tucker is behind me, wrapping his arms around my neck.

"Everything okay here?" Tucker asks, kissing the side of my face.

"I apologized to Daisy. We're good. I'd like to see you both at Sunday dinner. That should be enough time to kick the jet lag."

"We'll be there," I say. As he leaves, I turn in Tucker's arms to face him.

"Are you okay?"

"Yes." Things with Tuck's dad may not be perfect, but

they're good enough for now. I only hope that it stays that way.

"What happened?"

"He apologized. Said it wasn't his place. Told me you're a good man."

"He did?"

I nod. We start toward the exit, trailing a few feet behind our parents. Tucker looks down at me, and the smile that lights up his face reminds me of summer bike rides and late-night swims under starry skies. He is the boy who kissed me when we were 16, and he is the man I've loved as long as I can remember. He stole my heart a long time ago.

"I think you're right. It seems like he's changed. He seems to genuinely feel bad for how he acted."

Tucker holds out his hand and I lace my fingers in his. He brings my knuckles to his lips for a kiss.

"Did you ever think you'd see the day?" I ask him.

"That my dad has something good to say about me? No, never. Is this real? Am I hallucinating?"

"It's real, Tuck. He's proud of you."

I'm hopeful this is a new start for Tuck and his dad. I hope that Uncle Mark will want to be at his games, that next season he will be in the stands, on his feet, cheering for the Outlaws just as loud as the rest of us.

I'm not sure exactly what my future with Tuck looks like. It's still too early to tell. But I'm hoping forever is in the cards for us.

I choose to believe it is.

THIRTY-THREE

MY GOD, I SOUND LIKE A CHEESY FUCK

Tucker
3 months later

"That's the last of it." Holden wipes his hands on the front of his jeans after loading the last box into the moving truck. "I'm going to order pizza if you want to eat before you head to the new house."

"Yes, please," Daisy says. "As long as there's no—"

"Onion," Holden says, cutting her off. "I've got you, Dais. I know what you like."

"I feel like I'm intruding on a private moment between you two," I grumble, crossing my arms over my chest and looking from my best friend to my girlfriend. "Is there something I should know?"

Holden tips his head back and laughs. "She's all yours, bro. You won't have to worry about the third wheel anymore."

"Never, Holden," Daisy says. "We have loved living with you. We're going to miss you, you know." Daisy wraps an arm around Holden, hugging him from the side. "Who else am I going to watch reruns of *Gilmore Girls* with?"

"Hopefully not this guy." Holden gestures at me. "He wouldn't appreciate Stars Hollow. He definitely wouldn't get Lorelai's quirky charm."

I look at him like he's speaking a foreign language. "Damn straight. I'll be changing the channel fast."

Holden scoffs. "Daisy is the boss. We all know who wears the pants in your relationship."

"Daisy is *not* the boss of me." I put my hand on her shoulder, and she knocks it off just as fast. I can practically feel her rolling her eyes at me. "Okay, fine, maybe she is," I add. The truth is whatever she wants to watch is fine by me. All I care about is that Daisy and I are going to be living together. Officially. And I'm determined not to fuck up the good thing we having going on.

"Don't worry, Holden. I'll only watch it with you." Daisy smiles at him. "We should make it a weekly thing."

"It's a date, Daisy," he says, winking at me. The guy just loves getting under my skin.

"In that case, I'm coming," I say.

Holden's eyes snap to mine, and he presses his lips together. "Take it easy, man, it's not that kind of show."

Daisy cracks up beside me, elbowing me in my side. I shake my head at the pair of them. "Get your mind out of the gutter, Dais."

She snorts. "Sorry, can't help it. But don't worry, the only person I will come for..." she kisses my cheek. "Is you."

"Yeah, definitely not going to miss *this*," Holden deadpans.

Daisy and I had been house hunting in Reed Point for a few weeks when we found an older two-storey home not far from RPU. We'd spent the last three months bouncing back and forth between her condo and my house on Haven Harbor. It worked for us for a while. We were just happy to be together after spending three months apart while Daisy was in Italy—well, I guess technically it wasn't quite that long, but it felt like a fucking eternity. But eventually we decided that we wanted some privacy.

The timing couldn't have been more perfect since the lease on Daisy and Briar's condo was up and Briar was planning a temporary relocation to Vancouver to spend some time with her mom. As for Holden, he was more than happy to have our place to himself.

Daisy and I didn't have to look for long. We put an offer on the first house our realtor took us to see. Daisy took one look at the colonial revival with shutter windows and a large front porch and fell in love. The home is just shy of 2,000 square feet and is in need of a facelift, but Daisy has a Pinterest board of ideas. And here's the thing about how much I love Daisy: I want to make every one of those dreams come true. Our plan is to slowly renovate every room, inch by square inch, until it feels like us.

Us.

I like the sound of that.

My god, I sound like a cheesy fuck. When I look at my life these days, I almost don't recognize it. A lot has changed, but the one constant now is my love for Daisy, and the deep desire I feel to make her happy.

I've got an eagle eye at a thrift store now, and I'm starting to know my way around a discount travel website. And Daisy has free tickets to any Outlaws game she wants, and I know I'll find her in the stands when football season starts up again next month. Until then, I plan on getting my fill of her in our new home.

Holden, Daisy and I head back into the Haven Harbor house for a beer. We're still sitting around the kitchen table when Jake, Everly, Birdie and baby West stop by a little while later. Grayson and Sierra show up next with baby Sadie and before we know it, the kitchen is full of our friends who have all come over to see us off.

"Haven Harbor won't be the same without you guys," Grayson says, holding his beer bottle up into the air. "It's going to be a lot fucking quieter with this guy gone. Nobody telling stupid jokes or bragging about what a big shot coach he is."

"Uh-huh, and don't forget about my incredible good looks. It's a shame you won't get to see them on the reg anymore."

"Oh my god," Daisy groans. "I apologize for my boyfriend's insane ego." Then she leans over and kisses me, because she knows it's all true.

"He's all yours now, Daisy. You sure you know what you're doing?" Grayson asks.

"Hey, if you need a place to flee to when Tucker won't stop talking about how pretty he is, just know that our door is always open."

I shake my head. "What the fuck?"

"What? You're a lot sometimes. It isn't a secret." Jake takes a pull from his beer.

"What these idiots are trying to say is that we'll miss you both," Sierra says with the cutest fucking baby in her arms. "But we're happy for you and your new home and we all expect an invite to see it very soon."

"We would love that, right, Tuck?" Daisy pats my chest, looking up at me with a heart-stopping smile.

My expression isn't half as cheery as hers. "I guess so."

We all clink our beer bottles together like we have so many times before. It feels like the end of an era. Haven Harbor has been my home for the last five years. I have loved it here, but I love the idea of making memories with Daisy in our own place even more.

"Let me take him," Daisy says, reaching for West. The kid is a spitting image of Jake, with ice-blue eyes and dark-brown hair. I watch her snuggle him into her chest, inhaling his new baby scent. She looks good with a baby in her arms. She looks happy.

When she looks up at me, a smile spreads across her pretty face. "What?"

I shake my head. "Nothing." I shrug. "You're fucking gorgeous, that's all."

The last thing I need is the guys giving me the gears about baby fever. I know it's coming. They're already all over me about when I'm going to ask Daisy to marry me. They say it's inevitable so I shouldn't fight it. That may be true, but these guys have never known when to stop. The last fucking thing I need is to listen to them talk about babies.

I yank a slice of pizza from the box, scarfing it down. The only thing keeping me here is the pizza so that when I take Daisy home —fuck, I just said *home*—we're both full, and we can christen every inch of it.

I circle my arms around her waist from behind and place a kiss on her neck. "Are you ready to go?" Cradling the back of West's tiny head, she turns to kiss me. "I love our friends, but I love the idea of getting you naked in our new house even more," I whisper into her ear.

I swear I can see her pulse start to race in her neck. I tighten the hold I have around her body, catching the way her skin shivers when the hard lines of my body press against her soft ones. My mouth sucks on the smooth skin of her neck over her pulse that races the same way mine is.

"What are you whispering about with my son in your hands?" Jake glares at me, licking pizza sauce from his fingers. "You watch your dirty mouth around my little man, Collins."

"First of all, your kid is like two months old and has no clue what I'm fu–dging talking about," I shoot back, catching myself. "And second, it can't be half as bad as the shit Grayson says to your sister while he's—"

"Finish that sentence and I will rip every one of your limbs from your body."

Grayson snorts then grabs Sierra's ass and winks at Jake.

"Don't look at me like that, Gray." Jake shoots a pointed look at his brother-in-law. "I will end you. This shit never gets easier. I don't want to ever know what you two do."

"Jake." Everly clutches his arm. "My God. We've talked about this. Sierra is a married adult. With a child. You need to get over it."

"Never."

"Is he always like this?" Daisy whispers in my ear.

"Always."

An hour later, Daisy and I are standing in the empty living room of our new home. Just the two of us. It's nothing near as fancy as what we both grew up in, which is fine by me. I won't have to search for Daisy when I get home from work feeling desperate for her and needy.

I follow Daisy upstairs, my gaze glued to her ass in those damn tights she wears, I swear, just to fuck with me. It's taking every ounce of my willpower not to maul her. When she reaches the second floor she turns right, and I follow her into the master bedroom.

"Our first home." I wrap my arm around her waist and walk us toward the large bay window and the view of our yard. "How amazing would it be to put a pool right there?" I ask, pointing to the center of the yard.

"We could swim at night in the summers, just like old times."

"Naked," I add with a wink. "Lots of pool sex."

"When can we start digging the hole, coach?"

"I'll call someone tomorrow." I rest my chin on the top of her head as my hands slide to her hips.

"Are you happy?" she asks, looking over her shoulder at me.

"Do you even have to ask that?"

"I'm happy. More than I ever thought imaginable." Her smile is soft. "You know I love you more than this house, right?"

"I do," I murmur back.

With that, I turn her in my arms and drop to one knee. "Daisy—"

She gasps. Her hands fly to her mouth as her eyes fill with tears. "Tucker, are you serious?"

"As a heart attack." I slide my hand into my pocket and pull out a small square box. My heart is racing when I open it, revealing an Asscher-cut diamond in a simple white gold setting. Her eyes widen as I take the ring from the velvet pouch.

"Since you've been back in my life, I've never been happier. You're good. You're genuine. You're mine, and I want you forever. I've always known it, Daisy. Even when we started the stupid pact and I kept telling myself it was just temporary, my heart knew you were my end game. I knew I was never going to be able to let you go." Tears fill her eyes. "I've loved you all my life. We belong together. Marry me, Dais?"

"Yes, yes, yes," she cries, and the euphoria that floods my body makes me realize yet again that my heart is under her spell. "I will marry you."

I slip the ring onto her finger with a smile, knowing that everyone within a five-mile radius will now know that Daisy belongs to me.

"I love you so damn much." My lips are against her temple. Everything feels too good to be true, but I know that what we have is real. It always has been, and I will live the rest of my life making Daisy Carter happy. "We're going to have a long and happy life, Dais. I know it." I tip her chin up, my eyes searching hers. "I thought I had everything I needed, but I was wrong. I only need you. You and me and this house and our future. You are what I want most in this world."

The truth is, it feels like I can't breathe without Daisy by my side. She sees me for who I am: the good and the bad. She's always been my home, and it blows my mind that I somehow managed to make her mine even though she was the one thing I was never supposed to have.

Tears well in her crystal-blue eyes before sliding down her cheeks as I pull her face down to me and kiss her.

She frames my face in her hands. Daisy is my past, present and future. That sounds perfect.

I want it to stay that way.

For the rest of my life.

DAISY'S EPILOGUE
ONE BIG HAPPY FAMILY

Daisy
    3 years later

"Daisy, are you almost ready? We need to get on the road. We're going to be late." Aunt Daisy's voice echoes from the bottom of the stairs. I tuck my blouse into my jeans, grab my bag and jog downstairs.

Tuck's mom is waiting for me by the front door looking just as nervous as I feel. We've waited for what seems like forever for tonight, and the last thing I want to do is show up late for my husband's first game coaching in the NFL.

"Your parents and Mark are already in the car with Evie. She looks so cute in her Cowboys onesie."

There probably isn't anything cuter on the planet than our 11-month-old daughter wearing her dad's team logo. It was a gift from the owner of the Cowboys after Tucker signed the 3-year contract.

Evie was only 3 months old when we moved everything we own from Reed Point to just outside of Dallas, Texas. We had been living in SoCal for a year after Tucker took the head coach position for the USC Trojans. When we got the call that a team in the NFL was interested in Tucker, we didn't believe it. It came as an even bigger shock when we heard the team was the Dallas Cowboys.

I'd never seen Tucker at a loss for words, that was a first for me. But after the initial shock wore off, Tucker and his agent flew out to Dallas to meet with the organization. I wanted to be there with him on one of the biggest days of his life, but I was pregnant with Evie and as big as a house, so I stayed home on doctor's orders. Two weeks after Tucker signed the contract with The Cowboys, we found our new house online, sight unseen, and made an offer. I had Evie the next day.

Pretty soon, she's going to have a brother. I'm six months pregnant with our son, Theo. We are naming him after my grandfather.

I'm pretty sure I almost fainted when I took the test and saw the two pink lines. Evie had just turned 4 months old, and we were in a new city. I couldn't wrap my head around having two kids in less than two years. Tucker, on the other hand, was instantly ecstatic. After we had Evie, he couldn't wait to start trying for another. Who knew Tucker Collins would want a handful of kids? Never in my wildest dreams. He's the best dad. No surprise there. No matter how long his day has been, he feeds Evie her dinner, gives her a bath and rocks her to sleep. He fell so hard and fast for his little girl. The week after she was born, he added a new tattoo to his collection: A little bird for Evie, next to the daisy he got for me.

I know it kills our parents to be so far away from their granddaughter, but they fly out every month for at least a few days. This weekend, all four of them are here to support Tucker. Thankfully, our house is large enough to fit everyone—that was a requirement when we were house-hunting. Six thousand square feet is not what I ever envisioned for Tucker and me; I was happy living in our little colonial just off Haven Harbor. But the extra space sure helps when you have two extended families who are as close as ours.

This will be our home for as long as The Cowboys organization will have us. This will be the place we raise our babies. I would like to think it's the home where Tucker and I will grow old together, but it is professional sports, and you just never know.

I lock the door and jog down the front stairs, quickly scanning the flowers I planted yesterday—two rows of white hydrangeas lining the path leading to the backyard. Tucker couldn't understand why I didn't just pay the gardener to do it, but just because he now makes a ridiculous amount of money as the youngest head coach in the NFL doesn't mean we need to spend it. When I tell Tucker that, he just shakes his head.

Forty-five minutes later, we're parked underground at the stadium. My dad is holding Evie tightly in his arms as we take the elevator up to the owner's box.

"Good to see you, Daisy." Bill, the owner of the Cowboys, greets me as if he has known me all his life.

"It's good to be here! Thank you for having us. This is Randy, my dad, Victoria, my mom and Tucker's parents, Mark and Daisy." I introduce them all as I lift Evie from my dad's arms. "And of course, you know Evie."

Everyone in the organization has been so kind to the three of us, inviting us over for dinners and spoiling Evie with Cowboys-themed gifts. There was a time not that long ago when I was so nervous to be around the coaching staff and the team, but everyone has gone out of their way to make us feel comfortable. To make us feel at home.

And it is amazing to watch Tucker accomplish his dream. After all of his hard work, he deserves it.

Sometimes, the last two years feel like a dream. I feel like I'm living in a movie, and I'm the lucky girl who married her childhood best friend.

We got married the summer after Tucker proposed. Neither of us wanted anything too big or lavish, but it was important to us to celebrate with our friends and family. So, we said our "I dos" in his parents' backyard, which in a way is the place where our love story began.

I wore a vintage gown that I found in a designer thrift store online, and Tucker wore a suit that threatened to kill me. He looked so handsome. I had never really been one of those girls who fantasized about her wedding day, but if I had, this would have been the wedding of my dreams. My dad walked me down the aisle, Briar was my maid of honor and Tucker's dad gave the most heartfelt speech.

My gaze drifts over to my father-in-law, who is standing next to the buffet table talking to the Cowboy's owner. I can hear him talking up Tucker from here.

Uncle Mark is like a different person. He's more relaxed and easy-going. He's an amazing grandfather to Evie and has been genuinely supportive and encouraging to his son. None of us are totally sure what changed his outlook on life, but whatever it was, we're all grateful for it. It has helped to heal a lot of old wounds.

We're one big happy family, just like we used to be—only now even happier thanks to the addition of Evie, and Cassidy, Addy and Jonathan's daughter.

Tucker jogs onto the field wearing navy blue, a star on the front of his ball cap. Like the rest of the stadium, I jump to my feet. I listen to the deafening roar of the crowd. I've never experienced anything like it.

LILY MILLER

I used to think the Outlaws fans were intense, but my god, this is wild.

The stadium itself is nine times the size of the one the team played at RPU. The sound of the drums shakes the stadium ground beneath your feet. There is a sea of Cowboys fans dressed in blue and white, screaming at an ear-splitting volume as the Cowboys cheerleaders hype the crowd on the field. It's sensory overload.

I adjust Evie's headphones, making sure they're in place, then lean into my mom's shoulder so she can hear me above the noise. "I'm so glad you're here for this."

"We wouldn't have missed it. This is Tuck's big moment."

"I really want him to win."

"That's what he does best."

The jumbotron zooms in on Tucker standing on the sidelines, a look of complete focus in his steel-blue eyes. There is something so intoxicatingly gorgeous about this man in his game-day gear. He was quiet all morning as he sat and ate the breakfast I made him. He only cracked a smile once, and that was for Evie. When it came time for him to leave for the stadium, he hugged me for longer than usual at the door, as if needing to steady himself. The stakes are high here, and Tucker knows he needs to prove himself. But now, on the field, he is the picture of confidence.

The Cowboys are leading the Broncos 17 to 14 at halftime. Both teams showed up to play today, and the close game has me so nervous that by the fourth quarter I can't even stay in my seat. With only two and half minutes to play we're up 34 to 31. If we can hold them off, Tucker will win his first game in the NFL. He tries not to get too caught up in personal accomplishments, instead always focusing on the team, but I know that deep down, a win here would mean the world to him.

Cowboy fans have big expectations of Tuck. I'm not sure how he handles that kind of pressure. But he knows this game inside and out and if anyone in this stadium has underestimated Tucker Collins up to this point, he will sure as hell prove them wrong tonight.

A bloom of pride fills my chest as I watch my husband in his element. He is making all of Reed Point proud today, but no one is prouder of him than I am.

Nerves spark to life in the center of my stomach as the clock slowly ticks down. The last two minutes are torturous as the fatigue on our guys becomes noticeable. Our offense jogs out to the field, taking their positions with our QB behind the center. Tucker signals the play seconds before the ball is snapped. The quarterback sends the ball directly into the arms of Garrett Moseley, our best wide receiver, who takes off running for the end zone. He's fast and he's strong, outrunning every Bronco attempt to take him down to the turf.

The stadium goes wild as he runs the length of the field. I watch Tucker as he yells from the sideline, waving Moseley on. He yanks his headset off in victory as the receiver reaches the end zone. Touchdown! When Tucker pumps a fist in the air, I know we've won the game.

The entire stadium erupts with a noise so deafening I can feel it vibrating straight to my bones. My throat is raw from screaming but I'm not about to stop. The next thing I know I'm jumping up and down with my mom's arms wrapped around me. Tuck's parents and my own dad descend on us in a giant group hug.

"We won!" I throw my arms up in the air as emotion stings at the back of my throat. I look for my husband on the field through blurred vision. It takes me a minute to find him swarmed in a crowd of his players and coaching staff, a cameraman capturing it all for TV.

My heart clenches.

For my entire life, it's always been Tucker Collins. For a long time, I learnt how to love him from afar, but life is so much better now that I get to love him up close. And I will love that man until the day that I die. This I know soul-deep.

I'm shaken from my thoughts when Tucker's dad reappears next to me holding an awake but sleepy Evie against his chest. "I went to get a bottle of water and noticed her just starting to stir in her playpen," he says as he gently presses her head of dark curls into his chest to soothe her back to sleep. "I guess she didn't want to miss her dad's big win."

All the air seems to rush from my lungs watching Uncle Mark hold Evie so lovingly in his arms as he smiles with such pride for his son.

He kisses the top of Evie's head before carefully handing me my sleeping beauty, and as if Tucker can sense the way my heart is overflowing in this moment, he turns to look up to the stands, his gaze searching the crowd until it lands on me and Evie in the box. The moment his eyes lock on us, he beams. A smile tugs at my mouth so fiercely I'm pretty sure my cheeks will be sore for days.

I raise my hand in a wave, then I blow him a kiss before he turns and jogs to center field to shake hands with the Broncos coaching staff.

I swallow the lump in my throat. Tucker Collins, head coach of the Dallas Cowboys, Reed Point University's treasured hero, girl dad and soon to be father of Theo, is mine.

TUCKER'S EPILOGUE
COMPLETELY OUTNUMBERED

Tucker
8 years later

"Our dinner reservation is in an hour," I yell from the shower as I turn the water to lukewarm. I upgraded us to a suite with an outdoor shower, and right now I am very thankful that I did. Daisy fought me on it, saying she'd be just as happy cramming us all into a 3-star hotel. She argued that she'd rather save the money for the kids' university education than splash out on a luxury vacation. Don't get me wrong, it's a lot of money to send four kids to college, but when will my wife understand that we have more money than we will ever need?

The plan was to stop at three kids, but it turns out we like the chaos. Two weeks after Theo turned three, Rosie was born, and not long after Rosie, we had Jack. It's hard to believe that Daisy and I are completely outnumbered, but I wouldn't have it any other way.

I close my eyes and let the water rush over me. We may be here on holiday, but there is nothing remotely relaxing about taking four kids to the beach. Even if that beach is in Greece, bordering the Aegean Sea.

After my shower, I wrap a towel around my waist and walk out to the private terrace of our four-bedroom suite. Every July, we cross a new destination from Daisy's bucket list of destinations, and this time it is Mykonos. Last year was Turkey and the year before that was a ranch in Montana. If my wife wants to see the world then I will make sure she sees every damn place on her list before I die.

I find my family soaking up the late afternoon sun on the patio. Evie is in the private plunge pool playing with Theo while Daisy watches them from where she's sitting on the stairs with her feet in the water. Rosie splashes beside her contentedly.

I walk over to the playpen just inside the suite, where Jack is napping. Sure enough, my little man is fast asleep, his arms above his head. Watching his chest rise and fall, I sigh, overcome with emotion. I feel grateful every day for the life I've been given.

Brushing a dark curl from his face, I head to the bathroom to trim the scruff on my face that I've been ignoring for days. I'm adjusting the small towel around my waist when Daisy walks into the bathroom, untying the strings on her bikini top, tossing it onto the counter. "The kids are all inside. Evie is watching them while I have a quick shower."

"Your little helper. She gets her maternal side from you."

"And Theo is all his daddy." She winds her long hair into a bun at the top of her head. "He's already a handful."

"He just needs to keep busy. He needs a football in his hand."

Theo is eight years old, and football is already his entire personality. He's showing some solid skills, and he begs me to practice with him in our backyard every chance he gets. He reminds me so much of me, it's scary.

Evie and Rosie are dancers. They like everything pink. Their days are filled with Taylor Swift music and arts and crafts. These days, Evie can usually be found making friendship bracelets while her little sister watches. Evie wears them in in a stack around her wrist. I wear one too, a pink and purple one that she made me promise not to take off. The guys on the team used to give me the gears about it, but I paid Evie to make one for each of them at the start of the season and now the entire team wears bracelets made by my 10-year-old daughter.

"I'll have a quick shower, then I just need 10 minutes to do my hair and makeup," Daisy says as she slips out of her bikini bottoms and steps under the warm spray. "Can you hand me a face cloth?"

I grab a cloth from the cupboard, then let the towel drop from around my waist.

"What are you doing?" She flashes me an amused look.

"Thought I'd keep you company."

"Nice try, Coach Collins. You already had your shower. Now I'd like some peace and quiet."

Both of our gazes drop to my dick, which is slowly growing hard. What do you expect? I'm a man and my wife has only gotten better with age. Her hips are a little wider, her boobs and ass are a little fuller. Daisy has always been irresistible, but this version of her— the mother of my children—is absolutely my favorite.

She shakes her head, laughing. "Not this time, Tuck."

I groan, but I get it, so I let her have her shower in peace. When she steps out of the shower, I hand her a towel and once she's dry, I watch her lather her bronze skin in moisturizer.

"Need some help?" I ask. She nods and I get to work, squeezing the coconut-scented lotion on her shoulders and working it in down her spine to the curve of her ass. She moans, letting me know how good it feels.

"Tuck?"

"Yeah, rebel?"

"I changed my mind." She turns in my arms, grabbing two handfuls of my ass, pulling me into her. My cock hardens in an instant and a shiver of lust climbs up my spine. Daisy glances to the door, ensuring our privacy, before removing the towel from around my waist, dropping it to the tile floor. I gently roll my hips against her center.

"Kiss me, Tuck."

I lean into her, brushing my lips over hers.

"Of course I'll kiss you, Daisy Collins." A smile curves my lips. "You never have to ask."

THE END.

CURIOUS ABOUT HOLDEN? HE'S UP NEXT! HIS HEA and the final book in the Haven Harbor series is available now. Read his spicy, forced proximity, surprise pregnancy, enemies-to-lovers romance here: Wish You Would.

TO FIND OUT RELEASE NEWS AND WHERE YOU CAN FIND LILY, follow her on instagram, @authorlilymiller and on her website. Make sure to sign up for her newsletter.

WWW.AUTHORLILYMILLER.COM

ALSO BY LILY MILLER

HAVEN HARBOR SERIES

One Good Move

Play For Keeps

Never Say Never

Wish You Would

BENNETT FAMILY SERIES

Always Been You

Had To Be You

Heart Set On You

Crazy Over You

DEEP COVE MILLIONAIRES CLUB

Deal Breaker

Rule Breaker

ACKNOWLEDGMENTS

The list is long but I will do my best to keep it short and sweet.

First and foremost, thank you to my incredible readers. To each and every one of you who have taken a chance on one of my books, I love writing happily-ever-afters for you. You continue to inspire me with your excitement and passion for my stories. Thank you from the bottom of my heart.

Thank you to my Beta readers, ARC readers, bloggers and bookstagrammers for sharing my love of romance and getting this story to readers. I am endlessly appreciative of every share, post, review and mention. It means the world! A special thank you to Melissa McGovern for always being there to run ideas by or help design my covers and to Jordan Lee for your support, friendship and gorgeous edits. I am endlessly grateful for you both.

Thank you to my editor and friend, Carolyn De Melo, for being on this wild ride with me. There is no one I'd rather work with. You always amaze me with your wit and humour, attention to detail and ability to make the banter so much better. Without you, there would be thousands of commas sprinkled in all the wrong places. I love you for saving me.

To my friends, my hype team, who I have fallen in friendship love with. You listen to me chat about my latest book boyfriend and story ideas non stop. Carmen, Mary,

Leah, Erin, and Brandee, you are among my favourite people in the world, my chosen family, and I hope you know how much I love you.

To my cover designer, Kim Wilson, for knocking it out of the park every time.

To Sarah Martin of Sarah Martin Photoartistry for allowing me to use the stunning image you took for my cover photo. It is seriously the cover of my dreams thanks to you.

To Annamarie and Zack for allowing me to use your image for my cover photo. The bow in your hair, the way Zack is holding you, and the fact that you two are picture perfect are cover dreams come true. Congratulations on your own happily-ever-after!

To Ellie of Love Notes PR for being so wonderful to work with and for getting my book into the hands of readers.

To Rob Moseley, my good friend, for talking football with me for hours upon hours and teaching me the game. I love your enthusiasm for football. You made Tucker the coach that he is!

To Emily Silver and Mickey Miller for being the best book friends an author could ask for. I look forward to our daily chats and celebrating our successes together. I have learnt so much from the both of you.

To my assistants Kait Miller and Anita Walker for everything you do for me. I would be lost without you both. I love you both so much.

To my family who allow me the time and energy I need to write. You give me the space to do what I love, and I could never do all of this without your support. I love you more than a lifetime.

Lily xx

AFTERWORD

Thank you for reading! If you loved the story, I'd be so grateful if you left an honest review—it helps more than you know. Your time and thoughts mean the world.

Want to stay connected? Join Lily's newsletter to get the latest updates, special sales, audiobook news, and first looks at new releases.

Lily Miller Newsletter

ABOUT THE AUTHOR

Lily Miller lives in Vancouver, BC with her husband—her real-life book boyfriend—and their two daughters. When she's not writing love stories full of heat, heart, and happily-ever-afters, you can usually find her in the kitchen cooking, sailing the Pacific Ocean, or with country music playing in the background.

A lifelong romantic, Lily has been hooked on happy endings since she was a kid, and now she channels that passion into writing small-town, contemporary spicy romance that celebrates love in all its messy, swoony, unforgettable forms.

www.ingramcontent.com/pod-product-compliance
Lightning Source LLC
Chambersburg PA
CBHW071150070526
44584CB00019B/2731